THE INTERNATIONAL
EXPERIENCES
OF FIRST-YEAR
TEACHERS

THE INTERNATIONAL EXPERIENCES OF FIRST-YEAR TEACHERS

EDITED BY
CAROLE RICHARDSON
AND **WARNIE RICHARDSON**

YOUNGSTOWN, NEW YORK

Copyright 2009 Carole Richardson and Warnie Richardson

All rights reserved
Printed in the United States of America

ISBN: 978-1-934844-12-0

No part of this publication may be reproduced, stored in or introduced into a retrieval system, or transmitted, in any form, or by any means (electronic, mechanical, photocopying, recording, or otherwise), without the prior permission of the publisher.

Requests for permission should be directed to:
permissions@teneopress.com, or mailed to:
Teneo Press
PO Box 349
Youngstown, New York 14174

To all of our students, but, in particular, to those of you who ventured outside familiar surroundings to embark upon a career that will touch the lives of so many. Your choices and resultant experiences will resonate throughout the lives of all your students: past, present and future

Table of Contents

Acknowledgments   ix

Introduction: Teaching and Learning Within an International Paradigm
Warnie and Carole Richardson   1

Chapter 1: Teaching in Nigeria
Rubinah Atcha   9

Chapter 2: Teaching in México
Stephan Barrett   31

Chapter 3: Teaching in Mongolia
Paul Cheevers   47

Chapter 4: Teaching in New Zealand
Anita Cunningham   59

Chapter 5: Teaching in St. Vincent
Miriam Drake   85

Chapter 6: Teaching in Kuwait
Neil Fairbairn   113

Chapter 7: Teaching in the United Kingdom
Kathryn Hillis   139

Chapter 8: Teaching in Thailand
Erin Hoover   151

Chapter 9: Teaching in Thailand
    Amelia Swanson   **163**

Chapter 10: Teaching in South Korea
    Nathanael Johnson   **181**

Chapter 11: Teaching in China
    Carissa MacLennan   **223**

Chapter 12: Teaching on a Caribbean Island in the Lesser Antilles
    Elissa Odgren   **263**

Conclusion: Learning Through Teaching: Narratives of Transcending Geographic and Philosophical Borders
    Carole and Warnie Richardson   **295**

Index   **305**

ACKNOWLEDGMENTS

Of course, this book would have never been possible without 12 of our former students, the voices of whom speak so eloquently within these pages. Amelia, Anita, Carissa, Elissa, Erin, Kathryn, Miriam, Nathanael, Neil, Paul, Rubinah, and Stephan, we are indebted to you for your unselfish commitment to and belief in this project when the only light was at the end of a very long tunnel. We hope that it has enriched your lives in the same way that you have enriched ours.

We would also like to thank our two former graduate assistants, Ian Galbraith and Sarah Robinson, for their work on the final stages of this book.

THE INTERNATIONAL EXPERIENCES OF FIRST-YEAR TEACHERS

Introduction

Teaching and Learning Within an International Paradigm

Warnie and Carole Richardson

Every year, a number of preservice teachers graduate from Canadian universities, are hired into international positions, and spend their first year of teaching adapting to a new career and a new country. In addition to adjusting to the expectations of a new culture, they must also deal with the stress and joy of the first year of teaching in their own classrooms. Individually, each of these experiences is life changing; together they represent a unique experience. Many of these students remain in touch with their professors and colleagues and tell stories rich with reflection and description of this first year in an unfamiliar country. Correspondence and conversations ring with professional and personal insights and choruses of "I wish I had known…"

Our belief in the importance of hearing first-year teachers tell their stories of international teaching and learning is rooted in our own practice. As preservice professors who taught in the public school system on a small Caribbean island, we have experienced firsthand the challenges and rewards of living in an unfamiliar cultural environment and teaching in an educational system much different from our own. When we moved from Canada to the Cayman Islands to teach in the public system, our world changed as we adapted to a very different way of life, both personally and professionally.

As seasoned educators, we were able to use our previous teaching experiences and ongoing reflective practice to identify and understand the dissonances, both internal and external, that resulted from working to fit into our new surroundings without losing ourselves or compromising our philosophical beliefs about education. We were able to recognize that certain conflicts within our classrooms related as much to our students' and colleagues' anxiety about our expectations for them as to our own anxiety about their expectations of us. Conversations with one another and with other teachers helped us to understand that our latent desire to implement our well-developed teaching practice in a new environment signaled an unconscious unwillingness to adapt to change; rather, we were assuming that our new environment would adapt to us.

As we began to acknowledge that change within our practice was vital to success in our new environment, we developed new expectations, new relationships, and new understandings that contributed to our becoming part of the culture and community. We also grew as educators as we began to appreciate that to effectively communicate with our students, we needed to validate their individual realities, even as we expected them to embrace ours. Conversations about our triumphs and disappointments grew more insightful as we reflected on how our teaching practices were changing to meet the needs of our students and the educational system. We realized that there was no right way to adapt to change; the willingness to expand our ability to see through the eyes of others was the key to successful teaching and learning—regardless of the culture.

Upon our return to Canada, we did not resume our public school teaching; we instead assumed faculty positions in a university preservice education program. We stayed in contact with many of our newly graduated students as they began their careers, and we began to hear fascinating stories from those who had opted to spend their first year of teaching in a country other than Canada. We offered advice based on our own experiences but were very aware that, unlike our students, we had been experienced teachers when we taught abroad. Our students were adjusting to their first year of teaching and an entirely new way of life; in many cases, they were so successful that they stayed beyond their first contracts. Some traveled from country to country and reported new challenges with every new classroom. Others felt the pull of home and returned, only to set out again the following year. In every case, these young teachers spoke of the richness of their experiences and the way in which the disappointments and successes had contributed to their professional and personal growth.

We know there continues to be some disagreement between the concept of radical constructivism advocated by von Glaserfeld, whereby knowledge is constructed personally, and social constructivism, rooted in the work of Vygotsky, whereby knowledge is constructed socially (Reagan, Case, & Brubacher, 2000). At the heart of the constructivist approach is the belief that students actively construct meaning based on "their past experiences and their personal purposes" (Henderson, 1992, p. 5). If students construct meaning largely based on their past experiences, the corollary then is that teachers do the same. Adrienne Rich said, "Until we can understand the assumptions in which we are drenched, we cannot know ourselves" (as cited in Beattie, 2000, p. 13). It is through reflection on beliefs, past experiences, present situations, and future intentions; on interactions with students, colleagues, and parents; indeed, on every aspect of our lives that we begin to identify the assumptions that frame the way in which we teach. Connelly and Clandinin used the term "personal practical knowledge" to define a teacher's way of knowing within her classroom (1988, p. 25). This concept holds the teacher as an individual with past experience and future intentions impacting the present situation. Just as one cannot understand a story by reading only its introduction, body, or conclusion in isolation, one cannot understand the experience of a teacher in a classroom by seeing or hearing or reading about only what occurs in the classroom. However, as teachers, this is what we often attempt to do. Forgetting that everything that goes on in the classroom is filtered through the subjective reality of the teacher, we attempt to identify problems, make decisions, and find solutions within the physical reality of the four walls of the classroom. Employing personal narrative is a way of reflecting that allows teachers to reconstruct their own stories, the whole story, and thus "contextualize the classroom experience" (Reagan et al., p. 25). When teachers are asked why they choose to do things in certain ways, they often reply with stories of how they were taught or lessons they learned while teaching. Focusing on themselves as people allows teachers to go beyond simply recounting an experience; they can reconstruct their personal narrative with all the accompanying emotions and insights. The opportunity to write autobiographical accounts of learning and teaching experiences enables teachers to link current preferences and practices to past experiences and become aware of long-forgotten or previously unacknowledged events that have influenced why and how they do what they do; to, in essence, identify the paradigm within which they teach. The voices of first-year teachers, regardless of the setting in which they teach, provide fresh and powerful insights into the lives of beginning teachers. This book allows these voices to be heard within a context that speaks to challenges beyond those experienced by first-year teachers working in a familiar cultural environment.

In our previous research, we examined the international relocation of teachers and measured the significance of self-esteem, self-efficacy, flexibility, and pay satisfaction in teacher outcomes (Kirchenheim von & Richardson, 2005; Richardson, Kirchenheim von, & Richardson, 2006). These quantitative data indicated that those who scored high on scales measuring self-efficacy and pay satisfaction "would appear to be the ones most likely to find success within the international relocation process" (Richardson et al., p. 883). Restated, from a purely organizational perspective, our research showed that the accurate appraisal of some very specific intrinsic and extrinsic factors could provide valuable information to prospective employers in seeking out employees who would

Introduction

be better able to adjust to the international teaching experience. With respect to these statistical endeavors, there is no question that surveys, questionnaires, and other quantifiable data can reveal much about the profession. For example, understanding has increased in regard to trends in education, attitudes toward change, specific demographics of teachers and their students, and myriad other issues informed by numerical findings. This knowledge has, without question, led to the development of new theories, precipitated policy changes, and informed the design and deployment of curriculum. However, at the front of every classroom and at the heart of the teaching profession resides the teacher: the storied individual who interprets and communicates the textual, contextual, and hidden curricula and through whose personal experience every classroom experience is distilled. Because we bring the essence of our own understanding to the classroom, we must know ourselves in order to truly communicate. It is through narrating our stories for ourselves and others that we are able to own our experiences and carry them forward as we seek to understand who we have been, who we are, and who we might be.

The narratives that follow honor the voices of the individuals as they tell the personal and professional stories that live behind surveys and numbers. They speak frankly of the difficulties faced and triumphs experienced while beginning a career in a new country. Each of the stories chronicles a very different journey, and we hear these young teachers begin to reflect on their personal growth and come to a greater understanding of what it is to be a teacher—regardless of the country and the educational system. Some of these narratives take the form of e-mails home to loved ones, while others employ a journal style with chronological entries. All the stories reflect the personal backgrounds and styles of their authors, and it is in these differences that this book finds its strengths. Day-to-day writings are interspersed with notes to self about questions to ask and things to consider for future teaching. As in any conversation, travel and personal relationships are discussed matter of factly among accounts of teaching and learning in new schools. Some who traveled prior to teaching seem more accepting of societies with different expectations and systems. Others express surprise at the profound changes they experience in both their personal and global perspective. Each narrative is followed by detailed lists of frank and helpful tips that may aid other educators who choose to be adventurous and follow in their footsteps. Ultimately, these stories provide glimpses into the lives of first-year teachers who venture beyond the defined borders of their country—and their comfort.

We invite you to laugh, cry, and learn along with them. We hope their stories will resonate far beyond the pages of this book.

> In listening to people, we demonstrate to them and others that they are worth caring for and about, and in valuing the stories of their lives, we assure them that their voices sing for us and tell authentic and meaningful truths as they know them. In this way, the concept of voice is collaborative. As we do not have experiences which are free from the influence of others, our voices cannot speak authentically if we value only our own words. It is in the silences and the resonances, amongst the harmony and the discord that we find parts of ourselves in the lives of others. In doing so, we rediscover the universality of lives lived and the human need for story to share them. (C. Richardson in W. J. Richardson, 2005, p. 201)

REFERENCES

Beattie, M. (2000). Narratives of professional learning: Becoming a teacher and learning to teach. *Journal of Educational Enquiry, 1*(2), 1–13.

Connelly, F. M., & Clandinin, D. J. (1988). *Teachers as curriculum planners: Narratives of experience.* New York: Teachers College Press.

Henderson, J. G. (1992). *Reflective teaching: Becoming an inquiring educator.* New York: Macmillan.

Kirchenheim, C. von, & Richardson, W. J. (2005). Expatriate adjustment: Predictors and outcomes of adjustment in international relocation. *International Education Journal, 6,* 407–416.

Reagan, T. G., Case, C. W., & Brubacher, J. W. (2000). *Becoming a reflective educator: How to build a culture of inquiry in the schools* (2nd ed.). Thousand Oaks, CA: Corwin Press.

Richardson, W. J. (2005). *Voices from the margins.* Burnaby, BC: Aydy Press.

Richardson, W. J., Kirchenheim, C. von, & Richardson, C. (2006). The effect of self-esteem and pay satisfaction on adjustment and outcome variables. *International Education Journal, 7,* 883–894.

Chapter 1

Teaching in Nigeria

Rubinah Atcha

Teaching internationally, especially in my first year, was a roller coaster of an experience during which I went through stages not unlike the stages of mourning. I was filled with excitement, fear, anger and resentment, regret, and then back to excitement. Teaching in Nigeria my first year after graduation was, without a doubt, the greatest experience of my life, but it was certainly not without its challenges. For the most part, I felt like a student more than a teacher. So many things were new to me, and so little was directly explained. Not only was I exploring the lands, I was exploring the culture, the expectations, the educational system, and especially the ways of the people. While many told me I wouldn't survive living in a developing nation, especially one that was in the news for its instability and corruption, I did survive and have been back to Nigeria since then.

General Information

When I did find myself teaching, I was teaching in a nation with four languages: English, Yoruba, Ebo. Nigeria also has 36 states divided into three major sections, the Southwest, the Southeast, and the North, and three main religious groups. Because there are over 500 dialects, English is the official language used for education and business, so you might think this would make it easy for me to get around. You would be wrong. Their accents were very difficult for me to figure out as was mine for them. I found myself using short, simple sentences and small words. I reached the point where, in my e-mails home, I was having difficulty putting together complex sentences because I was using simple sentences on a regular basis. I began learning the local language of my area, Yoruba, which is spoken in the Southeast.

The three religious groups represented were Muslims (50%), Christians (40%), and those with traditional beliefs (10%). The Southwest was almost evenly divided between Muslims and Christians, the Southeast was about 85% Christian, and the North was nearly completely Muslim. Religion is vitally important to the Nigerian people. For every Tim Horton billboard in Ontario, there were 100 church billboards in Nigeria: Baptist, Redeemed, United, Catholic, Evangelist, Seventh Day, and the list goes on. I was intrigued to see that there were nuns everywhere. In fact, I was a Muslim teaching in an all-girls Catholic boarding school run by nuns! Religion was a major theme of my experience.

The elements of this experience that made it most interesting for me included the boarding school environment, the religious setting, the culture, and the curriculum. I'd never been to a boarding school, as either a student or a visitor, and I'd never known anyone with much experience within them, so the way in which girls lived in this highly conservative environment was of great interest to me. They were not able to make or receive calls, keep personal mementos such as photographs, send or receive letters, or receive visitors, and their days were scheduled from 4:50 a.m. to 10 p.m. The seclusion of the girls and the cultural traditions left a large hole for me to fill as far as being an adult role model or parent figure in the lives of my students.

I know I had a positive impact on the students both directly and indirectly by offering my opinions and advice to the principal as to what changes could be implemented in the school to help improve the environment for the students. I realized, however, that there was a fine line between sharing ideas and imposing my views. While teaching abroad, I had to force myself to accept practices that might be considered abuse at home. I was a guest. It wasn't my place to judge their culture. Nigeria was changing in regard to its cultural views and had to be left to change in its own time. Even the principal at the school, who was Nigerian, didn't always agree with how the students were treated, but she told me she was seeing changes in a positive direction. Change cannot be imposed. As a guest teacher, I often told others how we did things at home and explained our rationale without accusing them of being wrong. I found this approach to be an effective way of influencing the thinking of others.

One of the philosophies advocated when I was completing my teaching degree, which I felt was sorely lacking in the Nigerian school where I taught, was the idea of educating the whole student. On this point, I stood alone. Teaching life skills was not a priority, and the results were clearly evident in the local teachers themselves. They had gone through the same educational system and lacked certain life skills. To be fair, they made good use of the knowledge they had and performed to the best of their abilities. I am not laying blame but simply making an observation.

As Westerners, we value privacy when it comes to our beliefs, religious or otherwise; but in Nigeria, privacy does not exist at the same level, and the rules of political correctness just don't apply. Dealing with the issue of religion was a major aspect of my experience, and it touched virtually all elements of my stay. I was a Muslim Canadian with Indian ethnicity in a Catholic missionary school run by nuns, and the teaching staff held a variety of Christian beliefs. In Nigeria, one of the first things people seemed to ask about was my religion since I don't have a Christian or Muslim name. They would look at me disapprovingly, ask me why I was a Muslim, and then proceed to try to convert me with leaflets and illustrated versions of the Bible.

To be honest, growing up in Canada where, for the most part, your faith is your business, it irked me to be harassed and criticized for my religious beliefs. Interestingly, it was Sister Rita, the 6-foot-tall, intimidating Catholic principal with seven siblings in the church as nuns or priests who came to my defense. At one point during a staff meeting she said, "Even as a Muslim, Rubinah is a better Christian than most of you who read your Bibles every night!"

In regard to curriculum, the educational system in Nigeria is closely tied to the British system. It hasn't been that long since the British left Nigeria, and many remnants of British culture remain. The system was not explained to me by the school staff, so I was left to learn about it on my own, which initially I found irritating and rude. I was expected to teach without being instructed on the objectives and intended outcomes of the curriculum. But I think being able to absorb the system from a Canadian viewpoint rather than having my perception filtered through a local perspective actually worked to my advantage. I noticed differences in grading rules and curriculum content; in particular, I found the sheer volume of content being taught was far greater than what we would teach in Ontario, at least in some subjects. I would assume the trend continues into other subject areas as well. While teaching chemistry to 13 and 14 year olds, I found myself preparing lessons with content I would normally teach to students in Grade 12.

Although the expectations of student performance in terms of rote memory were high, the expectations when it came to higher order thinking were incredibly low. Thinking outside the box and creativity in general were very difficult for the students. In speaking to the principal, I realized she could see an impact of this deficiency in the larger society. I truly didn't expect a local Nigerian to see that weakness; however, because she had studied abroad, she had a much more open mind than others with whom my path crossed.

Cultural differences were tied into many other aspects of my experience. The differences in the level of respect a person was given based on gender and, more obviously, age were striking to me. Differences in more minor things like dress, food, and language were obviously part of the experience as well. One of the most trying aspects of my stay, something that really tested my patience, was the question of simple courtesy. Things I take for granted in terms of courtesy are nonissues for them. For example, if someone was in my presence who didn't speak the local language and I was able to speak theirs, albeit with a bit of difficulty, I would usually attempt to speak in that language. Although all the teachers were reasonably fluent in English, they would insist on speaking in their native tongue in my presence and would not even take a few seconds to give me a short summary of the discussion. Oftentimes, the conversation would be work related and of importance to me, but no one would tell me; then, when I didn't complete a task (because I didn't know about it), they would say, "Why didn't you get it done? You were there when we were talking about it." Looking back, I can see the humor in this situation, but at the time the frustration brought me to tears.

In contrast, there were other cultural practices in which they took great care to be courteous. Nigerians cannot be accused of not greeting people. They have a language of greetings. In addition to the usual greetings of "Good morning," "Good afternoon," and "Good night," there are the greetings you offer to people when they are working, eating, sitting, or standing, when they trip or stumble, enter a room, and so forth. They work very hard at making people feel wanted and cared for, whether that person is a foreigner or a local. Just as I found them rude for not speaking in English in my presence, they made mention of my rudeness when I failed to greet someone who just tripped.

On one occasion, I was with a colleague walking across the courtyard, and he took a minor stumble. I ignored it thinking if it were me in that position, I'd be embarrassed enough and wouldn't want someone to draw attention to my clumsiness. If he had fallen and hurt himself, I certainly would have offered help. As it turned out, my having ignored his stumble was interpreted as rudeness and a lack of care and concern. As with so many other things, courtesy is relative.

THE STORY BEGINS

My journey began in January when my sister drove me from Mississauga to Ottawa and back on the very day I was to leave for Nigeria. There had been a problem with my visa, and we had to make a last-minute, 4-hour trip to Ottawa the morning of my flight. Visas are important and not always easy to come by, at least in my case. After an exhaustingly tense drive and a few-hours wait at the High Commission, I finally got my visa and then had to get back to Toronto to make my flight. We drove through a January snowstorm and just made it back in time for my flight to a tropical African nation of which, in all honesty, I had little knowledge.

The night I flew over Lagos, the former capital of Nigeria, I found my heart ready to jump out of my chest. I was a very naive Westerner looking out the window of a British Airways plane at about 8.30 p.m. and peering down at the Nigerian city of Lagos. This highly populous, congested city was once the capital of the West African country. Having flown into other large cities, albeit not in Nigeria, I'd noticed that these large municipalities are usually lit up to the point that one cannot even see the stars in the night sky. The night of January 27, 2004, I was horrified to stare out my plane window at Lagos to find a pitch-black city with only a few flickering lights. I can only assume they were fires lit at individuals' homes. Panic struck—hard. At this point I heard the voices of everyone I knew who told me I couldn't survive teaching in a rural town in Africa. What was I thinking?

Before I left, I made sure I didn't know too much about where I was going because I didn't want to have expectations that would later be dashed. For me it was a good way to remain open-minded and flexible, two characteristics needed for international teaching. But when the plane was circling above Lagos, a city of millions, and it was pitch black, I felt rather foolish for not doing my homework. Looking back, however, I am glad I left my home relatively ignorant. It was the right move for me.

For the next 15 minutes, as we circled above the airport, my heart was pounding painfully, my palms were sweating, and my head was spinning.

Nigerians on the plane were talking *at* me, telling me stories about life in Nigeria. I was completely oblivious to the words exiting their mouths. I just thought to myself, "Where's the light? Oh my God. Oh my God. What the hell was I thinking?" I cannot express to you the magnitude of my insecurity and fear. I think the pounding of my heart was audible to the other passengers. The expression on my face that conveyed my fear certainly was.

What was worse, however, was that the terror was only to intensify. The landing was great, one of the smoothest in my experience, but stepping off the plane I was hit with a wall of hot, humid air and was lodged in the middle of a crowd of sweaty bodies all headed for customs. I wanted to cry.

Two flights had arrived at the same time, both delayed, and passengers were all in a hurry. To put it into perspective, I had left Canada in the middle of a winter storm and arrived in a tropical country with 40 °C weather, plus humidity. The pushing and shoving didn't help the heat situation, nor did it help my sense of safety and comfort. To my relief, however, I saw a group of men with American passports. I was never so happy to see Americans! That relief was very short lived.

In character with their limited knowledge and experience with developing countries, these oil workers began telling me about the horrors of Nigeria: the lack of civility and abundance of violence. They asked me what I was doing in Nigeria. I said, "I'm a volunteer." They laughed and said, "God help you in this jungle." In the next 30 minutes, as we pushed on trying to find our way to the immigration officers, they told me about Nigeria and how if I were smart, I'd go back home right now.

I arrived at immigration. The officials didn't want to let me into the country when I stated that my reason for coming was to teach as a volunteer. Nigerians are very suspicious of the idea of working for free. Finally, they changed their minds and I was off to luggage claim. After some time, the crowd began to disperse because they, unlike me, found their luggage. I waited and panicked and waited and came close to tears. I found my luggage, began walking out, only to realize I had no clue what the people picking me up looked like.

Before leaving Canada, I tried to exchange my money to acquire some naira (Nigerian currency) but was told that I would have to get American dollars and exchange that money in Nigeria. At the time, I thought waiting would not pose a problem. But at the airport, I was trying to carry my luggage, and my sweaty palms didn't make that task an easy one. And since people are not permitted to enter the airport unless they work there or are holding a plane ticket, I had to make my way out of the airport alone with my bags. Since I didn't have any Nigerian money, I couldn't pay for a trolley.

By the time I stepped out of the airport, it was about 10 p.m. It was dark, loud, and polluted outside. I looked into a crowd of people, trying to find a red-and-white sign from Student & Youth Travel Organisation, the group through which I was volunteering. My vision was greatly impeded by the scores of taxi drivers, security people, and God knows who else trying to get a piece of me or the wads of American currency they assumed I was carrying. I finally got a glimpse of the people who I thought were going to pick me up. "Miss Davies?" I asked one of the two rather kind-looking women waiting for me. I got the right people, but before any more words could be exchanged, the younger woman grabbed all of my luggage and started running away with it. Holy cow! Who were these people and where were they going with my luggage?

So many thoughts ran through my head in the next 60 seconds. Did I have my passport on me? My money? Were they in the carry-on luggage that woman just took from me? If I were left stranded in Nigeria without money, would my parents look for me? Bad was turning into worse. I didn't know what else to do but follow. I figured I would be safer with two non-threatening-looking women than with multitudes of strange men. To my relief, these people were the real thing. The rush was simply because they'd been waiting outside the airport for me for 3 hours, and it wasn't exactly safe for three women, one being white, to be outside so late in Lagos city. In Nigeria, if you are not black, you are considered white, no matter whether you are Hispanic, Asian, or Caucasian.

We got into the car and Miss Davies told me that we'd get something to eat before heading to the hotel. All I wanted was water and air conditioning, but food was a good idea too. Driving through the congested streets, if one can call them that, I was taken aback by the sight of children as young as 6 selling food and other items on the side of the roads. Aside from being overwhelmed by this unfamiliar setting, I was choking on the air entering my lungs, and my eyes stung from the exhaust fumes in the car. Our taxi stopped. I was told to exit. I opened the door, put one foot out of the car onto the road, the second foot out of the car into the…what? One of my first acts in Nigeria was to step out of a car and nearly fall into an open sewer!

I had serious doubts about my sanity. In spite of all this, my panic, fear, and doubts lasted for no more than 2 hours. A sense of confusion did take over, but even that lasted for only a few days. Nigerian people as a whole were the most hospitable people I had ever met. Everyone worked hard to ensure I was fed and had company, and they were curious to learn about me as well.

My first week in Nigeria was spent in the city of Ibadan. I was spending my nights in a church-run hostel and my days participating in an orientation program. I found the orientation to be tremendously helpful. It included lessons on history, culture and language; an opportunity to try Nigerian food; and information about the prices of items and how to get around. In addition, guides showed me the sights, and I happened to arrive during the Muslim festival of Eid. I was able to partake in the local festivities and even witness the slaughter of a ram, which isn't commonplace for a city girl like me.

During that first week, I hardly had a moment to myself. Nigerian hospitality is a bit like Indian hospitality—smothering. People often asked me how I could stand to be by myself so much. The individualistic culture of the West is not compatible with Nigerians. They are social and family-oriented people with little emphasis on individual activities. I had a very difficult time adjusting to this cultural difference, and at those times when I felt most alone and homesick, it bothered me even more. Their intention was to cheer me up, and I appreciated the thought, but I longed to be alone with my thoughts and to be free to feel sorry for myself—an activity that became commonplace during the beginning of my time in Nigeria.

After a week of sleeping under a mosquito net, I hadn't received any bites. I had not been bothered by food or water poisoning. My skin was becoming tanned, and I was no longer embarrassed by sweat spots; they were unavoidable. I did begin to lose weight quickly because it was too hot to eat, and, while at home people always told me I was too thin, in Nigeria I was considered on the heavier side and weight loss was welcomed. The local people told me many stories of fat white people and wanted to know what we did in America that made us so fat!

When my orientation period was over and it came time to leave Ibadan for my work placement, I was sad to leave my many new acquaintances. I was escorted from the city to the village of Ijebu-Ife, where I was to teach. Ijebu-Ife is a rural community about a 1-hour drive from Ibadan. It was quite a shock moving from a highly congested city with lots of noise, people, traffic, and pollution to this small, sleepy community with few cars and little else that is typical of modern society. There I was, a hijab-wearing Muslim Canadian being taken to an all-girls boarding school run by the Sisters of St. Louis.

A rather tall and intimidating Nigerian nun wearing an outfit like Maria's in *The Sound of Music* and a large cross around her neck greeted me at the gates of the school. I was beside myself, wondering what on earth I was thinking. Second guessing myself would become common practice over the next 4 weeks.

When I arrived, I was somewhat taken aback by the environment. The school was located on a large compound, mostly undeveloped, and had just over 500 students ranging in age from 10 to 18, onsite staff quarters (where I lived), a chapel, and a convent. But I felt very welcomed and comfortable. Sister Rita, the principal, put her arm around me and said with pride, "You are our first and only Muslim staff member."

I was taken to the living quarters for the teachers, where I met my suite mate, Joy. I opened my room door, and hanging above my bed was a Jesus is Lord plaque. I was invited to afternoon Mass, then evening Mass, and morning Mass. I had never been to Mass in my life. I am used to being the odd one out; after all, I am of East Indian descent, wear a hijab, and went to university in Northern Ontario, and yet, I had

Teaching in Nigeria

always found myself among people who had had the opportunity to see the world outside their own town, city, or nation. But to be the odd white Muslim person at a highly religious school in a rural village in Nigeria where most people have never seen or touched an oyinbo, or white person, made me homesick for the first time in my life.

I felt out of place, misunderstood, and ungrateful. Everyone from Sister Rita to Joy and the other staff members were amazingly friendly. They wanted me to feel at home and welcomed, but I somehow resented them for trying to help me all the time. Part of me was confused and needed assistance, but the other part felt helpless and stupid because everyone was showing me how to do things that I already knew.

That evening, I got to know many of my new colleagues over dinner and discussions in a room illuminated by flashlight. I tried to be involved, but I was nervous because I was to start teaching chemistry the next morning, and I had no information about the curriculum, the textbook, the school standards, or the rules. That night my mind was racing and the resentment increased. Why had no one explained anything to me? How could they expect me to teach when they had told me nothing? How many students did I have? Where were my classes? None of this was told to me. It was rude and it was unfair!

What I didn't stop to think about was that just as it seemed like common sense to me that someone would explain things, it was common sense to them that if one had a question, one would ask. The first lesson I learned from international teaching came even before I stepped foot in a classroom. There is no such thing as common sense. That revelation is something I carry with me every day, and it gives me a great deal of peace and patience while teaching, even in other places. Common sense is not universal in the way that I once thought. In every culture, what is common varies. We take for granted that people will understand what we mean; people will at least comprehend our point of view even if they don't agree. This is not the case when you decide to live in someone else's world.

I finally slept that night only to wake up at 4:11 a.m. to an uneasy feeling in my belly that was followed by cramping. I first thought that what

I felt was just nerves. It was my first day of teaching in a new country. Nerves were normal. But as the projectile vomit came flying out of my mouth and landed on my bedroom floor, I discovered this was more than nerves. Without electricity, I stumbled in the dark looking for my flashlight to assess the damage to myself and my floor. Let me tell you, being sick is a great way to get to know strangers very well.

I had known Joy for only 12 hours, and yet there she was cleaning up my mess at 4 a.m. She called the sisters, who got me to the hospital. My blood pressure had dropped, and my first week at the school was spent lying in bed. At the time, I was actually hoping I was sick with malaria only because it makes a better story than "I went to Nigeria and got food poisoning." Unfortunately, it was just heat stroke or something boring like that.

I was in and out of consciousness with either Sister Rita, Sister Christie, or Sister Mary Therese looking after me at all times. I can't express how well these three women took care of me. My resentment faded, but I felt so embarrassed. There I was, a Western do-gooder who couldn't even manage to feed herself, let alone carry water from a well or wash clothes by hand. How was I to be of any use?

When I finally recovered and began teaching the next week, I fell in love—with my life, my profession, my country, and my new students. The girls I taught had no adults to support them. They were at a boarding school for 80% of the year and were entirely cut off from family and everything that existed off the school campus. They were not allowed letters from home, nor could they keep pictures of their families. They only had each other to rely on, and it wasn't enough. In the evenings after school, I would go visit my girls and listen to their stories.

Some were from rich families that wanted their children to learn about hard work and discipline. Others were from poor families and relied on the Catholic Church to help them where possible. About one third of the girls at the school were Muslim, but they had to give up their faith, at least outwardly. My presence brought it back to them. I had never before felt so needed and admired. These girls gave me so much in return for just a few minutes of attention, and it broke my heart.

Teaching in Nigeria

I was teaching senior secondary 1 chemistry and the girls, who were wonderful, were the age of Grade 9 students but had a very different curriculum. Their regular teacher was Sister Christie, who they described as a disciplinarian, so they rather enjoyed having this oyinbo taking over. There were several things that were difficult to get used to, however. In Nigerian culture, a great deal of respect is shown to elders. All over campus the girls would curtsy and greet me every time they passed by. In class, they would come in, remain standing, and in unison say, "Good morning, Miss." The first day I didn't realize that they would remain standing until I gave them formal permission to sit.

Nigerian students were much more disciplined than the ones at home, perhaps because they knew they would be caned if they were not following rules. But the formality made me uncomfortable. Overall, the girls were very curious about me, but since it was not considered proper to ask teachers questions, they were very shy. The students carried my bags, books, everything. It was like having my own army of servants. I actually felt awkward letting them do things for me, but I needed to abide by the cultural and school rules.

I adjusted to the cultural expectations at my school in most ways, but there were a few things that never got easier. The difference in views regarding the roles and rights of women were always hard to swallow. This is the one area in which I never gave way to their culture. Without a doubt, however, the most difficult practice to accept was the way adults spoke to and physically treated children. In this respect, I felt helpless because it wasn't my place to interfere.

During the spring holiday, I had assigned some work for my girls to complete. In retrospect, I realized the girls were unclear about my expectations, but out of respect they did not ask me to clarify. As it turned out, what was, in my opinion, a simple task was made difficult due to the girls' lack of previous experience with critical-thinking exercises. In what I believe was an attempt to avoid disappointing me, the girls cheated on their assignments. Without anticipating the consequences of my actions, I reported the cheating to the principal. The next day at the morning assembly, after the anthem and before the closing prayers, each of my girls was caned three times in front of the school. The guilt of knowing I could have prevented the caning by not reporting the cheating was excruciating. As it turned out, the girls didn't blame me, and a few actually came and apologized that their actions had forced me to witness the caning. This heartbreaking experience actually worked to break down the walls between me and my girls.

After the incident, they were much more open with me, sharing all their thoughts and feelings. I became the on-campus counselor. Most days I worked until 10 p.m. because it was outside of class hours that I felt I did the greatest amount of teaching, and what the girls were learning had a big impact on their lives. In the evenings, the girls left the dormitories to do their homework in the classrooms. I spent a lot of time with the students during those hours. I was told by both the students and the principal that no other teacher had ever made an effort to know the students as I had. Of this accomplishment I was proud.

The number of students who had trusted me with their most personal thoughts, feelings, and experiences in the short time I was at the school was staggering. The problems they faced were even more overwhelming. The Muslim students at the school were gravely mistreated by one of the Catholic sisters, as were students of different Christian denominations. For example, Muslim students in her class were made to stand and were told they worshipped the devil and were the source of evil in the world. They were even physically punished for being Muslim. Even though their parents knew of this, a better situation would be difficult to find. Although there were certain obstacles to being a Muslim at a Catholic school, these schools were among the best in terms of the education they provided to Nigerians. There were many Muslim students who hid their religion, and they told me they were ashamed of telling their classmates they were Muslim until I came and they saw I wasn't ashamed. As I said earlier, as guests, it is not our place to impose our beliefs, but I found that by being myself, I was able to open a few eyes and minds.

During my entire stay at the school, no one ever made me feel incompetent. As embarrassed as I often felt as I stumbled through each day, the teachers at the school were actually in awe of me. They were so impressed that someone who had everything was willing to come to Nigeria to live in a room with electricity only 4–5 hours a day, lizards in the beds, and ants in just about every piece of food that was swallowed. The word volunteer wasn't one that most people were familiar with in Nigeria. Why would one work for free? And work so hard, at that? This is a logical question to ask when working all day doesn't bring in enough money to have a meal.

There was a huge problem in Nigeria when it came to perceptions of the teaching profession. Granted, even at home the perception isn't always positive. But in Canada, we can find comfort in knowing that, for the most part, we are appreciated. Imagine being a university graduate, spending your days teaching young people who are barely teenagers and who look down on you at the end of the day because what you earn isn't enough to support you; it's an enormous blow to one's ego. This was the reality faced by most teachers at my school. As a result, teachers were not motivated to work hard. In Nigeria, people who don't value teachers oftentimes end up becoming teachers because there is no other available job. Students at the school feared their teachers but didn't respect them in the way I think of respect. Teachers knew they weren't respected and thus resented the students and their jobs and showed little dedication and care toward their students. This treatment of the girls by their teachers in turn caused the students to not respect their teachers, and the cycle continues.

I found myself torn between supporting my fellow teachers, who I knew were not paid fairly or treated with respect by the school, and feeling the frustration of the principal, who believed the teachers didn't take initiative. I agreed that oftentimes the principal was stingy with her compliments and with the school's money, but I got to see another side of her that respected me for my initiative and hard work. To this day, I wonder whether Sister Rita would have given the other teachers more money and more respect if they had worked harder. Being in a place for three months makes it very difficult to properly assess the situation.

Unlike the other teachers, I found Sister Rita to be an outstanding person for whom to work. She possessed the same sense of generosity and warmth that I was lucky enough to come across everywhere else in the country. On one occasion, I went to her office and asked her if she needed any assistance with things. While I was working with her, I asked if she could provide me with transport money to attend the staff meeting that Monday. The return cost was about 500 naira (C$3). Sister Rita went into her drawer and gave me 7,000 naira, more than 10 times what I needed!

Just as it is hard to fairly judge people, it's hard to judge a culture and nation. My feelings at times were very negative. I can be a judgmental person at the best of times, but, in the end, when I returned to Canada completely broke and unemployed, the only thing I could think about was returning to Nigeria. Despite the turbulent beginning and sinking middle, the majority of my trip was breathtakingly awe inspiring, especially the end. I saw the strength of the human spirit as people worked hard just to stay afloat; I experienced the charity of poor families who would scrape together money to offer me a cold drink when I visited; and I witnessed exceptional students who wanted nothing more than to learn and be more than their parents were able to be.

On my last day at the school, the students, staff, and reverend sisters gave me a send-off unlike anything I'd experienced in my life. At morning assembly, the head girl read a speech singing my praises, another girl read a poem she wrote about me, others spoke and gave me presents, and the entire school body sang a song they'd written for me. The things my girls said touched me because they commented on the ways in which I was able to positively impact their lives. There were tears all day long, both from me and my beautiful girls.

I had been warned that, despite her hardened exterior, Sister Rita was a softy. I didn't know how much. Not only did she cry at my send-off, she wept on my shoulder, holding me so tight I thought I'd stop breathing. I was amazed, and still am, by the love everyone expressed toward me. It's hard to fathom why they cared so much, because I didn't feel like I did anything special. In truth, being at the school felt like a vacation to me. Nonetheless, their love for me was certainly reciprocated. What floored me even more was what I found in an envelope Sister Rita handed me that day.

Teaching in Nigeria

I had no intention of opening my presents because I knew I would just begin to cry. But something the sister said to me about her desire for me to continue to be a good person and her wish that I accept the Lord Jesus Christ made me curious. To be clear, Sister Rita never once criticized me for my religion. In fact, she showed the utmost respect. But out of her pure love for me and my soul, she wanted me to convert, which I would expect from any nun.

After speaking with her, I went to my room to open my envelope. Inside was something that left me speechless. First there was a card from Sister Rita, with a $10 bill attached to it. She wanted me to buy myself a Bible. I thought her gift was extremely sweet. In addition, there was $600 in U.S. currency, which I still cannot believe to this day. There was a note that went along with the money saying something to the effect of

> *Please accept this small token of our appreciation for all the hard work you did, without ever asking for anything in return. You made a huge sacrifice coming to our school, and we would like to offer you something to help offset part of your student loans. We wish we could do more.*

That sum of money was nearly equivalent to 4-months salary for a teacher at that school, and had it been given to me as salary, it would have been appreciated; but to receive it out of Sister Rita's understanding that I was a recent university graduate with piles of student loans made the money worth so much more. She told me that if she could have afforded it, she would have offered me a job. Furthermore, she said that if I wanted to work in Nigeria at a high-end private school that could pay me substantially more, she would make the necessary phone calls for me.

Putting work aside, I was made to feel very at home by the people I met. I received more than 70 letters, cards, and poems from the students at the school. I received warm wishes and love from my fellow teachers, and I was welcomed into the homes of many other Nigerians who barely even knew me. That kind of hospitality is what Nigeria is about. Despite the clashes and violence we see on the news, Nigeria is a warm, welcoming, and wonderful nation. Granted, it has its work cut out for it; there is great corruption and injustice, but the public is essentially good and rich in character.

It was a bittersweet departure. Despite finally contracting malaria during the second half of my stay and not have running water sometimes for more than 24 hours, I never felt more at home than I did during my semester in Nigeria. Even though I often picked ants doing the dead man's float out of my cereal during breakfast, my first international teaching experience left me addicted to Africa. Never in my life have I felt so loved.

While at the school, I was given some of the most valuable gifts of my life. One girl whose name I didn't know and who was not in my class of 45 students came running toward me and handed me a paper pouch filled with something. She was risking being caned, as it was against school rules for students to give teachers anything so as to avoid favoritism. The paper had some flowers drawn on it, and when I opened the pouch, I found about a tablespoon of milk powder. This little girl had saved some of her food rations to give to me. She knew I had food, but there was nothing else she had to offer. It was this kind of generosity that I came across in Nigeria time after time—not just in the school, but even when I went exploring the country on my days off—that made all my negative feelings melt away.

On May 1, 2004, as I entered the gate at the airport, I looked back, not at a strange and dangerous nation but at my second home. It's difficult for me to believe how quickly and deeply I fell in love with Nigeria. Its people, culture, land, and anything else you can mention feel like family and home to me. I was able to give while there, but I also gained in terms of maturity, tolerance, acceptance, and, of course, friends.

When I arrived home to my clean, quiet, middle-class suburban Canadian neighborhood, I didn't feel a sense of relief. I didn't even mark the contrast between my current surroundings and those of the previous few months. Being home in Mississauga was as normal as being away in Nigeria. People are people. And yes, there are differences, some welcome and some thoroughly annoying in both cultures, but that's what makes life and this experience so rewarding and educational.

Rubinah's Tips for Traveling Teachers

What to Know and How to Prepare Before Going to Nigeria

I think the first thing to do before heading to Nigeria, as with many African nations, is to ensure that the country is not experiencing an unusual amount of political unrest. Also, vaccinations are extremely important, and some need to be received months in advance. Even vaccinated, you still have to be careful with your health, because although I had all the vaccinations and was taking my malaria-prevention pills, I still was exposed to mosquitoes and contracted malaria. It was generally easy to find clean water, but it is not uncommon to be sold water with the claim that it is clean when in fact it isn't. Here are some other useful points:

- It is important to pack a variety of over-the-counter medications for everything from diarrhea to cuts and scrapes
- Sunscreen and allergy medications are a must
- Bring something for headaches and cramps and some bandages. Women should bring sanitary supplies. Although pharmacies are readily available, you never know if the medication you are getting is the real thing, so bring extra prescription medications
- Contact lens wearers should bring extra sets
- My experience with visas was not positive, but in speaking with others, it seems my problems were not typical. Nonetheless, for people who have only traveled to countries where Canadians can get their visas upon arrival, it is important to note that in Nigeria there is an application to be filled out even by tourists, and long-term visas are not provided. My initial visa was for a month; thereafter, it was renewed while in the country. I received help with the renewals, and although I had every legal right to have my visa renewed, we still had to bribe the office worker. As I said before, corruption is a problem in Nigeria, and bribery is not uncommon
- It is also a good idea to carry a copy of the picture page of your passport and the page with your visa on your person at all times
- It is important to hide any signs of wealth, like expensive jewelry and watches. It is assumed that oyinbo, or white people, have money, so it is best to dress simply. Furthermore, I wouldn't recommend traveling at night, as there is a problem with bandits on roads. Even most Nigerians avoid night travel

- You can expect strangers to come up to you and make conversation. Sometimes it is a sign of friendliness, but if someone continues to follow you or insists upon helping you even when you've declined their help, he or she may be looking for money. I wouldn't recommend giving out contact information until or unless you really get to know and trust the person; it's not a dangerous thing to do, but you will start receiving calls or e-mails asking you for money—I learned the hard way
- Nigeria has two main seasons, one is wet and the other is rainy. In my opinion, both are hot, so appropriate clothing is a must. Wearing light clothing, both in color and weight, is smart because when things get dirty and you have to hand wash your clothes, jeans just aren't fun to have!

Most of all, I feel that if you are taken care of in terms of your visa and health care, Nigeria is a welcoming and safe place to work and visit. It's far less scary than you might think from how it is portrayed in the news; there are, however, some areas (primarily in the oil regions) in which you may not want to travel without a local guide or friend.

WHERE IS RUBINAH NOW?

Now considered a veteran teacher at my school in Bahrain, I am actually the most senior individual in my department after a full 4 years in the business. As such, I am often asked by new teachers what it's like to teach internationally. Some of these teachers are new to international teaching, while others are new to teaching altogether, but in either case I offer the same two pieces of wisdom: first, be patient; and second, there is no such thing as common sense.

For me, teaching has always been more than just a job or career. My interests lie in teaching in the developing world, not only to help others but also to help me gain a better understanding of the world, thus allowing me to share what I have learned. Having taught now in four different countries outside of Canada in paid and volunteer positions, I can't imagine a better way to learn to respect and understand different people than by living among them and living like them. Every aspect of my life becomes intertwined with being a teacher; it has become a way of life. My very purpose in being where I am is to teach, and if I were at home, I think my perspective would be a little different.

I never imagined myself becoming a teacher; in fact, teaching was at the bottom of my future careers list because I was so shy. In high school, I would have rather taken a zero on a presentation than to speak, but now I feel at home at the white board at the front of my class, in a foreign country no less! For me, teaching in general, and international teaching in particular, is the greatest high. When I'm not teaching, I feel as though something is missing. What I value most about teaching is the opportunity to broaden my students' perspectives as well as my own. Living in a different country, with different values and different beliefs, makes you both stronger in your own values and more accepting of the values of others.

Chapter 2

Teaching in México

Stephan Barrett

My New Names

Steve pronounced in Spanish is EBeev...no thanks. My nickname Stevee Bee is personal and impossible to say. Stephan becomes Estephan or Esteban. Preschoolers address me as Estephanie; the 1st through 7th graders address me as Mr. Stephan; and the 8th through 12th graders use Mr. Barrett. In regular practice, the students use our version of *sir* which is simply Mister (or Miss). It takes some time to get used to being called just Mister; "Mr. who?" is commonly my reply. Another option the students learn is to call their teachers *teacher*, *maestro*, or *maestra*. The only time our students tend to call me by an appropriate name is when I play soccer with them, and then it's Mr. B.!

Learning Spanish

My wife, Natalee, and I have made some excellent friends here who are between the ages of 3 and 6. Many people are familiar with the research on the rapid ability of the human brain to learn languages at a very young age. It is a pleasant surprise to hear our kindergarten (through third grade) students speaking complete Spanish after 7 months of schooling. More surprising, however, is the ability of two senior students from Canada and the United States to become fluent after having arrived in México only nine months ago.

Talk, Talk, Talk

Our school is so small (400 students total) that we build close relationships with our students; ideally, we guide them through their education and toward their future. Not so ideal are issues of discipline and management, which a teacher begins to notice when the students finish kindergarten and enter pre-1st grade (an extra grade is provided so that the students can practice their language skills and also perhaps because the school receives an extra year of income). Part of the culture is to talk—a lot! Students will chat from 1st grade through 12th grade. In fact, they don't ever stop! Overseas teachers at the school, who account for 70%–80% of all teachers, are perplexed by the amount of in-class talking. The students, regardless of status (high achievers, academically struggling, popular or not), love to talk, even in the class the principal teaches. Consequently, I am grateful for my former associate teachers. They taught and showed me effective management skills. I did not predict that I would be using my management skills with even the keen students.

Nowhere to Hide

The American School of Puerto Vallarta has two gates, both guarded by security. Surrounding the property is a high concrete wall, which was funded by the American Defense Department along with the one-way mirrored windows in each room (15,000 U.S. dollars). Having said that, I believe our school is probably one of the least-guarded American schools in Latin America. For example, last October when the staff visited the American School Foundation in México City, the security was equivalent to that of a vault in a major bank in Canada.

Our high school students cannot skip a class unless they want to sit in the cafeteria or in the courtyard, which means they will be seen by the principal because the property is so small. The cafeteria is outside, the hallways are outside, and all doors lead to the outside. One of our 10th-grade students was successful in skipping class last week. He walked to the primary area and climbed the wall using a tree to assist. His peers from another school were waiting for him and asked him to purchase some liquor at the plaza across from the school. To his dismay, when he was purchasing the liquor, our principal walked by on his break! The week following included meetings with the director, the student's parents, the school counselor, and others. When he was finally allowed to go back to class, I was the one teaching. He walked in, sat down, and was about to burst with his story. I could see the words virtually tattooed in the veins on his forehead. Noticing this, I asked him if he wanted to tell us something, and he replied, "Yes." I then asked him to come to the front of the room and tell his story. To my surprise, he told us his entire story, which was 20 minutes in length, something similar to what you might expect from an adult disclosing at an Alcoholics Anonymous meeting.

GARBAGE OR TREASURE

Our groundskeepers are incredibly tolerant and do a great job. Our students, however, have a difficult time placing their refuse into the garbage bin. This behavior is partly learned from the culture, but, more significantly, it's also partly due to our students being used to having someone else picking up after them. At 7 a.m. the grounds are clear of garbage. By lunch, the groundskeepers are clearing off the picnic tables and combing the soccer fields. By 4 p.m., the after-school students have again dropped most of their bottles and cans around the school. Our primary science teacher has introduced a recycling program. Grades 5 and 6 are responsible for implementing this program throughout the whole school. The teacher's goal is to teach the students to throw away their garbage and to separate what is recyclable. The program has been moderately successful. The students have started to put more of their garbage in the bins and to separate it. The science teacher wants the students to learn how to recycle, but unfortunately Puerto Vallarta doesn't officially recycle, so students do not receive much reward or feedback for their efforts.

Aluminum cans, however, are recyclable. The night-cleaning staff separates the cans from the garbage because they can sell the cans themselves for extra money. This practice reminds me of how little money they make compared with teachers.

Almost all cans in Puerto Vallarta end up being recycled due to economic motivation. People take cans out of street-side garbage bins behind restaurants, homes, and so forth. Even if the cans make it to the garbage dump, people living in the community adjacent to the city dump collect anything that is salvageable. To them, finding an aluminum can is like finding cash.

BREAKING DOWN THE DAY

In Grades 7 through 12, each student has seven periods that are 45 minutes long. There is one 30-minute break in the morning and one 45-minute break in the afternoon. Each full-time teacher is responsible for teaching four periods and, as a result, has three prep periods. The day begins at 8 a.m. and ends at 2:30 p.m. Most teachers don't arrive until about 7:45 a.m., however, and they leave the grounds by 3 p.m. These are the same hours kept by the primary school and the administration.

The term *extracurricular* is known here, but a very small number of teachers are asked to contribute their time after school for extracurricular purposes. Many students do stay after school, however, for paid services. For example, students can receive coaching, tutoring, assistance with homework, and after-school supervision (my job) from paid staff. If I am booked to supply teach, I work from 8 a.m. to 6 p.m. If I do not teach a particular day, I still go to work from 3 p.m. to 6 p.m. to supervise the after-school programs and provide services that may range from security to first aid. When our school performed the musical *Guys and Dolls* in the evenings before the spring break, I was typically at school from 7:30 a.m. to 11:00 p.m.

THE AFFLUENT HOOLIGANS

My favorite level to teach is high school. It is interesting to teach students, mostly Mexican (about 15% are American or Canadian), who are well traveled, speak multiple languages, and often have parents with lots of money. Moreover, the experience of teaching high school students who are always in the same classes is unique to me. Some students meet in preschool and then are together until graduation. Imagine the social dynamics of this situation. Each high school class consists of all the students in that grade. The 11th and 12th graders are very close to one another, but there is a lot of peer pressure in middle school; the hormonal 7th and 8th graders have pressured each other into bringing their own bottles of spray deodorant to classes following physical education (PE).

CASH IN HAND

Early one month, our secondary students took the U.S. standard tests (SAT-9). A ninth-grade student was going to be absent during the testing days, so he (and his parents) asked the principal and counselor if he could take the test before the other students. The staff agreed and requested that I administer the tests to the student after school hours; I was chosen because they know I am always on campus after school, and I don't have any direct responsibilities or engagements (coaching, tutoring, etc.) with other students. During the student's last testing day, I asked the counselor about how to receive payment for my services since I was aware of the non-extracurricular-pay policy; his reply was, "The student will pay you." Somewhat confused, I went to the principal and asked what the protocol was for the student to pay me. I asked, "Do they pay at the accounting office?" and "What kind of paperwork is necessary for this transaction?" I was shocked when he replied, "No, the student will give you cash: there is no paperwork to do." When the last test was complete, the student said, "Thanks, Mister," while placing 500 pesos (50 U.S. dollars) in my hand. I know that I am new to the teaching profession, but a student paying a teacher in cash is probably unique to many.

HAVING BACKUP

Most of the time when I am asked to substitute teach, I use the regular teacher's lesson. Sometimes there is no teaching work at all; then my responsibility is just to assign certain work and then simply manage the class (which is not necessarily simple). This situation is no surprise to most substitute teachers. It also is not unusual for a substitute teacher to need a backup plan when the lesson isn't going as anticipated or there is no lesson. The latter is the most applicable in my experience at the American School of Puerto Vallarta. Because I am called on to teach nursery through Grade 12, I have experienced many surprises. The biggest surprises include having been placed in a high school Spanish class (my Spanish is at a 2-year-old level) teaching German under a tree (after my elementary-level knowledge of German had been replaced in my brain with 2-year-old-level Spanish); teaching prekindergarten PE (not knowing Spanish means doing all the actions with the kids and ensuring myself of a workout); reading Grade 12 British literature out loud so the students can explain to me what I am reading; and administering a Grade 12 calculus test while using my Grade 7 algebraic knowledge to answer the students' questions.

Consequently, I have three important backup plans: bringing out my soccer ball, bringing out my entire collection of colorful white-board markers, and telling tales from my wonderful travel experiences. Allow me to elaborate. In México, as in many countries, soccer (or football) is almost a religion. On Easter Sunday, the U.S. team played México in a match to qualify for the World Cup. Throughout the streets of downtown (the centro) there were shops, bars, and restaurants with large-screen televisions showing the match. Right before the spring break, our high school math teacher took ill for 3 days, and so there were no lesson plans for any of his classes. In effect, his math students and I played a lot of football that particular week. Sometimes the students notice when there is no lesson prepared for their class, and they call my bluff. When this is the case, they always ask if they can play football. But soccer is something I reserve for special backup days, even when it would be my first choice as well. Instead of immediately pulling out the ball, I try to hook them with whatever comes to mind, and from there I go into some far and wide story/tale/fact/adventure of my life's journey, trying to make it as interesting for the students to listen to as it is for me to tell.

March 17, Saint Patrick's Day, was another day when I found myself without any lesson plans. This time I reached for my white-board markers (since I was in a classroom with a white board). That morning, by coincidence, I read a short history of the life of St. Patrick, and so I decided to share it with the students. On the board I drew the British Isles (geography); I compared the different amounts of time St. Paddy had spent in different places (math); I explained the hierarchy of the priesthood (religion); I talked about the commonality of saints and the use of white to depict their halos (spirituality, philosophy, and Eastern mysticism); I mentioned St. Paddy's achievements, experiences (history), and modern day effects (politics). The success of these lessons was very satisfying, as I do not teach many lessons of my own. I believe the success of the lesson can be partly attributed to the wonderful colors of the markers.

FIELD TRIPS: WHY ME?

Not knowing what you will be doing at work from one day to the next does have some benefits, such as being selected (or volunteering) for various field trips. My attitude is "If I am not booked to teach, I ought to take advantage of a school-related adventure." When my wife, Natalee, organized a day trip to the local refugee orphanage with her 3 and 4 year olds, I couldn't resist going. We also brought along a couple of friends who were visiting us from Ontario at the time. The success of this trip has resulted in weekly visits to the orphanage for my wife and me, where we donate our time to the 34 extremely needy children who currently live there.

The canopy tours are very popular. If one goes on the tour of Mismaloya (where the movie *The Night of the Iguana* was filmed), one may also see the location where Schwarzenegger's movie *Predator* was filmed. Luckily, I was able to attend the jungle tour in the mountains with the fifth and sixth graders. I love it when education is tied to adventure!

I also went with the seventh graders and a friend visiting from Ontario on a 3-hour bus ride inland to climb an inactive (but still steaming) volcano. The climb to 6,000 feet took an hour and a half in our huge luxury bus, which struggled with the low-grade cobblestone road. When we reached the top, my friend and I (along with our guide, the students, and their teacher) made the 2-hour journey to the crater's face, where we had a wonderful view of the surrounding mountains and their valleys. On the way back to the bus, some of us were sucking on rocks to overcome our thirst (try it, it works!), while others were munching on candies found deep in their pockets. We arrived back at the school at exactly 9:39 p.m. (there was a competition on the bus to see who could guess our arrival time), 4 hours and 9 minutes late. (Incidentally, my visiting friend, Kraeg, won the time-guessing competition. His guess was 9:40 p.m.; amazing!)

WHY WEDNESDAYS ARE MY FAVORITE DAYS

Soccer! Football! Futbol! Füsball! Yes, every Wednesday the best soccer players at the school play together in a friendly match after classes. I remember when I was asked whether I wanted to accept the job of after-school supervisor. Only 2 days before the proposal, the school's PE teachers and coaches (along with the security staff, grounds staff, and some students) asked me if I was interested in playing soccer on Wednesdays; after swallowing the nervous lump in my throat, I agreed (only to be presented with the job proposal a week later). When it was time for me to respond to the job offer, I asked the important question in my most professional and assertive manner: "Would I still be able to play soccer on Wednesdays?" I am happy to say I still have my after-school job.

What is it like to play soccer at our school? Playing *futbol* against the students is quite a challenge in two respects. First, they all have been playing since they were very young, in many cases since they could stand! Second, their cardiorespiratory function supersedes that of any adult who is not a marathon runner or cross-country skier. Playing futbol with (or against) the Mexican staff is also extremely humbling. Their cardiorespiratory function may not be what it used to be, but their skill level is magical! Our school's athletic director and soccer coach is Eduardo Espinosa (also known as Lalo). He is a native of Sicily, Italy. He has played professional soccer in Italy, Germany, Argentina, and México. Now he belongs to a coaching association that includes coaches from around the world. He also is one of the nicest and most genuine people my wife and I have met. From our youngest student player to our oldest groundskeeper, all the players try their best when playing futbol, because if Lalo is not acting as referee for the game or coaching the students, he is playing with us! When he shoots, the view of the ball is reminiscent of the biblical story of Moses parting the sea.

Grades 3 Through 6
If a student enrolls in the nursery class, he will have experienced 4 years of school by the time he enters Grade 1. As a consequence, our pre-first-grade and first-grade students who are in their fifth and sixth years are completely bilingual. We have learned that our school models Ontario's French immersion program, except that we have a 45-minute Spanish lesson and preschool students have instruction in English all day. The primary grades receive instruction in English half of the day and Spanish the other half, and so each primary student has two classroom teachers. In addition, art, music, PE, library, computer, and science are all taught by nonclassroom teachers.

I previously was trained as a high school teacher with a small amount of experience teaching Grade 7. Most of the knowledge I have attained for teaching at the primary level has come from Natalee, who has taught kindergarten through second grade for many years. I greatly commend Ontario's primary teachers, who put a great deal of time into their teaching schedules, their minimal prep-time (or lack thereof), their extracurricular responsibilities, and their curriculum content. A primary teacher moving to our school would find the opposite experience. Every primary teacher has a 45-minute lunch break. In addition, on average, every primary teacher has at least 1 to 1½ hours of prep time each day. I also have already mentioned the very minimal extracurricular responsibilities of the teachers and the typical workday schedule; therefore, I believe our teachers are significantly less busy than those in Ontario.

Beyond the Schedule

Early in the school year, most of my substitute teaching was in the secondary school (for which I was thankful). The first time I was assigned to the primary school was when I filled in for their science teacher, and my days consisted of 1-hour intervals of teaching Grades 1–6 in a seemingly random order. Shortly thereafter, word went out that the school's new first-year and first-time-contracted substitute teacher (me!) survived well with the younger students; a short time later, I was asked to teach PE and art for the primary school.

But the true understanding of primary teaching comes into play in English and math. The students begin each day with their morning routine, which includes calendar work and journal writing. The teacher then initiates whatever lesson is planned in spelling, English, or math and continues working with the same students until recess. When working with fourth, fifth, and sixth graders, I can simply administer alongside the lesson plan, however, working with pre-first through third graders is a huge challenge for me!

Getting Younger All the Time

My time spent with prekindergarten and kindergarten students has been mainly teaching (or rather, performing) PE. I admit that I am most nervous with the younger students, yet they are the least critical of my lessons; swinging my arms and running around the field while the students try to catch me works well with them. Twice I have been asked to substitute full days for the prekindergarten teacher. Her class consists of 22 students, and she has two teacher assistants. When I substituted for those 2 days I had to exercise my authority by insisting on a role reversal: I became the teacher assisting the teacher assistants.

In the Nursery

The nursery class consists of 17 students, all of whom speak Spanish as a first language. Two intelligent, kind-hearted teacher assistants and one jovial, saintly, genius, guru teacher named Natalee head up the nursery. Of the whole school, this class is the only one where I know all of the students' names, I presume because my wife is their teacher and because the 3 and 4 year olds are the most adorable creatures I have seen on this planet (I expect to see other life-forms on other planets soon). I attribute my ability to speak Spanish to help I received from those little language-learning experts, because Natalee speaks only English with them (translated via her assistants), and her students speak only Spanish with her. I then learn my Spanish from Natalee, who learns it from 3 year olds...perfect!

I immensely enjoyed playing the role of grandfather with Natalee's nursery students by dropping in from time to time saying, "Hola," and playing games with them, which was shortly followed by a grandiose Seinfeld-style exit. However, the days of playing grandfather are now over. Nowadays when I visit the nursery, I enter the door as teacher or assistant or as a teacher assisting the assistant teachers (as I mentioned before). Natalee puts me to work with the little ones, whether it is puzzle building, coloring, reading, or waking them up from their naps.

When and why did this transition occur? Last year, when Natalee and I were signing our contracts to teach in Puerto Vallarta, Natalee would joke about waking up in the morning and saying to me, "I feel like sleeping in today, why you don't go in for me?" As funny as it sounds, this scenario became a reality once we began teaching at the same school and I was the school's contracted substitute teacher. Before last March, Natalee had not missed a day of work, and so she was permitted a week off, during which she left to see one of her best friends get married. After diligently trying to find an experienced preschool teacher to teach her class, she had to settle for the nursery's grandfather as the substitute.

Gradually, the fear within my bones left me and was replaced with a great joy. My days as teacher assistant teacher became more and more comfortable for me. I spent the mornings on gate duty, watching the little ones trickle out of their parents' beautiful Hummers (I could write much more about this) and enter class, where they would place their belongings in the cubbies and start their morning activity. Six and a half hours later, I would watch them do the same thing in reverse. With some clever planning and schedule manipulation, my week in the nursery ran as smoothly as the afternoon breeze blowing through the palms. I may not have learned many skills that I could transfer to a high school setting, but if I am to be a parent someday, I will owe a big thank you to those adorable Spanish-speaking 3 and 4 year olds for the lessons they taught me.

FINAL INTERESTING TIDBITS ABOUT OUR SCHOOL:

- We have a full-time irrigator; therefore, our school has the greenest grass in all of Puerto Vallarta (light rain has fallen only about 10 times since October)
- Our computer lab is the largest network in the city
- The bathrooms are shared by everyone—director, staff, students, irrigator, and others
- One of our property lines is shared with the international airport. As a consequence, picking up any family or friends who may visit

is a convenient 10-minute walk. The airport also serves as a resting place for the soccer balls that soar high enough to make it over to federal land
- The one-way mirrored windows make for great laughter when visitors or new students walk by and fix their hair and clothes while looking at their reflection

Stephan's Tips for Traveling Teachers

These tips are specific to my situation here in Puerto Vallarta, México. Please use them only to guide you and help to generate more questions and answers of your own. The most reliable and integral way to gather information about your specific situation is to contact the teachers (via e-mail or telephone) who currently are working or have worked at the school you are interested in. Traveling here with my wife, who is a teacher as well, has made all the difference to me because of her companionship. If you are traveling alone, be sure that your soul will be satisfied with the solitude.

What to Bring

- If you can, bring a teaching spouse; or get to know your roommate (via e-mail, etc.) before you relocate
- Ask yourself: "How much do I want to simplify my life?" If you want a carbon copy of your current lifestyle, then bring it all! If not, make a tally of what your apartment comes furnished with, and find out what can be purchased nearby at a reasonable price. This will save you time, effort, and the cost to ship items
- Think of what brings you safety and comfort, and bring those items (e.g., clothes, medicines, music, accessories, first-aid items)

Questions to Ask

- What is the current political state of the nation? Remember, safety first!
- Do you require any vaccinations or precautionary medicine for the area to which you will be traveling?
- How will you be compensated? Ask about salary scales, currency used for payment, travel allowances (keep all receipts), shipping and moving allowances, frequency of payment, and when your first payment will come
- Where will you be staying? Ask lots of questions about your accommodations: relative location, immediate surroundings, neighbors, etc.
- What is included and what isn't? For example, find out whether items like phone, cable, Internet, utilities, laundry, cleaning, pest control, and security are included

- What is the standard of living in the area? Find specific answers, and do some research on your own. Reading a couple of travel guides is helpful
- Will you need travel insurance? What about health insurance (coverage, deductibles, and limits)? What is the school calendar? What resources should you bring?
- What will be a typical day for me at school? What is there to do on the weekends and holidays? What are the local people like? What are the societal norms and customs? Where and when is it safe to travel? What is the tempo and rhythm of the city?

What to Expect

- An expansion of your comfort zone, including your personal, professional, and social limits
- A holistic adventure and journey, which can only be realized if you *live* this experience

Important Paperwork

- Ask the school for clear instructions on what you will need to bring
- Photocopy all your identification papers and documents twice. Leave one copy at home with someone who is reliable. Put the additional copy with your checked luggage, and keep the originals on your person
- Entrust someone at home to run your financial matters while you are gone

Financial Considerations

- How much money will you need to carry you between the time you tie up the loose ends at your current place and the time you make your first international pay deposit? Not including all the reimbursable expenses, how much money do you need for your settling in period?
- Once you start getting paid, will you make enough money to live comfortably, travel on the weekends, travel home for summer and holidays, and pay student loans?

If I Had to Do It Again, I Would...

- Do it again! Saint Augustine said those who do not travel read only a page in the book of life. The opportunity to combine travel and adventure with the professional pursuit of teaching, the love of children, and the humbling experience of embracing a new culture is hard to resist

Things I Would Like to Have Known

The answers to all of the previously listed questions would have been helpful. Remember, think about safety and shelter first. Then open the lotus flower of questions regarding finances, accommodations, and lifestyle.

Where Is Stephan Now?

Stephan and his wife stayed 3 years in Puerto Vallarta, México. At the time of writing his first-year journal, Stephan was beginning to realize that it could take a whole year just to get used to the change in lifestyle of teaching in a new country. Not long after his realization, it became obvious that it would take another year of adjustment if he were to uproot from one country to live and work in another. With this experience and wisdom attained, Stephan and his wife decided that a 3-year term was essential to having a more complete international teaching experience; they needed a second year to just *be*, and not be preoccupied by either first-year adjustments or last-year planning.

    Stephan and his family are now living in Southwestern Ontario. Stephan is taking time off from teaching at an adult learning center to take care of the most precious and special of all Mexican souvenirs—their México-born daughter, Noelle Faith! And Natalee is using all of her many teaching skills and abilities instructing English-as-a-second-language learners.

CHAPTER 3

TEACHING IN MONGOLIA

Paul Cheevers

WHY MONGOLIA?

Throughout my life, I have always enjoyed undertaking challenges that cause my peers, my family, and basically anyone who cares enough to give it a second thought to ask, "Why?" During the chaotic and stressful final months of teachers college, the chance to once again prompt others to ask this question arose. At a time when all of the fresh-faced, newly graduated teachers were eager to snatch up any teaching opportunities that came their way, I wanted my first teaching choice to stand out. Many of my friends chose international job locations their first year—England, South Korea, and China, to name a few. But none of those appealed to my need to be as different as possible. I was starting to worry that I was not going to find my ideal teaching location and that I would have to settle for one of the more frequently chosen spots.

It was the end of March. The school year was coming to a close, and I was about to return to Brantford, Ontario, to finish my teaching practicum, after which I would be off to Kenya for an international teaching placement, and I knew that I did not want to return home for my Eddie (Faculty of Education) graduation without a head-turning job to talk about! I needed to make a choice soon. Then one day, out of the blue, I received a phone call from a friend who had turned down an interview for a teaching position in a school in Mongolia called the American School of Ulaanbaatar (ASU). My friend did not want to teach overseas alone and asked me if I wanted the contact number for the school. Mongolia? Sure, why not? It sounded like a head turner to me! I jumped at the opportunity. I called the school, and within a week I had an interview and a job. I was going to be a Grade 6 teacher in Mongolia.

My first thought was, "Now that I have my unusual location for my first teaching job, I need answers to all of the *whys* that are sure to come. What do I really know about Mongolia?" My answer was short and probably similar to many people's basic general knowledge–it's cold and there are a lot of deserts and mountains. I love the outdoors, mountains are a great challenge, and I was well acclimatized to a cold region in North Bay, Ontario, where I had spent 5 years at university. As expected, the questions came. Whether or not they had been interested in my life before now, people wanted to know why I chose Mongolia, and I enjoyed every minute of answering those whys!

WELCOME TO MONGOLIA

I arrived in Mongolia at the Genghis Khan Airport and was greeted by the head of school and the school driver. Both were extraordinarily friendly and very eager to tell me about the school. As we drove away from the airport, I listened to the head of school tell me about how wonderful the school was and how friendly the people were here. As we left the airport parking lot, one thing quickly became evident: there was nothing around me that showed any signs of life. It appeared that I was driving into a desert surrounded on all sides by mountains. Then suddenly, on the horizon, a large city appeared. I was relieved to see the first signs of recognizable civilization outside of the airport. We continued to drive through the city and out the other side, down some bumpy dirt roads, and past some herds of sheep and cows. I began to panic and think that the pictures on the school's Web site were all a setup and that I would spend the next 10 months living and teaching in a Mongolian traditional ger (yurt)! Then, just as quickly as the city of Ulaanbaatar had appeared on the horizon, a beautiful bright building appeared. It was the school! My fears of living a nomadic teaching lifestyle were quickly relieved, and I was comforted by the bright, modern-looking building situated in a valley and surrounded by large mountains just begging to be climbed. It looked like a perfect setting for my first-year teaching experience.

The next 10 days were spent meeting all of the teaching staff and preparing my first classroom of my very own. Little did I know at the time, but these 25 teachers (22 of whom were at this school for the first time) would be an amazing source of workplace assistance, comfort, and friendship during the next teaching year. We all bonded quickly, as most of us had never been to such a place as Mongolia before, and we all came from similar situations with one major thing in common—we were teachers. Most were from Canada and the United States, with one from the Philippines and one from New Zealand. I also met the person who I eventually realized was the most valuable asset to my classroom—my program assistant. She was a Mongolian woman about whose role I was confused at first, but I would quickly come to realize that she was in my classroom to ease the cultural differences such as the language barrier and any issues that the students were not comfortable discussing with the new foreign teacher. This cultural barrier worried me a little. I had taught in Kenya for a month and had quickly experienced the difficulties of teaching students who barely spoke my language. Lessons had taken three times longer than planned, and many students were reluctant to discuss their school work, let alone any personal issues, with a foreign teacher. I knew that for the 10 days before school began, I could worry all I wanted, but I wouldn't be able to answer my own questions or calm my fears associated with being a first-year teacher in another country until school had truly begun.

And It Begins

I had prepared for this day to the best of my ability. The classroom was stocked with supplies, I had tried my best to properly pronounce the students' names—Dulguunyam, Enkhjin, Munkhjin—but putting the letters K, H, and J beside each other in a word was a tough concept for me to grasp and was even tougher to pronounce! My living quarters were on the school property, so I could walk to my classroom each day in a matter of minutes. As I exited my apartment building and walked up to the front of the school, I was amazed by the scene in front of me. The entrance to the school was covered in balloons; there were reporters, cameras flashing everywhere, dignitaries, politicians, and even a red carpet! I felt like I was at the Academy Awards. Apparently someone had neglected to tell me that the first day of school was a greatly celebrated event in Mongolia and that the parents of the students were very appreciative of foreign teachers making the leap of faith necessary to come to Mongolia to teach. Parents had done their research to find out who their child's teacher would be and had even looked at our pictures on the school Web site. I was swarmed by children and parents handing me flowers, chocolates, and various other gifts. Suddenly I thought, "Maybe this won't be such a difficult transition after all!"

The first few days of school went as I had expected, with lots of icebreakers and difficulties properly pronouncing names. Other than being able to see gers being built outside of my classroom window and the odd herd of sheep or cows crossing the soccer field during gym class, everything was pretty much as I had pictured it. Another thing that surprised me was the lack of a language barrier between me and most of my students. I knew the students had to pass an English test to attend the school, but I was still very surprised at the high level of proficiency in English demonstrated by most of my students. I would later find out that this was because most of my students' parents were government officials and business people who traveled a lot and brought their kids with them for extended stays in English-speaking countries. A few of my students had lived for a period of time in America, England, Japan,

Germany, and other places. I felt like I was teaching in a multicultural classroom that could be anywhere in the world!

THE MOST IMPORTANT WORDS FOR THE YEAR: ADAPTATION AND ADJUSTMENT

As September progressed, I began to notice a few major differences between teaching in Mongolia and teaching in Canada. It was Friday afternoon, and I decided that I would take my class on a science field trip to the nearby Tuul River to observe some of the Mongolian wildlife. Throughout my training as a teacher in Ontario, the notion of "Safety First!" was always emphasized, so as my class of 10 and 11 year olds approached the river, I reminded them not to get too close to the water. Knowing that I also had my program assistant to help supervise the children, I turned my attention to a group of children who were trying to catch an insect for observation and went to assist them. Shortly after helping catch some large, previously unknown (to me) bug, I turned around to see the rest of my class—along with my program assistant—playing on an island about 30 feet from shore in the middle of the river. Led by my program assistant, they had hopped on stones, with varied success, to get themselves there. I thought to myself that if I had allowed such behavior with one of my classes in Ontario, I would have received many angry phone calls from parents that night telling me I had endangered their children. I looked around me to see all the children playing on the island, a car parked in the middle of the river with three men washing it, and the usual herd of sheep and cows drinking from the same river bank that I was standing on. I was finally hit by the complete realization that I was teaching in Mongolia, not Ontario.

The ASU teaches The Ontario Curriculum, which is a major reason for hiring Canadian-trained teachers. Traditional Mongolian teaching consists purely of teacher-directed learning, with lots of memorization and repetitive work. Canadian teachers are taught to be fun, innovative, and flexible, and so we are prepared to handle the many challenges that come with teaching in diverse situations. As the year went on, the words flexible and innovative began to stand out as reasons for my hiring. The

Ontario Curriculum puts a large emphasis on hands-on learning, especially in science, where experiments are necessary to ensure student understanding. Experiments require supplies, and although this relatively new school was fairly wealthy, Mongolia simply does not have a lot of these supplies—this is where creativity and innovation came in! Substituting coffee grinds for brown sugar, making my own play dough, using balloons as makeshift globes, I did whatever it took to attempt the various science experiments that my students were expected to complete. Growing up in a city in Canada where you could find basically anything you needed by going to the nearest Wal-Mart, this lack of access to supplies was a big adjustment. Mongolia does have many stores, but they do not cater to educational needs. Anything ASU needed in terms of school supplies was shipped from North America, which could take months.

Even on days when I felt my creativity and innovation were at their best, I hit snags that brought my lesson to a complete halt. One science period in early November, my class was doing an experiment on shadows, and we were making very basic sundials. We went outside around 10 a.m. on an extremely cold day to test our creations. Up to this point, the sunlight in Mongolia had been very bright, and I had only experienced one or two cloudy days in Ulaanbaatar. Mongolia gets very little precipitation since it's a desert. But on this day, the sky looked cloudy and no sunlight made it through. We returned to the classroom and decided we would test our sundials the following day, since consecutive cloudy days were unheard of up to that point. The next day we went outside and it was extremely cold once again, and, sure enough, it was cloudier than the day before. I commented to one of my students that I found it so strange for it to be cloudy two days in a row. The student informed me that I was seeing smoke, not clouds. Apparently once it gets cold in Mongolia, people burn cow dung and various other materials to heat their gers, and most days the sky will remain filled with smoke. That night when I returned home from school the Weather Network Web site said, "Ulaanbaatar, Mongolia, −29 degrees with Smoke"—and I thought I already understood the differences between teaching in Ontario and teaching in Mongolia. Little did I know!

Teaching in Mongolia

I found the differences in resources available to such schools go far beyond difficulties such as a lack of science supplies and the delayed arrival of books. Positions such as guidance counselors, which we would consider to be standard in Ontario, are still unheard of here. There are no systems in place to identify children with special needs. I have no official qualifications to formally identify children with learning or behavioral disabilities, but through my experiences working at a summer camp specifically for children with these disabilities, I have learned to recognize some of the obvious signs, and they are apparent in many children here. There are no special classes, teachers, or extra help set up for them; as a consequence, these students are expected to perform at the same level as any other student in the classroom. This puts additional stress on me, as I feel the moral obligation as a teacher to ensure the best learning environment for all of my students. In my classroom, there is huge variation in the students' learning abilities. I am often caught between the needs of the higher achieving students who are ready to move on to new material and the needs of the few students still trying to grasp the basic concepts of the lesson.

The students at ASU do not represent a sample of the general student population in Mongolia. My students all come from high-income families, and many rarely see their parents, who tend to be too busy with their business affairs. This void really deprives the students of an authority figure who sets and enforces rules and discipline. Teaching students whose main authority figure is their driver or nanny has shown me that they seem to think they can do what they want. This attitude has created issues in my classroom; for example, some students don't do their homework because there is no one home to make them do it or even question whether they have any. I have also found that the students here become very clingy and needy, as many of them do not see their parents much and look to me, their teacher, as a role model. Being viewed as a role model is a nice feeling but worrisome at the same time.

The students can also be an amazing resource. They tell me of life outside the school, which sadly I do not get to experience much since the first year of teaching is a full-time job and more! Only the younger population of Mongolians can speak English, so getting around in the town is difficult. I often have my students write out directions in Mongolian that I can hand to a cab driver or write the names of things I want to purchase from a pharmacy or other specialty store. They teach me about the geography of the country when they explain where they traveled on the weekend and what they do outside of school for fun. My students have become one of my greatest resources for understanding life outside of the school in Mongolia.

Inside of school, the students have their issues in terms of loving to talk all the time and roughhousing with each other, which can be attributed to Mongolian culture since wrestling is their national sport—but the kids are amazing. They want to learn, and they love to have fun while doing it. One thing I love about Mongolia is how students and parents truly appreciate teachers, and they let you know it. I often have parents come and tell me that they appreciate what I do and how happy their children seem to be since coming to ASU. They often bring me lunch or gifts after school and invite me to their homes for dinner or to their child's birthday party. I truly feel appreciated as a teacher here in Mongolia.

Whenever a challenge arises inside the school, I have found that the best person to use as a resource is the other Grade 6 teacher. She has been teaching internationally for 25 years. When the school is missing a book or math manipulative, I turn to her for materials. When I am having problems with a student's behavior or a student is having a difficult time picking up a new concept, I know I can always turn to her for advice. I have learned that experienced teachers are the best resource. I have gained more practical information from actually teaching and watching or questioning other teachers this year than I did sitting through any class in teachers college.

Challenges Outside of the School

The end of summer and beginning of fall here in Ulaanbaatar are beautiful. Hiking in the nearby mountains every weekend, shopping in the open-air markets of the city, and going to outdoor restaurants for dinner several times a week were just a few of the activities I enjoyed in my spare time. The challenges began once the weather turned cold. I had researched the challenges of Mongolia in terms of the weather. The temperature drops down around –30° at night, and with the windchill factor it frequently hits –50°. With the cold comes smoke! The air isn't fresh, but the school is raised up above the city enough that the smoke does not affect the air quality around the school and living area. With the extreme cold also comes boredom and cabin fever! Many days (too many) are spent indoors because of the intolerable cold. There is one major motivating factor to go into the city on even the coldest of days: living here is cheap. The Mongolian currency is very weak, and since the international schools in Mongolia pay in U.S. dollars, teachers have a lot of financial freedom. Dining out, grocery shopping, travel and tourism, and visiting the Mongolian pubs and clubs are within any budget. Another issue is the language barrier. The Mongolian language is a tough language to learn, but once you master the basics (simple directions, questions and counting to 10) it is possible to survive in the big city.

I am often asked if I would come back to Ulaanbaatar, Mongolia, to teach again. My response is easy: most definitely. The children are amazing—they love to have fun, they love to sing and be active, and they accept challenges with open arms. Teaching here has fulfilled all of my expectations for my first year of teaching. It has been rewarding, challenging, and an amazing learning experience. Many times I have called and e-mailed home to complain about the –40° weather at night or the smoke-filled air in the city during the winter, but these issues are offset by the amazing experiences I have had and act only to ensure that people will continue to ask me my favorite question, "Why?"

Paul's Tips for Traveling Teachers

What to Bring

- My school supplied me with a list of what to bring to Mongolia to prepare for the weather and living conditions. Bring lots of warm clothes, and I am talking about hats that cover most of your face. It gets very cold!
- I would also recommend bringing any materials that might assist in your lessons. Teaching resources and materials for activities and lessons are hard to find in Mongolia. Stores here concentrate more on essentials for living such as clothing and food. Stationery stores are poorly stocked
- The children here love music and singing, so bring music-related resources
- The winter months can get boring (I can only put up with the extreme cold and explore the same mountains so many times), so bring lots of activities to keep you busy such as board games, books, video games—anything that you can think of to stay busy. The winter here is long and there is not much snow, so outdoor sports like hockey are very popular and are great for staying active

What to Expect

- In September, early October, late May, and early June, it's beautiful and warm outside. The rest of the year is very cold with very little snow. Other than the extreme cold and lack of teaching resources, which have already been mentioned, you need to think about whether you want to return home or travel throughout the year. Mongolia is a great place to travel, but there are also many (warmer) nearby countries, which are great to explore
- Flying home to Canada takes about 24–30 hours, and there is a time difference of 12 or 13 hours, depending on daylight savings. If it's Saturday at 1 p.m. in Ontario, it's Sunday at 2 a.m. here in Mongolia! It costs approximately $1,600 to fly round-trip to Ontario. Be prepared for jet lag and flight delays in the wintertime

Teaching in Mongolia

IMPORTANT PAPERWORK

Schools here will bend over backward to ensure you get all of your paperwork filled out on time and will even pay all of the fees.

- The most important paperwork that you are expected to take care of on your own is an HIV test, which is required to get your Mongolian visa. The school will send you all of the paperwork that you need for your work visa and Mongolian entrance visa. These fees will be around $150, but the school will reimburse you once you arrive

FINANCIAL CONSIDERATIONS

Living in Mongolia is very inexpensive. Going out for dinner and a drink at a nice restaurant will cost you about 7–8 U.S. dollars. Like most international schools, ASU pays for your living expenses (except for food and telephone), so your only expenses are food, leisure activities, and any travel that you plan on doing.

IF I HAD TO DO IT AGAIN, I WOULD...

I would have traveled more within Mongolia. Outside of the major city of Ulaanbaatar, which is smoke filled and dirty, Mongolia is a beautiful country. The landscape is incredible, especially the Gobi Desert, which is gorgeous and very diverse. I spent all of my holidays traveling to warmer locations within Southern Asia such as Thailand, which was also a very highly recommended trip.

THINGS I WOULD LIKE TO HAVE KNOWN

- More information about the health system in Mongolia would have been helpful. Health concerns have arisen with several people at my school. There is no emergency number (like 911) that you can call here if you have a serious emergency, so knowing the right people and the right numbers to call is essential!
- The school will provide you with information and a health plan for free, but the accessibility of these health facilities still seems sketchy at times, since the doctors at hospitals often do not speak English

- Mongolian currency cannot be exchanged anywhere in the world except within Mongolia, so before you leave, make sure to change all your currency into U.S. dollars or some other currency that would be more useful

WHERE IS PAUL NOW?

I recently signed another 1-year contract to stay and teach in Mongolia. As much as I would love to continue to travel and see the world, I feel a very strong obligation to stay at my first teaching job for at least 2 years. I am told that every other international school requires their new teachers to sign 2-year contracts and that it would not look good on my résumé to leave after only 1 year, especially given that it's my first year of teaching. However, demonstrating a 2-year commitment to my first teaching job is definitely not my sole reason for staying in Mongolia for another year. I have contemplated going back to school in Canada to complete my masters in education, but I have found several international schools that offer this degree to their teachers for little to no cost. Many of these schools are in much warmer locations, so this option is appealing to me; but as I stated before, I do truly enjoy it here. The students are great, the country is very interesting, and I love the challenge of being here. But it's a big world, and soon the time will come for me to continue exploring it, and what better way to do so than to combine travel with my passion for teaching!

CHAPTER 4

TEACHING IN NEW ZEALAND

Anita Cunningham

During my bachelor of education year, while on Christmas vacation, I was perusing the Internet looking for alternatives to the Ontario school system. The lack of job prospects was disheartening, as was the notion that I would have to supply teach to earn my way into a full-time teaching position. I was confident that I was worth more. I found a New Zealand government Web site that was encouraging foreign-trained teachers to come to New Zealand and teach its wonderful students (http://www.teachnz.govt.nz). I was hooked! The Web site talked of offering relocation grants and a virtual signing bonus. This was a far cry from Ontario school boards' offers of supply teaching 2 days a week! I quickly e-mailed the link to my new boyfriend with the subject line "What do you think?" He thought it was great, but I knew he would go along with any plan I had as long as it meant he could get away with not being the organizer! The Web site also included some fantastic links to the New Zealand Ministry of Education, with information about the curriculum and some facts about the regions of the country. Full details of our fascinating job search can be found at the end of our story.

AND IT BEGINS

We believe our teaching experience in New Zealand was unique due to the isolated location and the socioeconomic situation there. We do not assume that our experiences would have been the same in every part of the country.

DECEMBER 14

We are officially employed as teachers! The only thing we still need to do is apply for work visas, but we shouldn't have any problems now that we have a job offer and a principal who knows how to pull some strings. As you can imagine, we are both excited to finally have some good news and to start making plans.

The Okaihau College is in the Northland (a 3- to 4-hour drive north of Auckland) and has 500 students and 35 staff members. The town itself has a population of approximately 200 people, but there's a larger town about 30 minutes away. The town isn't on the coast, but a 30-minute drive to the east is the Pacific Ocean, and 30 minutes to the west is the Tasman Sea. I think we may learn how to sail and scuba dive! Andy will be the new math teacher, and I will be teaching English and some social sciences (history and geography). We don't know much else about the place or school but are looking forward to the next part of our adventure. I'm just glad we won't have to count our pennies anymore. I think the principal was impressed with my glowing references and the fact that we weren't deterred by the small size or remote location of the school.

So now, it's time to prepare lesson plans and figure out how to pronounce these funny names of towns and people (the school is 65% Maori, so we will have a lot to learn)!

Early January

The first day of school arrived and I was warned to be tough. Apparently my version of tough isn't really tough. I can honestly say that day was the worst experience of my very short teaching profession. Will it be the worst I experience? I sure hope so. The day started with the staff being confused about the opening ceremonies that started in 20 minutes. I couldn't remember anyone's name, and at the last minute before the welcoming ceremony, or *powhiri*, I was told that I would have to give a speech introducing myself to the entire staff, student body, and parents. Public speaking is not my favorite activity and actually brings me to tears (and sharp shooting pains in my stomach, not to mention the profuse sweating). We entered the hall to the mournfully beautiful wailing sounds of the traditional Maori singers. We were being welcomed into the school with an official Maori Welcome Powhiri. I was moved but too overwhelmed to soak in the significance of this moment. I floated up on stage where I worried my sweat stains would show and took my seat along with eight other new staff members. The speeches were made, prayers were said, and after 10 minutes I found the courage to look at the audience. So many people were packed into a small hall and all were looking eagerly at the new staff; they seemed to be in awe. Gavin (who became a close friend) started the speeches and of course mentioned rugby—the crowd cheered. What was this, a high school popularity contest again? When it was my turn, I must have spoken. I must have introduced myself and my country, mentioned my family back home that was missing me, and said something about wanting an adventure in a beautiful country. I know this only because my students told me months later, when they were nervous about their public speeches and I attempted to placate their fears by revealing my own nervousness and my inability to remember my opening speech. They giggled.

So, I took my 29 seventh-grade students back to my classroom, which was next to my partner's (Andy) classroom, thank goodness. Being close to him brought me huge comfort. Our rooms were joined by a door—I thought of it as an emergency door to safety. My seventh graders listened attentively for 10 minutes and then couldn't handle it any longer. They were almost bursting out of their seats after a summer holiday of running and swimming, but I hadn't finished my talk. My thoughts began to spiral, "Well, I'll just give my stern teacher look and that will stop them. OK, that didn't work; maybe if I move closer to them while continuing my teacher look. Oh, too bad I can't maneuver myself to them in this maze of tightly packed desks. If only I knew their names!! More realistically, if only I could pronounce their names!! Ah, thank God for short classes!"

There were about 50 parents present to support their seventh-grade students on that first day. It was an amazing feeling to see these smiling parents. I had one parent come up to me and give me a half hug and say how glad she was to have her daughter in my class. I had another couple walk their child to class, and when I invited them in, they beamed. I sent a letter of introduction home with the students that day and called all the parents the next week. Apparently that kind of contact is rarely made by teachers, but it's an extremely good thing to do with the Maori parents. I've been reading up on Maori culture; I still can't pronounce their names, but we'll get there!

My 29 seventh graders are nervous and full of energy and questions about Canada. We need to work on the blurting out of questions and answers, but that's a typical challenge. I have a nightmare class of eighth graders who seem to think speaking constantly and grabbing at each other is okay. I guess that behavior is typical of eighth graders who are bored, so I need to move forward instead of going over rules. I wish they'd just come to school knowing all those routines.

We've experienced the confusion of handing out all the paperwork one needs to distribute to a class of kids who still just want to be on summer vacation. I must admit I forgot a number of things to hand out, but oh well—nothing major like tuition fees! I took my students on a tour of the school and got us all lost. I answered a million questions; I just hope I didn't give out any misinformation. I had one sweet boy come up to me and say he was sorry his uniform wasn't right and hand me a note from his mom about not having enough money for the school-regulation shoes. I really think there's a problem when the school system makes kids buy a certain type of shoe or notebook. Maybe they think a *Lord of the Rings* binder might distract the kids from my English lesson! My Grade 8 English class was a nightmare. While playing a good get-to-know-you game of classroom bingo (for you nonteachers, that involves walking around collecting signatures on a bingo card of random things like who likes to eat pizza or who knows how to surf), one boy was trying to pull over my metal shelving unit. I asked him what he was doing and he said, "Miss, it won't fall over on me, honest." I didn't take his word for it. Maybe some seatwork is a better way to start?

Now that I'm home, I am more exhausted than I have ever been and am relieved the day is done. The important thing is that I'm alive and so are all my students, and at the end of the day that's all we can ask from the first day of school! I am a teacher getting paid to do what I love, and it feels good.

FEBRUARY

There are so many things I take for granted. My students ask me constantly, "What language do they speak in Canada?" and when I say English, they are surprised because they can't fathom why I have a funny accent. My students are fascinated by North American schools that they see on television. "Miss, what are lockers?" someone asks. One boy in the class shouts out, "It's where they store their winter boots in school. I know because I have cousins in New York." Good answer, but not totally true. They are fascinated by the idea of school being in only one building, not understanding that students wouldn't attend classes if they had to go outside in 30° weather! The idea of a snow day baffles them; "So school's just closed?" They get so confused when I show them a map of the world and put a pushpin where I live in Canada (near North Bay) and a pushpin where I live in New Zealand. They see the size difference of the countries and ask if the map is wrong.

My class has some unique students about whom I need to have more information. One student has anger-management problems. He is a clever student with poor social skills and seems to be teased by some of the girls. I can never catch the teasing, though, and he doesn't want to talk about it. The other day he was on his way to the bathroom, and as he was walking by my window outside, he turned and came running back in the doorway, grabbed a chair, and raised it over his head. It was like a movie was playing in front of me, but I did snap out of it quickly enough to grab the chair from him. Thank God he is only 11 years old and not yet very strong. I had to restrain him and force him out of the classroom. All I could think about was the rule of "Don't touch the students," which was drilled into our heads in teachers college in Ontario. I know I did the right thing; I protected the class, even though some of them were bullies. Of course the young man was suspended and the bullies received no consequences. Discipline in the school is flawed.

March 10

We are now 6 weeks into school, with only 5 weeks until the first-term break. I've had more ups and downs than ever in my life. There have been times when I've felt useless and others when I've felt pleased with my skills and compassion. There have been times when I felt a student's poor behavior was all my fault and others when I realized that I was responsible for putting a smile on someone's face. Sometimes I feel there is not enough of me to satisfy all these needy students, and other times the kids manage to do something wonderful that helps me—makes my life easier—and they give back to me.

I'm teaching Grade 8 English to 25 students (8MG is how they are referred to) 1 hour each day, 5 days a week. The students are very needy both academically and socially. Many are living in difficult family situations: some are being raised by grandparents, single parents, or drunken fathers; some have been abandoned by their mothers; and some have illiterate parents. But some students have marvelous parents who check their homework every night and make a point of coming in to meet me (the new teacher). The class is filled with 25 students, all of them reading at least two grades below grade level. One of them reads as low as Grade 1. They also have difficulty with common social tasks like listening to their peers and entering a classroom quietly. All the teachers and administrators got together and brainstormed ways to deal more effectively with the students. Our solution was to post "Respect is…" signs in all our classrooms. Now we just have to wait and watch. Change takes time and optimism, and I'm trying hard to be optimistic. On a good day I feel I'm on a roller coaster with them. Some days when they leave my classroom, I think, "What have I done to deserve this?" Until I can get their behavior under control, I am stuck having them do a lot of reading and independent projects. I find it ironic that all those teachers in my life and in the school who warned me, "Don't smile until Christmas" were right. But that kind of sternness just wasn't in me. I wanted to be like a big hug, ready to motivate and teach with compassion and patience. My situation now is so far from where I intended to be.

I'm also teaching a Grade 9 English class of 25 students (9CD is how they are referred to). I teach them 1 hour a day for 4 days each week. This group seems to completely lack motivation to succeed, complete a project, or listen to their teacher. The girls are tough and give me attitude over any type of request. The kids call them *the evils*; in my day it was called the glare. But whatever you want to call it, it is like a death stare meant to show utter indifference. Teenage girls seem to have mastered that one! The boys seem to refer to everything as gay: my projects, the reading material, and each other, and they do not view this as a positive thing. I resort to giving out detentions for late projects and refusal to do work during class time. I spend my lunch hours chasing kids down and forcing them to sit in my room and not do work. I'm giving so much of my time to this class and feeling like I'm not making progress. One boy was encouraged to leave school by the administration after he repeatedly tried to intimidate me when asked to get to work. He would stand in my face, arms crossed, a look of anger and hatred beaming down on me. He entered my room this way. After he left, it came out during a staff meeting that the boy (14 years old) had physically abused his own mother. Yikes.

My original form class is a Grade 7 class of 29 students (7AC is how they are referred to). I was not eager to be assigned a junior class, but the more I am at this school, the more I realize being assigned this group was a saving grace. I don't have to worry about standardized testing and national exams. I teach my form class English and social studies for a total of 10 hours a week. The students' abilities are so varied that I find I must give at least two lessons, and some days I do four different activities with four different reading levels and give four different assignments. My classroom is so small that there isn't enough room to have 29 desks and maintain aisles. I have a hard time keeping the noise level down and the disruptive kids separated; there are just too many of them for me to be effective. The hardest part about being a form teacher is the management and care of so many students. While one was asking where to drop her clothes from physical education (PE), another was handing me money for something about which I had no idea.

After 3 weeks, the administration saw the need to split the three Grade 7 classes into four separate classes and keep the students they considered the high-end academic achievers in one class. Luckily I had an ally who said I should get the top Grade 7 form, and the administration listened to her. I doubt I would have made it otherwise. My new form class is 22 students—18 above average and 4 average students. I have 4 students who are classified as gifted. What a treat to be given such a class in my first year! The class is chatty but bursting with energy. When they are given a task, they dive into it. They are bonding and getting used to my rules. The beauty of the class is they want to succeed and to be liked by their teacher, so it only takes a look from me to get most of them to stop being disruptive. I have 2 students who are disruptive, and they challenge me daily. One has enough pride for 20 adult males and becomes angry and defensive at the drop of a hat. For example, if I ask him to put his desk down on its four legs, he looks at me as though I've insulted his manhood. I've worked out ways to communicate what I need from him without speaking, and I enjoy teaching him now. After I had acknowledged his intelligence, he began to respect me more.

I am thankful today for my administrative support. If my Grade 9 boy who was trying to intimidate me had remained, I don't know what I would have done—but the administration supported me and believed me and took decisive action quickly. I am thankful for my vice principal, who knows I'm struggling with my eighth-grade students and their behavior and will randomly walk by to make her presence known. By doing so, she communicates to the students that she is on my side and they need to follow my instructions. The dean in charge of seventh and eighth grades and has even come into my classroom to show her support. Their presence means more than I can communicate here. Imagine a rambunctious class, where students are constantly throwing paper, shouting out, talking, and doing very little work. When I would speak, so would the students—over top of me. They test the new teachers, especially the young ones (just like in Ontario schools, but more so). When the respected older staff, like the dean and vice principal, entered the room, the atmosphere changed, as if the students were acknowledging that what they were doing was wrong. My vice principal has listened to me complain after school and has given me pep talks. She has cried with me and supported me, and it has only been 6 weeks!

March 30

I've never met such a welcoming group of people before. From the first day, we were given the household goods we needed: couch, lounge chairs, kitchen table and chairs—essentially everything we needed to furnish our empty house. Over time we've been given even more: a dehumidifier, videos, a television, etc. They offer these things along with dinner invitations and wood for our fireplace as though it's nothing. But it's not just the material goods we appreciate. They have listened on our bad days, shared worksheets and lesson plans, provided help settling a class, and dispensed advice on students. I've found a companion and mentor in our head of the Department of Special Needs, who is a fellow

Grade 7 form teacher. She understands me. She laughs at my jokes and listens to me complain. We make each other giggle during boring staff meetings. I think it has something to do with her reminding me of my mother.

I'm frustrated at the moment with the assessment system in place in New Zealand. It doesn't make sense to me. I wonder how I would have liked this system as a student, and I always come up with the same answer—I would have hated it! To be more specific, the Ministry of Education establishes criteria for marking the many different types of English tasks (strands). The levels are established by what you should be doing at each grade level. So, a Level 1 marker is for Grades 1 and 2, Level 2 is for Grades 3 and 4, and so on. There are still 2– and 3+ markers, but for the most part a student should be moving up at least one full level for each grade from the beginning of the school year to the end; if not, something is wrong. So during a regular school year, a teacher should assess formal writing (newspaper article, essay, structured paragraph, or research report) at least three times. There are six different strands, and all six strands have to be assessed each term (four terms). I am drowning in so much marking, and it's only the first term.

The other part of the level system that bothers me is that the rubric used is for all junior classes (Grades 7–10). So, my Grade 7 students are being compared to all junior students, and they end up achieving only a Level 3 or 4 even though their assessment rubric goes up to Level 6. I feel like they are being set up to never achieve 100%. Last week I had a paper submitted by my Grade 7 student, and I thought it was a Level 5 (Grade 9). To check myself, I took the paper to the department leader and was informed that it was close to impossible for a Grade 7 to achieve a Level 5. I was interpreting the rubric incorrectly. The problem with the rubric is that it is so vague and open to interpretation that I was using my professional judgement. Apparently that was a mistake.

On the flip side, one of my Grade 9 students received a Level 2 for his creative writing (descriptive writing) piece and was furious at me for giving him this mark when he discovered that it translated into his work being at a Grade 2–3 level. I never received another piece of creative writing from this student—why would he hand in anything after such an insult? The students don't take the news that they're working six grades below their peers well; they become discouraged and begin to hate the subject. I would, too.

April 4

Birthdays were always a huge event in my family, with fancy cakes and streamers. My siblings and I always felt special on our birthdays. Typically the day started with a computer-generated banner hung in the kitchen to welcome in our day. It was slightly funny because the dot-matrix printer would run all night, so we knew the sign was coming! Later, when birthdays became more about friends, I recall many fun birthday parties involving a craft or adventure. So, being away from home for my 27th birthday was another reminder of how much I missed my friends and family. Andy surprised me with a wonderful present, and his parents purchased an Oprah magazine for me (my favorite, and something I couldn't justify buying for myself at $18). We had a wonderful dinner with friends and I spoke to my family. On Monday I arrived at school still glowing from the celebration. The day was normal until my third period (right before lunch) when my friend Lynne asked me to hang back in the staff room after morning tea break. "But I'm teaching!" I exclaimed. Lynne responded with a nonchalant "Oh well. They won't burn the room down." Eventually we walked over to my class (her coming with me was strange) to be met by a chorus of "Happy Birthday!" My Grade 7 students had arranged a surprise party for me. These students, who didn't have much money, had baked cakes and cupcakes and purchased enough sugary snacks to last a week. I felt honored that they had gone to all this trouble and cared enough to make my birthday special. We didn't do an ounce of work that period, but we chatted, played charades, and celebrated my special day.

April 12

New Zealand works on a four-term school year instead of using semesters. Term 1 begins at the end of January and runs for 11 weeks. And then comes the blissful term break—2 weeks off. Term 2 is 10 weeks long, and then we have another 2 weeks off. Term 3 is 9 weeks long with another 2 weeks off. Finally, Term 4 is 9 weeks long followed by 7 weeks of summer holiday, which falls over Christmas. I must admit that the idea sounds lovely, but when you're in the middle of Term 1, you're drowning. I did lots of counting that term—I always knew how many sleeps until Friday. The minute Sunday night rolled around, my heart sank and I became irritable. Andy and I filled our free time with short hiking trips to deal with our frustration and exhaustion. Luckily my parents came to visit in mid-February to brighten up my life.

When Term 1 break came, we were racing out of Okaihau at exactly 4 p.m. We had 2 weeks of adventure and abandonment planned in the South Island. Our partners in crime were our British neighbors and best friends, who were also new to Okaihau. We explored, hiked, challenged ourselves physically, and returned somewhat rejuvenated. I am optimistic that Term 2 will be an improvement, but I still carry a sense of dread. Is that possible? Can I survive 10 more weeks if they're like Term 1?

May 9

I am all for integration. I believe that when we are with motivated people who are high achievers, we become better versions of ourselves. When our peers challenge us to do better, we often rise to the challenge. However (you knew the *but* was coming), when the classes have 25 or more students without education assistants or resource help, a multilevel classroom doesn't work. Students here aren't identified like in Ontario. Only students with mental or physical disabilities get extra help, whether it's one-on-one instruction, withdrawal time, resource time, help from an education assistant, or even funding. In our school, *special needs* is a label for the students who are deaf, have Down syndrome, or are neurologically dysfunctional. So, the student who I suspect to have fetal alcohol spectrum disorder or attention-deficit disorder or even a learning disorder in processing information receives nothing. The New Zealand Ministry of Education does not recognize these identifications as serious enough issues to warrant funding and help. The students who may or may not have myriad disorders and exceptionalities are left struggling in the mainstream classroom with nobody but the classroom teacher to help. Do they fail? Yes. Is this a surprise? Not to me. The result tends to be that behavioral issues run rampant. Students act up, throw things, swear; anything to avoid doing the task they can't do. If the assignment is writing, many sit there and refuse to do work because they're dyslexic. Then, when confronted, they become defiant and throw something, are sent out of class, are given a few detentions, but ultimately get out of doing the impossible task of writing. If I couldn't read or write effectively, I also would be frustrated. Students lash out for attention so that maybe the teacher will help them, or they do it just to hide their inabilities. Teachers seem to lack any knowledge of how to help these students. I'm a first-year teacher, and I can honestly say that except for one of my colleagues, I know more about students with special needs than any other staff member at this school. It is difficult for me, knowing that some of these students could be helped immensely by spending 30 minutes each day in a learning-strategies session to help support them. I'm only here for 1 year, and many of my ideas are foreign to these people. So, I vow to be patient with my students.

May 18

It's getting cooler here, and our uninsulated house is getting cooler. Our fireplace is burning every night now, but the heat just escapes through the walls, the single-pane windows, the gaps in the window frames, or the holes in the floor. Our dehumidifier is pumping 24 hours a day to keep the dampness out of our house. We climb into bed at night, and everything feels damp. Nice. However, we are enjoying our teaching and our extracurricular activities. Andy is golfing and playing badminton while

I continue my jogging, circuit training, and reading. We're half way through Term 2; there are only 5½ weeks until I fly home for 3 weeks. But who's counting!

The school runs a cross-country race every year. The course is practiced during PE classes, and then all the Year 7–9 students race for a 1 hour, competing for house points. The course goes off school property in places—running through streams and forests. The race was 2 weeks ago. During the race, one of our more challenging students sat in the bushes and shot at the other students with a BB gun. Of course, we from North America think, "Yikes, that's a weapon." A BB may not be a bullet, but a BB in the butt still hurts! Luckily, the boy was a horrible shot and he hit only one student, who was not seriously injured. As a result, he was suspended for 5 days. I can't imagine such a light punishment would have been doled out in Ontario for that type of behavior.

I teach another group of interesting Year 8 students who are fine as individuals but as a group can be horrific. One Monday, one of the boys kicked a possum he found (in the boys bathroom) hard and long enough to kill it. Later on the same day, a girl picked up another possum, swung it over her head, and slammed it on the ground, killing it. Possums are rat-like creatures the size of a small raccoon and are considered a nuisance here. But regardless of whether the behavior is directed at raccoons or seagulls, showing blatant disregard for life should be highly discouraged! Animal-cruelty protections don't extend to possums, so there was no punishment for any of these students.

May 29

Andy and I received our bonus, NZ$3,000 each, for committing to teaching in New Zealand. I've decided to spend my money on a flight home for Term 2 break. A trip home is my salvation in this chaos; when I think of spending 2 weeks at my cottage surrounded by people who love me, I smile. Just the thought is so heartwarming that it brings tears to my eyes. My niece, Emma, will be 8 months old at the time of my visit, and

I am both thrilled and nervous to meet this precious person. I receive e-mails from my parents twice a week, and they always include pictures of home. The recent pictures were of the 24th of May long weekend at the cottage: raking the beaches, planting trees, and a huge barbecue dinner. My family was covered in dirt and mud and bug spray and their muscles probably ached from the manual labor of opening our cottages, and I balled my eyes out for more than an hour. Why am I here when I could be at home?

June 8

I managed to survive my first professional evaluation! My seventh graders were rangy today, which made it difficult to hold their attention. I had one boy sit there like a bump on a log staring off into space. He's coming back at lunch to talk about what was going on with him. I had one boy act silly throughout the lesson, despite my efforts to settle him down. I made it through. I haven't read the feedback yet, but that will come, sooner rather than later I hope. I was nervous for the first 5 minutes and the last 5 minutes, when the bell rang and we weren't cleaned up yet. I hate that! I am still not used to these short classes (54 minutes). It's no wonder these teachers can't get through the material. Anyway, the evaluation is done, and I know I could have done some things differently, but for the most part I am proud of the way it went. The kids got the content I wanted and got more practice working as a team. In the end, that's all that matters.

All else is well. We will have parent–teacher night tonight. I'm scrambling around trying to update my kids' portfolios. We keep all the standardized tests, writing, and other work in one place, so I have to make copies of things done in their books, which can be a pain. I'm looking forward to meeting with the parents but wish that the parents of my more difficult students were coming.

I will start taking a literacy course next Wednesday. It's a 10-week program that teaches strategies to promote literacy in my classroom. Apparently, the methods are quite useful for all subjects and really help make reading a fun activity. I will get a cute little certificate, which I will add to my portfolio when I go home. We have a literacy specialist on staff participating in a nationwide study this year; she runs the literacy course.

June 22

The weather has turned quite cold here. Yesterday we had hail pelting against the windows and the roof. All the buildings have metal roofs, so the noise was deafening in my class yesterday. It only lasted a few minutes, but it caused some serious chaos. The kids asked me if it sounded like that when it snowed in Canada. I tried hard not to laugh!

August

I will never complain of the rain in April in Ontario again. Never have I experienced weeks of continuous rain like this before. Never have I felt so gloomy from endless days of rain. Our lawn is under ankle-deep water. Our driveway is a giant swimming pool. I now drive in and park in a different location each night to avoid the car sinking! It's been raining for so many days that I'm actually used to the pounding of rain on our metal roof. I don't even hear it anymore. I am learning to hate the rain with all my being. Not only do I hate it for limiting my activities and dampening my mood and molding my house. I also hate it for the way it makes my classroom smell. Imagine 25 students sitting in a closed room, dripping wet, in uniforms that are washed once a week but worn daily. The students are so used to being drenched by the rain that it doesn't stop them from playing rugby in the field at lunch or walking slowly to classes. It is a part of their life. They don't wear waterproof jackets or cover their hair with their sweater; they just accept it. I find myself thinking back to when I was a kid in school—playing with the snow, rolling in it, eating it, and throwing it. I immersed myself in the stuff. That was a normal Canadian childhood to me. Maybe being soaking wet is part of a normal New Zealand childhood?

August 8

Andy and I have been very busy this weekend. Andy was in Whangarei at a basketball tournament. He arrived home around 7 p.m., just 20 minutes before I did. We were preparing for an evening of cards with the neighbors when we heard a knock on the door. We opened it to find two angry parents. It turned out that one of Andy's basketball players on the senior team lied to him about where he should get out of the school van. He got off with his friends in Kaikohe, telling Andy he lived down the street, even though the student knew that his parents would be picking him up at the school in the next town over. The mom became hysterical, yelling and swearing at us, and then finally the father threatened Andy with a bash (party). And he didn't mean a party. Apparently all of the Okaihau teachers know where this family lives and know that their son is dropped off at the school. His mother was completely irrational. I wasn't scared so much as disbelieving that this woman had the nerve to come to our house and be abusive on a Friday night after Andy spent his entire day coaching her son. Eventually we got them out of our house and we called another basketball player (who, as it turned out, hadn't arrived home either, so obviously there was a party going on). I don't want Andy to ever drive that boy anywhere again.

SEPTEMBER 13

We had a student die on Sunday. He was in a car crash involving a head-on collision with another vehicle. His mum is said to be paralyzed (not confirmed by the family), and the student who was driving died instantly. He was in Year 12, so the school is in shock and upside down with kids leaving for the tangi, a 3-day funeral. Neither Andy nor I taught him. It was shocking to see the kids do the haka (warrior or spiritual dance and song) at an assembly with tears flowing down their faces. The boys-don't-cry attitude so prevalent in our culture is not present when the emotion is for a worthy warrior here in New Zealand. I had tears in my eyes just watching them.

September 16

My teaching career at Okaihau College has gone from "Get me the f--- out of here!" to "I can handle this" to "Hey, I think they've learned something!" One of my Year 8 boys has gone from not being able to spell *where* or *used* to writing a great story set in medieval times. We worked hard together with the spelling, but the ideas are all his. He even typed the correct spelling of words he hasn't had much luck writing, which makes me wonder if he might have a learning disability.

With only 9 weeks of teaching remaining, I can see how I might actually miss these kids! My seventh graders are writing pen-pal letters with one of my fellow Nipissing University graduates up in Nunavut (Whale Cove, to be exact). My kids are loving this activity and are creating a book about our culture here in New Zealand.

October

Progress is being made. It may have been due to the large number of students absent today, but I made progress with my Grade 8 students today. We've been building toward this day. They entered the classroom in a civilized manner, sat down, and did some work. Is there hope for tomorrow? Now that they're finished testing me, I'm learning that positive reinforcement works.

December

The end is upon me. Today is the last day of school and I have such conflicting feelings. One part of me is just counting down the days until I am home and it is Christmas and I am surrounded by my family and friends. The other part of me wants to cherish every moment of this good-bye so that I can grow from this experience. I think back to last February, when I thought that I couldn't go on here and that I'd made a mistake, and I understand that what doesn't kill you makes you stronger. I feel stronger from this experience.

My last day of school has arrived, and I have so many things to do. I made individual cards for my form class with a picture of our class on the front and a personal note inside to show the students how unique and important they are. When I handed them out, they lowered their eyes and shyly snuck glances up at me. Instantly I thought, I wish I'd done a better job at communicating this message earlier to them. We watched movies and gorged ourselves on popcorn. My Grade 8 students arrived in their usual loud fashion, bursting with energy and vying for my attention. After a few games of hangman, the good-byes started. The students gathered in a circle to sing a waiata (traditional song with hand gestures and movement). This one was a leaving song. The boys performed the traditional haka (like an intimidating warrior dance with pounding of fists on chests, stomping feet, and belting out of foreign words) for me, and the windows rattled. The emotion poured out of them and the tears ran down their cheeks. That's when it hit me that I would never see these young people again. Not on the street or accidentally in Georgian Mall, and I cried. I cried big, sloppy tears and did not try to brush them away. If they could show their appreciation for me, then I could do the same for them. Together we had grown so much, teaching each other valuable life lessons.

Anita's Tips for Traveling Teachers

How to Find a Teaching Job in New Zealand

Through a Web site, http://www.teachnz.govt.nz, I learned that there is another government-sponsored Web site that shows all education-related job postings across the whole country (http://www.edgazette.govt.nz). The *Educational Gazette* is a magazine that includes job postings. The Web site breaks down the postings by geographic location, making the job search easy. Schools are autonomous entities in New Zealand, and applications are made directly to the school principals for all jobs, even supply work; this system is very different from the school-board system in Ontario. Because the schools operate individually, principals in a region don't necessarily talk to each other like they do in Ontario, so it makes sense to apply for everything that fits your skills and qualifications. However, we found that there is very little hope of obtaining a job by applying from the comfort of your Canadian home. You will have to make the leap of faith and go to New Zealand to actually secure the job. Our British-trained teacher friends were hired over the phone, but the school was desperate, and one of them had 3 years of experience as a senior teacher.

The Web site (http://www.teachnz.govt.nz) encourages you to apply to the New Zealand Teachers Council for registration. The registration costs money, but without it, you will not even get an interview. The council is similar to the Ontario College of Teachers in that this organization is a new government organization designed to standardize the country's educational system, which is especially important since the schools are all separate. The schools try to deliver the same curriculum, but they have very few checks and balances. Applications should be completed and mailed before you even arrive in New Zealand. This way, if you are missing any Canadian documents, you can quickly send them off in the post with minimal headaches. The teachers council does not investigate your qualifications as a teacher, so submitting your provincial certificate of qualifications and registration is useless. The teachers council simply gets a report from the New Zealand Qualification Association (NZQA) and uses that information to grant you a teaching license.

The same Web site can also link you to NZQA, another government department that will take your money and determine your pay. It's crucial that you submit the correct documents and as much documentation as possible to show your education and experience. New Zealand is similar to Ontario in that you get more money as a teacher if you have a higher level degree (honors, masters, etc.). Sometimes the New Zealand equivalent of your degree does not exist; if that's the case, you're out of luck and you may have to settle for less money. But you should appeal the decision! An appeal costs extra, but it will be refunded if it is determined that you deserve to have your degree recognized. Again, send your documents before you leave to lessen the pain of this slow process, and send them at the same time as you send the documents to the teachers council. If requested, the findings of the NZQA can be faxed directly to the teachers council to save time.

The next step is to find a job and then apply for a work visa and permits. You must submit your letter of appointment or contract, application form, passport, and, you guessed it, more money. The forms are all available online (http://www.immigration.govt.nz) and are pretty easy to fill out. We did not secure jobs until we were in New Zealand, so the process may be different when you're overseas applying from outside the country. You send your passport through the mail (scary but safe) along with your forms. We didn't bother getting a work visa since we couldn't afford the extra cost at the time. If we wanted to leave the country later in our adventure, then we could reapply and have that additional visa added to our record. The work permit is what you need. We were quickly and flawlessly granted permission to work. Most principals will allow you to work while your paperwork is being finalized; in our experience, teachers do not get turned down for permits.

The next step is applying to the Inland Revenue (IRD) for your IRD number (equivalent to a social insurance number). You need this number in order to be paid, so don't leave this step undone or your first paycheck will be held up. This link is available online at http://www.teachnz.govt.nz. The school that hires you will apply on your behalf for your Ministry of Education employee number (MOE #), which is also required to be paid, but getting this number happens quickly and painlessly once you have your paperwork done for the NZQA and teachers council.

FINDING A TEACHING JOB IN NEW ZEALAND: THE HARSH REALITIES

In reality, the *Educational Gazette*, by law, has to post all jobs—even the phantom postings for jobs that really are already filled by someone who has experience and knows the students. You don't really have a chance at obtaining more than half the positions posted on the Web site. You can apply and get rejected, like we did for more than 4 months. It is disheartening, but it's important to keep a positive attitude. When things got tough, we broadened our search for employment to more remote areas. Some of the job postings included the tag line, "No actual position available." Don't even bother wasting the money for the fax on those postings, as it really has been filled internally.

Our biggest mistake was in our handling of the registration paperwork with the New Zealand Teachers Council and the NZQA. We brought our paperwork with us to New Zealand and dropped it off in person only to discover we didn't have the correct documents. When we were thousands of miles away from home, this mistake felt like the end of our world. Our police checks were to expire in 2 weeks, which would make them invalid. However, the teachers council would not accept our North Bay Police Department police checks because the wording was not specific enough. The Web site states a police check from the Royal Canadian Mounted Police (RCMP) or your local police department was sufficient. But in reality, New Zealanders don't quite understand the concept of multiple police departments—their country is too small to need such odd things. In the end, we had new police checks done through our local Ontario Provincial Police (OPP) offices but had them type another letter for each of us on (OPP) letterhead that included the date and our names, birth dates, driver's license numbers, and a sentence or two saying that a criminal record check for the "above mentioned Canadian citizen" that "checked the Canadian national and United States suppository for criminal activity showed no criminal record." The letter we received had the signature of the staff sergeant. We were thankful the New Zealand authorities accepted these since a police-records check with the RCMP can take up to 3 months and involves fingerprinting.

Our other problem was in assuming the request for proof of graduation meant sending official transcripts from all our universities. Apparently in New Zealand you must supply a notarized copy of your diploma. We giggled about this turn of events since our diplomas were lying under our beds at home (dusty, never looked at) in the fancy frames our parents splurged on at graduation day. So, 3 months later, after spending a few more dollars on notary fees and post fees, we had met this requirement. Through the relentless assistance of our parents, the paperwork was faxed and delivered by courier to the appropriate offices, and we qualified to teach in New Zealand.

Another problem was that our 4-year honors bachelor degrees were not recognized by NZQA as honors degrees. Instead they were recognized simply as 4-year degrees. Apparently, to receive an honors degree in New Zealand, you must finish a 3-year program and then apply for the honors year. Another discrepancy is that an honors degree in New Zealand requires completion of a thesis. This difference translated into my partner and I losing NZ$8,000 per year. We appealed the decision (paying an additional $250) and submitted letters from our university registrar offices, course descriptions, and transcripts. Despite our best efforts, the NZQA did not, in the end, recognize our degrees.

The Money Situation
You will not become rich teaching in this country. Teachers are paid on a similar scale to Ontario teachers. A beginning teacher with a 3- or 4-year university degree is paid about NZ$37,500 per year. If you are lucky enough to have your degree recognized as a 4-year honors degree, you will be paid $40,000 per year. If you can prove that you have years of experience, you will see your pay increase. Keep in mind that teachers' salaries top out in New Zealand far sooner than they do in Ontario. The maximum pay is about $55,000 per year, compared to Ontario's $80,000 per year.

Teachers are paid twice per month via direct deposit, and taxes come off directly. In New Zealand there is no need to file taxes, as the Inland Revenue determines your tax rate correctly in the beginning. At the end of the year, our records showed that we paid about $6,200 in taxes—far less than we would have paid in Ontario.

Bank fees were steep. Customer service was a foreign concept to these multi-million-dollar companies, which we found frustrating. We began to appreciate our Canadian bank, with its friendly faces, answers to our questions, and low fees. The banks in New Zealand charge fees to deposit money, to withdraw money, to transfer money from one account to another, and to use bank machines (even if they are at the bank with your account). On a normal month of grocery shopping and gas fill-ups, we would spend NZ$15 on bank fees for about 20 transactions. Our account was supposed to give us 20 free transactions if we kept a balance of $2,000. We maintained that balance but never received clear answers as to why we had to pay so much in fees. In the end, after calling and being put on hold so many times, I gave up and enjoyed my stay.

One warning about money comes from personal experience. I brought (as recommended by my Canadian bank) a cashier's check for $5,500, which was my entire savings from summer employment, and my partner brought $2,000 in traveler's checks; that was all the money we had until we found jobs. We used his traveler's checks to purchase a car for $1,600 and had the remaining $400 to spend on food and gas for our car. We opened a bank account with one of the three banks in the country that will open accounts for *visitors* (anyone without New Zealand citizenship) only to find out that my cashier's check would be on hold for 30 business days until it could be cleared by my Canadian bank. So we actually had only $200 from the remaining $400 for food and gas that was supposed to last us 30 days. Not only were we angry, we were desperate. After much begging, we found a bank manager willing to release $2,000 so that we could live. Unfortunately, the release of the remaining money took more than 30 days, and we were down to pennies by the time the money was released to us.

One New Zealand dollar was worth approximately C$0.83. When we returned to Canada, we saw our New Zealand savings dwindle away on exchange rates. But while in New Zealand, our dollar could go a long way (if we forgot about Canadian prices).

New Zealand pricing includes taxes, so the price on the sticker is the price you pay at the cash register; there's no need to mentally tabulate taxes. Consumers still pay the sales tax of 12%, but this method seemed pleasantly different. Some things we found to be cheaper than they were in Ontario. For example, our rent in our school-owned, three-bedroom home was NZ$400 per month. A loaf of bread was only $1 (remember, tax is already included), and a bag of apples cost $2. There were some clothing stores where you could get sweatshirts for $15 and dress pants for $25, which we thought was cheap. The quality of the clothes was similar to what you would find at Wal-Mart. Our favorite cheap purchase was fish 'n chips. It became a ritual for Andy and me to have fish 'n chips from our corner shop every Friday night. We would get two large pieces of deep-fried fish and a huge helping of fries for less than $5. When we had returned from New Zealand and completed our first hard week of teaching back home, we purchased the same meal (slightly skimpier on the fries, in my opinion) for $22. We haven't continued that ritual. However, not much else was cheap. Here are some examples of prices we found to be shocking:

- Gas: $1.25–$1.37/liter
- 24 cans of Coca-Cola: $14.99
- Electricity bill: $80/month in summer and $200/month in winter; we did not have a dishwasher, washing machine, dryer, computer, stereo, or many lights
- School supplies: $5 for a pack of five regular pens
- American magazines: *Oprah* was $18

Helpful Hints on How to Find a Teaching Job in New Zealand

A few things we wish we had done when applying for these positions are:

- Make follow-up phone calls if an in-person meeting cannot be arranged. Some deputy principals (same as a vice principal) who do the hiring will take the time to discuss the job with you if you take some initiative and show that you're really interested in the position

- Make connections with the New Zealand curriculum in the cover letter (available online through links at http://www.teachnz.govt.nz) so that principals can see the similarities between The Ontario Curriculum and that of New Zealand
- Refer to the grade(s) you taught as *year* (Grade 8 = Year 8). It's a small difference, but it confuses the principals who are not used to *grade* being used to refer to the achievement level of a student. In New Zealand, *grade* refers to the student's mark. Knowing the lingo helps
- Have a phone number for principals to contact you. Not all principals are comfortable with e-mail; some want a more personal contact. We bought an old cell phone and used pay-per-use rechargeable phone cards. It is free to the cell-phone owner to receive calls. Using the cell phone was also a convenient way to keep in touch with family for free!
- Don't expect the traditional interview. Most principals will sell the school to you during the interview, leaving you wondering where you stand or assuming the job is yours. We discovered that the principal is interested in your reaction to the information and in the questions you ask about the school. Ask informative and educated questions about things like opportunities for co-curricular participation, the community socioeconomic effects on student achievement, literacy strategies employed by the school, and so on
- During the paperwork stage, make sure you give them exactly what they're asking for. If in doubt, ask the teachers council or NZQA directly via e-mail or phone; believe me, the extra effort will prevent many headaches
- Arrive in New Zealand with a working holiday visa (if you qualify), which will allow you to supply teach temporarily until you find full-time work. It will also allow you to start teaching at your school on a moment's notice. Without this type of visa, you will have to get letters from all the schools that agree to put you on their supply lists (with dates you're on the list, contact information, position you will fill) and submit that to immigration services. This process is long and allows you to work only for those schools and only as a supply teacher. You'll have to pay again when you find full-time work

Where Is Anita Now?

I've returned home and, thankfully, have obtained employment with Simcoe County District School Board. I've had the opportunity to teach a variety of

English classes and to be a special-education resource teacher, and a student-success teacher. No longer do I have 25 to a class; now I have 32. No longer do I have unfailing administrative support in my classroom, and no longer do I have to explain that English *is* my first language! I miss many of the staff members who helped me get through the toughest year of my life, and I miss my vice principal, who offered emotional and professional support. Luckily, I have found a school that has a caring, supportive staff; it is a place I can now call home.

Andy and I got married a year and a half after our return and are settling into life in Simcoe County, just outside of Barrie and Orillia. I'm about to begin maternity leave for my first child, and I'm adjusting to this new life away from teaching by creating to-do lists and pursuing my masters of education degree. Andy is now a daddy, and though he still doesn't plan much, he still goes along with all my crazy ideas for adventure!

CHAPTER 5

TEACHING IN ST. VINCENT*

Miriam Drake

In August 2003, I took off with great eagerness for St. Vincent and the Grenadines. I didn't know this tiny chain of islands, located in the Caribbean just below St. Lucia, even existed until I replied to an advertisement in the *Toronto Star* and got the call for an interview. Leaving the security of home and jumping at the chance for adventure, I took a 1-year teaching contract. Arriving on the island, I quickly realized that I was no longer in Canada and that there would be no orientation; it was sink or swim. With everything jammed into two suitcases, I decided to swim. As the new Grade ½ teacher coming from Brantford, Ontario, I quickly encountered many new and strange things, from cockroaches and centipedes to hand-washing clothes and torrential rains; I didn't know if I would last a week, let alone a whole year. This is my story of leaving home, bridging a cultural divide, and experiencing a year of teaching that would change my life forever.

---

* Names of people have been changed for privacy.

How It Began

I had the same ritual every morning: get up, have breakfast, and then use the computer to search for a teaching job. Newly graduated from the Faculty of Education at Nipissing University and eager to make some money, I scanned the many job boards, newspapers, and school-board sites for a full-time teaching position. It was mid-July and I was sick of hearing family and friends ask, "So have you got a job for September yet?" So when I read the ad, *Small private school in Caribbean looking for primary/junior teacher*, it occurred to me that living in the Caribbean for a year might be a welcome change after having spent five cold winters in North Bay, Ontario. I had always wanted to travel, and this experience would look good on a résumé. The job seemed like an interesting opportunity, so I faxed them my cover letter and résumé, assuming that, as with the hundreds of other jobs for which I had applied, I wouldn't get a response.

A few weeks later, I received a call from one of the directors of the school asking me if I would come to an interview. Excited at this prospect, I immediately said yes and quickly wrote down the information he provided about the school and the island. That evening I went on the Internet to look up St. Vincent and the Grenadines and found that there wasn't a great deal of information available. What I did find out was that St. Vincent and the Grenadines is a small chain of islands south of St. Lucia and north of Grenada. The island of St. Vincent gained its independence from England in 1979. The capital city is Kingstown, and the language spoken is English.

A few days later, I went to the interview and asked more questions of my interviewers than they asked of me. They showed me pictures of the school and told me that it was the only private school on the island. A Canadian couple had opened the school 8 years earlier after retiring from the Toronto District School Board. They told me that the school only had 35 students from Junior Kindergarten to Grade 10 and that students were mostly local children, with a few expatriates. The staff was a mix of local Vincentian teachers and foreign teachers. The school provided teachers with accommodations, round-trip airfare, and pay in local currency. They stressed that conditions were very basic and the work would involve long hours because there were only a few teachers and very few resources. The school and accommodations were outside of the main city, but public transportation was good. They gave me a letter from a previous teacher that I read, and I was so excited that even the part about the cockroaches didn't bother me.

Reactions from friends and family were mixed when I told them what I was thinking about doing. Most were excited for me, but others had many questions and were worried about my safety, natural disasters, and what I would eat. I didn't have answers for most of these questions, and that made me nervous. Could I really do this? I had traveled across Canada and through a little of the United States, but I had never flown anywhere off of mainland North America.

I accepted the job and, along with signing the contract, realized there were many things to organize in a very short time. I needed to get a passport, a police check, inoculations, plane tickets, travel insurance, health insurance, and supplies for teaching. My parents' living room soon became a mini-warehouse, and my list of supplies got longer. I spent hours waiting on the phone to get quotes on tickets and insurance and spent the rest of my time at the drugstore, the grocery store, camping outfitters, and teacher supply outlets. I also had to go to the doctor's office to get blood work and shots every couple of days. I had to try to buy summer clothes while the stores were stocked with back–to–school clothing. I accumulated a mini-drugstore stocked with prescription drugs, Gravol, drugs to relieve diarrhea and constipation, and cold and sinus medications. There was equipment to buy: flashlights, a good water-filtration system, mosquito nets, batteries, and film. I also packed cookbooks, Ziploc bags, and powdered skim milk. I had no idea what I would need as a teacher, so I began to accrue another pile; this one had stickers, markers, pencils, scissors, glue, construction paper, and a few storybooks. My parents laughed as I packed my bag, found that it was too heavy, unpacked a few more things that I thought I could leave behind…repacked…too heavy…unpacked…repacked…weighed…until I finally had my two bags down to 70 pounds each. While preparing for the trip, I tried to fit in as many visits with friends and family as I could. Even though I was well organized, I was to find out that nothing could prepare me for the adventure upon which I was about to embark.

The night before my departure, with everything packed and ready, I went to bed hoping I hadn't forgotten anything. The next morning my parents drove me to the airport. We hugged and cried and I told them, "It will only be a year and we can e-mail and phone each other. A year isn't very long." However, after I got on the plane and put on my seatbelt, I broke down, admitted to myself that I was scared, and wondered what I was doing.

Arriving

The flight from Toronto to Barbados seemed long. As I awaited my connecting flight from Barbados to St. Vincent, I learned my first lesson in the Caribbean: nothing ever happens on time! I arrived in Barbados around noon and then had to wait 6 hours for my flight to finally leave for St. Vincent (I was only supposed to have a 3-hour layover.) The people at the help desk were tired of me checking as to whether I had missed my flight or not. With no way of calling my contact in St. Vincent, all I could do was wait and hope my ride would be there when I arrived.

When I got to St. Vincent, the immigration officer inspected and then stamped my passport. A customs officer opened the exit door for me, and I rolled my two 70-pound suitcases into the heat and blackness of night. A sea of brown-skinned faces looked at me strangely. Suddenly a woman approached me and said in a thick accent, "Are you Miriam? I'm Erica." Thank goodness I had found my roommate, or rather she had found me. I had arrived at 8:30 p.m., 3 hours after my flight had been scheduled to arrive from Barbados. We jammed my suitcases into the vice principal's tiny jeep and we were off, whipping around hairpin turns on the wrong side of the road, with me having no idea where I was being taken. As we drove, I could see the odd store; people sitting outside on their porches chatting with neighbors; dogs, goats, and cows on the side of the road; sailboats rocking back and forth in the dark ocean; and little lights on the hills where houses were. I realized I was a long way from home.

THE FIRST DAY

My first night on the island was not a restful one, even though I was exhausted from the trip. The heat and humidity were a lot to get used to, as were the sounds of dogs barking, traffic, and roosters crowing at 2 a.m. We only had slats for windows, so it didn't keep out the noise, and I wanted them open to catch the breeze from the ocean.

I got my first daylight glimpse of the island in the morning. Wow, what a sight! Green hills everywhere. What a difference from the brown flat landscape of Barbados. From my balcony I could see the ocean.

Erica, my roommate, was born in St. Vincent, although she had just moved back in the past 5 years from England. Her West Indian–English accent was very strong, and I had a hard time understanding her, but she was great about telling me all about the school and the island. I am glad that I shared accommodations with her.

Erica took me on my first van ride to Kingstown, which was a life-changing experience. The driving on the island was insane, but I still had all my limbs so I was thankful. Kingstown was very busy, as it was the main shopping day for locals. People were everywhere with carts trying to sell fruit (mangos, green oranges, and bananas), root vegetables (dasheen, sweet potatoes, and carrots), rice, fish, milk powder, and sweets. The sights and smells were more than my brain could take in. We did some grocery shopping but I didn't buy much, as I was still trying to get used to the currency exchange, and the ways the stores sold food was very different from the ways in Canada. The government market for fruits and vegetables had lots to offer, but my bartering skills were not good and I often paid too much. Erica also took me to the market for fish and meat. What an experience to see men with machetes hacking at carcasses. I thought I might just have to become a vegetarian as the smell and hygienic practices made my stomach do loop de loops. Because of my fair complexion, I stood out in the crowd, and many people came up to talk to me and to try to sell me things; however, due to the strong West Indian accent, I could understand very little of what was being said to me.

Preparing to Teach

We started at the school on Monday. My classroom was small, with four bare walls and a few dusty desks. The vice principal told me I would now be teaching Grade ½ instead of Grade 2/3 and that I now had 12 students instead of 7, so this changed the game plan quite a bit.

Monday and Tuesday were mainly spent cleaning my classroom, as the custodial staff didn't start until the following week. I was thankful for all the posters I brought to decorate the walls. The window markers were useless, though, as I had shutters for windows—no glass.

We seemed to have a pretty good set of math manipulatives, and there were books in the library, but craft and physical-education (PE) supplies were very minimal. The photocopier was broken, so I had to be creative with some of the activities I had wanted to do with the kids on the first day.

On Wednesday and Thursday, I was finally given my curriculum. It seemed pretty disorganized, but a lot of the topics were similar to those covered in a Grade ½ class in Ontario, so I was able to muddle through.

On Friday there was a school open house so that students could come to register, meet their teachers, and buy their school uniforms. I met most of my students, but they were fairly shy, as were the parents. It would take some time for them to warm up to me. One little boy was very excited to see my wall about Canada, and he kept asking me questions about polar bears and killer whales. The students were all adorable.

The school had five classes. Erica taught Grade Junior Kindergarten (JK) and Senior Kindergarten (SK), I had Grade ½, another Canadian teacher from Toronto taught Grade ¾, our vice principal from Michigan taught Grade 5/6, and two Vincentian teachers taught Grades 7–12.

The First Week

I survived my first week of school. There still wasn't a working photocopier or computer. I felt like I was in a *Little House on the Prairie* episode, where the kids had to write out everything by hand, which, in Grade 1, can be quite a challenge.

We started every morning with a schoolwide assembly, during which we sang the national anthem and made announcements. The assembly usually started at 8:45 a.m. but could begin at 9 or 9:30 depending on when all the students were dropped off at school. This variation made it hard to get a routine going.

One thing I noticed right off the bat was that the students were very polite, always answering with, "Yes, Miss." My students had a wide range of backgrounds. Most were born in St. Vincent, but two children were from Taiwan (and English was their second language), and one child was from Canada. I also had a developmentally delayed child. Most of the parents were working class, but I also had the governor general's child in my class.

I had 12 students (5 in first grade and 7 in second grade), mainly boys. They were a very talkative bunch but were well behaved. My students ranged from those with advanced abilities to a couple with special needs, so I had to learn to plan three lessons for each subject. The school had some resources, so I didn't have any trouble planning. I also became the music specialist in the school. So I taught music to grades 1–6 and led the choir and recorder groups.

It was truly an international school, as the teachers came from England, the United States, Cuba, Canada, and St. Vincent. The children were also from all over the world, so it made for a nice mix of cultures.

Getting Into the Swing of Things: September

St. Vincent was amazing. The island was made up of green, rolling volcanic hills and was surrounded by the beautiful blue–green waters of the ocean. I lived about a 20-minute drive from the main city, Kingstown, in a small village called Calliaqua (meaning calm sea).

My apartment was very nice; it had a living room, dining area, kitchen, bedroom, and balcony overlooking the ocean. My roommate joked that while it may have been third world outside our doorstep, inside our house it didn't need to be. So I had lots of comforts from home, like satellite service for the television (yes, I could still watch *Survivor*), a stereo, a DVD player, Internet service (although it took awhile to get), and a microwave. I was so grateful that Erica had all these luxuries. I only wished we had a washing machine, as every day I had to hand wash my clothes.

I slowly adjusted to island life. The weather was warm, with temperatures ranging from 26 °C to 32 °C most days, but my body was now used to the heat and the large amounts of water it needed to replenish itself. I felt better knowing that even the locals sweated, so it was not just me.

The hurricanes headed north of the Grenadines that year, so I thankfully didn't see the result of one. We did have 20 minutes of rain almost every day, and when it rained, it poured, so you didn't want to be outside. One evening we got 6 inches of rain in a matter of 30 minutes. I got caught in one downpour on the way home from church, and I was only a 3-minute jog from home, but there wasn't a dry piece of clothing left on my body when I got home.

I figured out the van system and eventually found it quite normal to squeeze 22 people into an extended minivan. The drivers drove very quickly and played their music very loudly. I had a couple of experiences with drivers thinking they could pass on a turn with oncoming traffic; I just closed my eyes and hoped we would make it, and we did make it safely to each of my destinations.

We usually went to Kingstown on Fridays and Saturdays to shop, and it was always packed since the shops were closed on Sundays and by 5 p.m. most days of the week. I got better at bartering and had certain vendors in the market that I would visit for my produce. I also learned to stomach the meat market. Boneless, skinless chicken breasts didn't exist in St. Vincent. The grocery store stocked most things I would eat or buy in Canada, but some things cost a bit more since they had to be shipped in (e.g., C$7 for a bag of Doritos). Even the President's Choice brand had made its way to the Caribbean.

Erica, my roommate, introduced me to the local food. I tried the traditional callalou soup, pig's tail, breadfruit, green oranges, pumpkin, and the fish, but I am definitely not a fish fan. My favorite dish was the sweet potato pudding (sort of like cake); it was very sweet. I decided that Vincentians didn't know how to make Pepsi, although they seemed to do well with Coca-Cola. The local beer, Hairoun, was comparable to Canadian beer. I was careful with the 80-proof rum, as it was known to knock your socks off.

The beach was very nice, and the nearest spot, known as Villa Beach, was only a 15-minute walk. It was a bit crowded on Sundays but generally quiet; but, being in the hotel hub of the island, it would become very busy in peak tourist season. The water was very warm and sharks weren't a worry, but jellyfish could sting, so you had to watch out for them. Erica and I would also go to a pool at a hotel just down the street from our house after school sometimes to relax.

Mosquitoes in the rainy season were a big problem. Despite sleeping in mosquito netting every night, I had bites covering my legs. But after I had been bitten for a few months, the mosquitoes didn't like my sweet Canadian blood any more. Cockroaches were gross but manageable. I got the technique down: spray…poison…stomp…spray…pick up with Kleenex and flush down the toilet. I put duct tape on the hole we thought they were coming from, but it didn't seem to stop them. We also had little geckos (lizards) that came into the house, but they ate the mosquitoes, so I didn't bother them. They ran away as soon as anyone came near them anyway.

In the first month I did a bit of traveling. I went to Bequia, the next island over. The hour-long ferry ride over was rough but worth it for the beach. I also was able to visit a private resort island called Young Island for a student's birthday party (a perk of having the governor general's child in your class). A room costs $400 (U.S. dollars) per night, so going over for an afternoon was quite a treat.

I had my first meet–the–teacher night at the end of September. I was busy getting my classroom prepared and getting my kids ready for their presentation, which went well despite the fact that I was missing half my students. The school choir also presented their first song and did a great job.

I learned that red eye (or pink eye, as we call it in Canada) is like the plague on the island. One weekend at the pharmacy, I needed to pick up some Visine for my eyes. My roommate went in to ask the pharmacist where we might find some and just mentioned the words *red eye*. People backed away from her so quickly that it was humorous. You would think she had said she had leprosy. The experience at the pharmacy seemed funny until later that week, when a student of mine got red eye and it spread like wildfire in a primary class. I had students dropping like flies.

Our school had an environmental focus that year, so we had a switch-off day, meaning we turned off all the lights, the photocopier, and the computers for one day. I managed to get my photocopying done ahead of time, but some of the teachers struggled with this concept. I also started a composting program, hoping we could plant a garden later that year.

Rain: October

On Sundays I usually spent the day at the beach with a few of the other teachers and their families. We would go to one of the local hotels in Villa Beach for lunch and a swim in their pool. Then we would go into the ocean for a dip in the sea. It was always a nice afternoon. I was able to work on my tan and get away from the planning and books.

It was a good thing that I got my vitamin D quota early on because I soon learned what they meant by the rainy season. Rain, rain, and more rain was the weather forecast. My raincoat was put to good use. I had a few minifloods in my classroom near my doors, and during one senior music lesson I had to move desks very quickly, as a crack in the windowsill decided to open up and allow streams of water to come down on my students' desks. Needless to say, when the sun did shine, I washed and dried loads of laundry during the small window of clear weather we got (boy, did I miss washing machines and dryers).

Mother Nature was certainly showing herself. The rain continued, and Erica and I found out where all the leaks in our house were. We had pots all over the living room, and Erica was hoping that the puddle in the middle of her bed would dry before she went to bed; the funny thing was that she moved the bed from the other side of the room earlier in the week because of one leak, only to be troubled by another one.

A Long Weekend for Independence Day: Late October

It was now late October, but my weeks were still full of lots of adventure. One day during PE class, I had local school kids join the class. They had, apparently, been kicked out of school, had seen our class in the field, and wanted to join in. I said it was okay as long as they followed the rules. I laughed so hard because I am pretty sure that by the end of the class, these kids thought I was crazy. I was having my students act like race cars to keep them running around the field. The local boys couldn't figure out why I kept telling my students to rev their engines and hit the gas, but they were good sports and kept running.

One morning I awoke to find I had caught the red-eye plague. My right eye was completely swollen shut. Because our school was small, there were no supply teachers, so I had to go to school feeling horrible and looking worse. I tried to hide it with my sunglasses, but by 9 a.m. most of my kids knew that, "Miss had red eye." I took lots of precautions to ensure that I didn't spread the illness, and most kids didn't want to touch anything I had touched. I was thankful that the eye drops from the pharmacist worked well, and even though I had red eye in both eyes, by the end of the week I was at least feeling better. But my eyes remained very bloodshot.

Independence Day is a national holiday in October, and each class had to prepare for an assembly. The students all worked very hard on their presentations. The kindergarten class was really cute with their presentation on the flag and the national bird, the St. Vincent Parrot (Amazona guildingii). My kids gave presentations about the historical monuments of the island. Unfortunately, no one could hear them because they didn't project their voices. We also presented a song, "Our Country's Birthday," which was quite well done. I was proud of them.

On Independence Day, we were out of school, so Erica and I spent the day in town running errands. We also went to the hospital to visit one of Erica's friends who had just given birth. The hospital visit was quite an experience. The maternity ward on the island is very different from one in a Canadian hospital. The windows were open, and there were no separate rooms, just a long room with beds and no fans for these poor women. They were also expected to provide their own food.

That evening I went with the other Canadian teacher and her visiting boyfriend to Calliaqua for *culture pot*. It was like a huge street party that took place every Friday night. We bought food from one of the many barbecue vendors on the street. For C$5, I got a huge plate of great food. We then went to the main street, where there was lots of dancing, loud reggae music, soca music, and dominoes. We had to leave early because of the rain, but the local people were just getting started.

The next day we rented a car and went up the leeward (western) coast of the island. We drove to the rainforest for a hike. Driving there was quite an experience. I felt like I was in a commercial for a Nissan Pathfinder (except we were in a Suzuki). Thank goodness for four-wheel drive. The rainforest was amazing, with huge trees and beautiful flowers. The highlight for me was seeing a cocoa tree in its natural habitat. We hiked up 1,350 ft above sea level to the parrot sanctuary in hopes of seeing the Amazona guildingii. This is a parrot found only on this island, and only 450 of the species are alive today because of poaching. Unfortunately, the parrots were hiding, but the view was worth it. We had just finished our lunch when we got to experience why they call it a rainforest. The rain was quite cool, and I think I was cold for the first time since I had arrived in St. Vincent. A change of clothes and another half-hour drive later, and we reached Barrouallie, a tiny fishing village in the northern part of the island. People here are very interested in white-skinned people, so as we drove through the village, all the people had their eyes on us and many children ran up to the car to shake our hands. We came to this village because Adam, a friend of ours, had been doing some fishing with the locals and met a tour guide by the name of Al who was going to take us around for the afternoon. Al took us for a drive and showed us the set for the movie *Pirates of the Caribbean*, which was filmed in St. Vincent. He also took us to see a view of La Soufrière (the volcano). We also saw Trinity Falls in the Wallilabou River, a small waterfall you can swim under. It was very peaceful and lovely to swim in fresh water, but the water was chilly since it runs off the mountain. We then went back to Barrouallie to the beach where the fishermen were bringing in their catch of tuna. They were huge fish. The people of this village normally fish for pilot whales (or *black fish*, as the locals call them). They use every part of the whale, from the oil to the skull. The trip was quite an experience. Al showed us his fishing boat and his house. I was very humbled to see that his home was basically a wooden shack on the beach where he, his wife, and their three children lived. The people in the northern part of the island live a very hard life.

The next day we got up bright and early to drive the windward (eastern) coast. The beaches on this side are quite dangerous for swimming, and with 3–4-m waves crashing, we could see why! Surfing would have been nice if there had not been coral underneath the waves. The beaches on this side all have black sand from volcanic ash. The drive up the coast was breathtaking, as we drove through the banana and coconut plantations. Banana trees aren't as tall as you would think. The road along this side of the island has many ups and downs; some roads were pretty close to 90° straight up or down, and there are very few guardrails in this country. The road also becomes very narrow, so we hoped for the best going around some corners. At the very top of the island is a town called Owia, where there is a salt pond. You have to walk down about 250 stairs (we counted) to get to this pond, which is surrounded by volcanic rock, so it is calm on the inside but you are surrounded by the rough ocean. There is one spot where the ocean crashes over the rocks, sends the water 10 m up, and makes a bit of a waterfall over the rocks. It was an amazing experience to swim in this pond surrounded by the coral and tropical fish that live there. Coral is very sharp, however, and one of my legs was sore after scraping against the coral. I now understood the meaning of adding salt to your wounds.

Halloween

Halloween was celebrated a little differently here than it is in North America. In St. Vincent, they celebrate All Saints' Eve and All Souls' Day (November 1 and 2, respectively) just as people do in many South American countries. For about a week, it sounded like fireworks were going off every evening as people lit bamboo with a bit of kerosene to scare off the jumbee (ghosts). On All Saints' Eve, many people went to the cemeteries and lit candles for their deceased loved ones. The belief is that the jumbee come and walk the earth on this evening. Erica tried successfully to spook me by telling me there were jumbee up at the school (needless to say I didn't go into the school at night). She also had us walk in the door backward at night so the jumbee couldn't follow us in. I didn't see any jumbee but told Erica if I did, I would be out of there.

At school we celebrated Halloween in a more North American style. We had a spooky assembly in the morning, during which all the classes presented a little something. My kids did a song and dance called I Monster Walk. The kindergarten class put a spell on the teachers to make bats hang from their armpits, and they were so surprised when the teachers stood up with paper bats hanging from their shirts. In the afternoon, all the students (and teachers) put on costumes, and we had a costume parade. Then the students broke into teams and visited the different classrooms, where the teachers ran activities. I conducted a potions class, a la Harry Potter, where we made slime (I was a wizard). It was a big hit, and I think the parents enjoyed it as much as the students.

National Testing and Report Cards: Mid-November

My Grade 2 students had to write national tests. The tests were supposed to be based on Grade 1 curriculum, but somehow they were expected to understand double-digit multiplication in Grade 1. As the teacher, it was very stressful because I couldn't help the kids, even though I knew they didn't have a clue what to do. Teachers in the Caribbean are also expected to mark their students' tests, so I spent a whole week marking the tests carefully because the answer sheets from the government had several errors on them. This experience made me realize I didn't want to be a Grade 3 or 6 teacher in Ontario.

We were still getting lots of rain. Our shower was solar heated, so I had cold showers many days in a row (I think one day my shower consisted of a 30-second run under the spray of water). The weather was so cool, I actually even wore a fleece sweater to bed one night and around the house the next morning. The winds were so strong that one day they blew the rain through my closed window slats all the way across to the other side of my room. I had black marks all over the walls and a big puddle in my room that I had to mop up. I hoped that I dry weather was coming soon.

Our school also celebrated Remembrance Day. We held a peace vigil in the assembly hall, and it was very nice. My class sang a little song, and my recorder ensemble premiered at this assembly with a song about peace (and it actually sounded pretty, not like saws on metal). The whole school worked hard at making origami peace cranes to decorate the hall. We made about 275 cranes, and they hung from the ceiling.

I was also busy trying to get my report-card outcomes to jive with those of the principal. We didn't see eye to eye on several outcomes, so it meant a lot of after-school meetings to try and come to a compromise.

The kickoff to Christmas had begun. In St. Vincent it is customary for people to buy new furniture and curtains at Christmastime, so every store has draperies in the windows. Christmas decorations also started to appear. Erica and I spent most of one Saturday trying to find the best bargains on ornaments to decorate our classrooms. Every store had a different price. I thought it was hilarious that they were playing Christmas carols about snow in the stores when there was no chance of it snowing; I thought a Christmas flood could have occurred.

Preparing for Christmas

The rain slowed down from the buckets we had been receiving. I started decorating my class for Christmas and the kids were thrilled. Of course, now the kids wanted everything we did to be related to Christmas, but I was trying to hold off the big festivities until at least December.

I started a carol club during morning recess so the kids could come in and sing for 15 minutes to practice for our Christmas barbecue fundraiser. I had a great turnout, but Frosty the Snowman just didn't seem the same in the heat we were experiencing.

Report cards turned out to be a bigger job than I expected. Thank goodness I only had 12 students. I kept dreaming about the numbers 1–6 (the national rating scale for grading). I didn't have a hard time with the comment part of the report cards since they only gave us four lines, but the scoring took awhile.

Our school went on a field trip to the circus. The circus was a big deal in St. Vincent because most kids had never seen a camel or tiger in real life. The circus had come all the way from France and was there for a month. It was fun to watch all the kids' reactions when the lions roared.

At a staff meeting in late November, the last item to discuss was reorganization of the teacher–class ratio, and we were all told we would know by the end of the week how this change would affect each of us. I came home convinced I would be packing up at Christmas since I had the least amount of experience at the school. On Thursday, everyone except for me had heard what to expect, which didn't do much for my stress level (or sleep). Finally, on Friday at 3:00 p.m. I found out that I was not fired; however, I would now be teaching a Grade 2/3 class starting in January. Erica was getting my Grade 1 students, so I would now have 10 students and an even bigger challenge as I gained 2 of the children who caused the most problems at the school (2 boys who were best friends but also couldn't stand to be around each other). I was going to have to do a lot of regrouping and program adjustment during the holidays, but I was just glad I still had a job.

We went over to Bequia to get away from all the noise of St. Vincent and relax after report cards. We got a head start on our Christmas shopping in the morning and found this great little place that made homemade ice cream (they even had chocolate; believe it or not, chocolate ice cream was a hard thing to find on the island). We had a wonderful afternoon at the beach. The crossing on the way back was a little rough, but we made it in one piece without anyone going too green and had dinner at Ocean Allegro, a favorite restaurant, to finish off the perfect day.

HOME FOR THE HOLIDAYS

I made it home to Canada for Christmas, but I arrived 2 days later than I had planned due to a huge snowstorm that hit the eastern seaboard. I flew out of St. Vincent to Barbados around 11:00 a.m. Saturday, and after many delays and an unplanned overnight stop in Philadelphia with −20 °C temperatures and no winter clothes, I made it to Toronto. Canadian customs officers probably thought it was strange when I kissed the ground in Canada, but I had never been so glad to be back home.

THE WINDS OF CHANGE: JANUARY

I arrived back on the island the first week of January. The trip back to St. Vincent was eventful, to say the least. I got there, but my bags slept over in the United States. The warm weather and green grass were a welcome change; I felt like Dorothy in *I Wizard of Oz* going from Kansas to Munchkin land; St. Vincent was in Technicolor.

I spent the entire first day back at the school getting my classroom together. I moved into a bigger room, and I had to dust, mop, and sweep everything because the dirt had accumulated over the holidays. I managed to make the room sparkle, even without the new toys that were in my luggage. Monday everyone was back to school. The kids were so excited to come back, and I must admit I was excited to see all their smiling faces again. My new class was wonderful and worked together very well. Monday also found me working as a bat chaser. It seemed that over the holidays, fruit bats decided to move in. There were 20 bats in the stairwell up to the senior teachers' rooms, so my umbrella and I went up to wake the bats and chase them out. I was glad when students offered the next day to help the senior teachers out.

I finally got my luggage (after a lot of tears and phone calls and Erica finally speaking a little harshly to the airline. It seems you need to be a local to get some things done). It was like Christmas all over again. I was thankful everything was still in one piece, except for my chocolate bars, which had melted somewhere along the line, but it was nothing the fridge couldn't fix.

I got to meet another critter of the islands in January when I picked one of my dresses up off the floor and a centipede came crawling out. If you are sprayed or bitten by a centipede, it is a painful experience (pain in all your nerves and swelling). I was lucky, because it didn't do either to me, but we did have to kill it, and those suckers are tough to kill. Erica made me burn the centipede because it's a superstition or old wives' tale that if you burn a centipede after killing it, you will be able to see them when they are around. So I found yet another use for strong rum—as lighter fluid.

It was fun to be back in the hustle and bustle of the market. The highlight was the gentleman who came up, full of compliments and looking for a quarter, and when I refused he then told me that my family and I stink like dogs. I told him that that comment definitely wasn't going to get him a quarter, and he walked off disgruntled.

My students had been pretty well behaved and were settling into the new classroom and new routines nicely. The school started a healthy heart club, so every Tuesday, Wednesday, and Thursday morning one of the teachers ran a 15-minute aerobics class for the kids and teachers. It was a lot of fun and good for the kids. We even had parents join us a couple of days.

My choirs and recorder clubs also got back into business. I was excited to see more kids turn up, and after a few squeaks everyone remembered how to play the recorder again.

We were now having nice weather most days, with only tiny showers here and there. I learned that my new classroom had a few more leaks than the other one. I had a nice water feature in my windowsill and over my only bulletin board. I also had to quickly move some desks away from the door when water came in and flooded the classroom. My students were very helpful, and the rain didn't disrupt their lessons too much.

We started noticing a strange smell at the school and the house. It was the stench of rotting lobster and fish guts. Someone had dumped them near the school in the bushes. We spent an entire week fighting with the Ministry of Health to come and get rid of the mess; however, they told us we had to find whoever dumped it and have them clean it up. Finally they came and burned the trash (which caused an even worse smell and caused black smoke to waft through the school). Erica and I thought this would let us sit in comfort in our living room again, but unfortunately they didn't quite get it all. Sanitation wasn't a high priority with the government.

Hiking the Volcano: February

A group of us who were friends went out to a new restaurant and club on the island, called Marcomay's, for a farewell party for Adam. It was a nice place. Luckily we got our barbecue before the electricity went out; so we ate dinner by candlelight and rain on the patio (we were sitting under a gazebo). After dinner we went into Calliaqua for culture pot (the big street party). A live band was playing, which we enjoyed. Carnival season was starting, so all the bands were getting ready by performing their new songs.

That weekend we headed out to hike La Soufrière, the active volcano on St. Vincent. We took a van to Barrouallie. I thought Barrouallie was one of the most fascinating villages on the whole island. The beach was beautiful with black sand, and it had its own distinct smell of fish and whale oil and seawater. Friends took us to the base of the volcano via the sea. It's a shorter hike from the leeward side of the island. We passed by the set from the movie *Pirates of the Caribbean*. On our way, I was totally blown away by the scenery of the coast, but the highlight was the dolphins that jumped up right beside our boat.

Landing on the beach at the entrance of the hiking trail was an interesting experience, as we arrived at high tide and we were coming in on good 2-m swells. The boat couldn't be beached, which meant we had to ride a wave in and then jump when it was safe. It took some tricky maneuvering by the driver, but we all made it to shore slightly wet but alive. We walked up the dry river to the trail. This part was cool, as we walked through tunnels of molten rock. Most of the trail was through the rainforest, which had lots of greenery and wildlife. Unfortunately for us, there was also lots of rain. I did okay with the hike for the first 45 minutes, but then the air became thinner and I started having problems breathing. Apparently, with my asthma, my lungs didn't like the pace we were going, so I had to slow down. Everyone was patient with me as I slowly made my way up. Because of the lack of oxygen, my muscles were protesting greatly, but I was determined to make it to the top. By 11 a.m., we had made it to the canopy of the rainforest and we could see just how far we had actually climbed. The boat on the coast was now just a little dot. We could smell the sulfur from the volcano. The last 45 minutes of the climb were pretty slow going. Each time I got to the top of a hill, I saw one more, and my legs were now making a very strong protest. Finally someone said, "At the top of this hill is the summit." I decided that the gods of this volcano did not want any visitors. Not only was it raining, but at 4,000 ft above sea level, the wind was very strong. There were several times we had to just crouch and wait for a gust to finish before climbing because the wind was strong enough that it could knock us over. When we reached the summit, we were completely surrounded by clouds, and it felt like we were at the ends of the earth. Needless to say, the view wasn't all that great. It was also very cold; I felt like I was back in Canada. We ate some lunch and managed to get a small enough break in the clouds that we were able to see down into the crater. The descent was much better for me as my lungs were happier. I still had sore legs, but I could deal with that. Going through the rainforest was slow because the rain had turned the trail into mud. We managed to slip and slide our way down the mountain, and when we got back to the dry river, the sun was shining again.

We then went up the coast another half hour to the Falls of Baleine. It was very impressive to see a 200-foot waterfall in the rainforest. We all had fun jumping into the pool of cool, crisp, fresh water.

Home Sickness

In February I had a bout of homesickness, which made things tough, but keeping busy helped. Things at school were still going well. I liked working with the Grade 2/3 class better because they had developed a sense of humor, and you could joke with them a bit more. The directors returned, which made everyone feel a bit more on edge.

Bad News and Good Times

In February, the Canadian teachers also asked the directors about the money for our plane tickets, which (according to our contract) we were supposed to get in January. They informed us that the school didn't have the money to pay for the term. The school already had to take out a loan to pay our wages. Needless to say, I was not too pleased. The directors finally returned my plane ticket and the passport that they had had for more than 2 weeks while trying to get our visas extended. I would be doing the next extension on my own, as I didn't like them having my passport for so long.

There were some fun adventures in February. The first weekend was the blues and jazz festival in Bequia. Some friends and I went and stayed at a resort owned by the parents of one of our students. Our stay turned out to be an escapade, as they had overbooked the hotel. When we arrived Friday night and got the key to our room, we opened the door to find someone else's luggage, but we got that straightened out quickly. The rest of the weekend was spent relaxing on the beach, eating lots of delicious food, and going to some amazing concerts. There were local musicians as well as groups from all over the world performing.

On our ferry ride back to St. Vincent, we learned what faith was truly about, as we had to cross during a storm. At first the boat trip was like some ride at Canada's Wonderland, but then it became a little scary with 4–5-m waves breaking over the deck and people losing their lunch all over the place. I didn't like the fact that when the boat dipped, the horizon disappeared, and all I could see was a wall of water. I was very happy to reach land.

The second week of February brought Valentine's Day. Our school was selling candy–grams for the students, so I spent most of the week making these candy-grams in my free time. My efforts paid off in the end, as I got quite a few from the kids. In my classroom, I had a cookie–decorating party, which the kids loved. I was glad to see 3 o'clock come around so that moms and dads could deal with the sugar highs.

During the last week of February, the work situation continued to go downhill when I asked for a reference letter. The directors decided they needed to do a formal evaluation, and that was fine, but they apparently missed the idea that when you give one negative comment you need to back it up with a positive one. I did not believe the evaluation was a fair judgment of my teaching ability, but at least I had learned who *not* to use as a reference.

March

We went to Bequia for a little rest and relaxation on the beach and to face our fears after our last ferry ride. I almost lost my cookies in the morning, but the ferry ride back was better. When we got off the boat in St. Vincent, I accidentally created an adventure for myself. I was getting into the taxi while holding my friend's child, to go home and I stepped on a metal grate that covers a manhole–type thing on the wharf. Apparently it wasn't covered properly because when I stepped on it, I fell all the way through. I was up to my waist in water, and my arms were stuck from the armpits up. Thankfully, the child who was in my arms was unscathed and I walked away with only a few minor scrapes and bruises. I was a tad embarrassed when it took three people to get me out of the hole. Needless to say I created quite a scene at the wharf.

STILL NO MONEY

In late March we asked the directors for a meeting, and they dodged the questions again; they kept saying it was out of their hands and refused to have a meeting. They also refused to pay us in weekly or monthly installments for our plane tickets, as we had asked for. Basically we had decided they were lying and had the money but weren't going to give it to us. So we now had to try and talk to the other investor in the school who was on the board to see if he would be able to help with the money. The more I learned, the more I heard that many previous teachers from Canada had left the school due to money issues and verbal abuse, so I wouldn't be the first. The directors left the country again without paying us for our tickets. I now wanted to go back to Canada.

A VISIT FROM HOME

I survived until the Easter holidays, which was a 2-week break. Report cards were completed on time; parent–teacher interviews took place with only a couple of difficult parents, and the end–of–term drama presentations went well with everyone remembering their lines and cues.

On April 1, my parents arrived in St. Vincent and we stayed very busy. The next day, a Friday, was the last day of school before break, and my kids were wired. Between my parents being there, the new sports equipment, a pizza party, and an Easter egg hunt, the kids were as high as the kites my parents brought for them. We all had a good time.

While my parents were there, we did lots of traveling. We were able to drive through the banana plantations and also see how pineapples grew. Pineapples are pretty amazing: one fruit grows per plant, and it takes a whole year to grow. I appreciated the free ones students had brought to me over the past few weeks. We drove to the coast, where we went to Black Point Tunnel. This stone tunnel was hand carved in 1815 by the slaves to transport rum and sugar to European vessels. We also went to Fort Charlotte, which is an old fort that protected the English from the Caribs. We saw the old leprosy colony and the women's jail, with only 15 women residing there. They don't hang women in St. Vincent (only the men) because the one woman they did hang took too long to die (there are some perks of being a woman). We went to the botanical gardens in Kingstown, which are the oldest botanical gardens in the Western Hemisphere. There we saw lots of interesting tropical plants: jasmine, mahogany, ylang-ylang, orchids, and others; we also saw the Amazona guildingii (parrot) rehabilitation program. They were trying to breed the birds in captivity and release them back into the wild.

My parents and I flew down to Union Island and spent some time in the Tobago Cays Marine Park. Snorkeling around the coral reefs was amazing; it was like swimming in a giant aquarium.

THE FINAL COUNTDOWN

By the time I had reached I third term, I felt like I was off to the races. It was hard to believe that I only had 43 more teaching days, and it didn't seem like enough time with my students, but somehow I would manage.

School was interesting, as always. We had a meeting with the other director to discuss staff issues. All I really wanted was my money. The Vincentian teachers were all up in arms about the possibility of more foreign teachers coming next year. The whole thing was like a big soap opera.

JUNE

I had only 20 more days until I went home, and I could hardly wait. We rented a beach villa in Bequia to enjoy our second-to–last weekend. I finished up my report cards so I could sleep by the pool all weekend.

The directors pulled a fast one on me and paid the other Canadian teacher for her plane ticket but told me I would have to wait until September. I was really angry, but I kept hoping the money would fall from the sky.

Culture Shock

Coming back home to Canada was harder than I expected. I was happy to see family and friends, but getting back into the swing of North American life took some getting used to. Suddenly I was supposed to be connected to the world all the time with cell phones and credit cards. It seemed to me like people were always rushing, and I missed the spicy food.

Miriam's Tips for Traveling Teachers

What to Bring

- A good water-filtration system
- A plug adapter
- Mosquito netting
- Batteries
- A digital camera
- Your passport and copies of it
- Some local currency to get you started

Things to Prepare for

- Make sure you visit your doctor and get all the necessary inoculations for the country
- Internet services are available but it takes some time to get set up
- Things are never on time; bring a book and relax
- Drink lots of filtered water when you arrive because your body will need to adjust to the heat
- The accents are strong, but if you listen carefully, the locals are speaking English
- If you're female, be prepared to hear lots of catcalls in town. It is a cultural thing, and they are complimenting you. However, be smart and don't give out too much information
- Be prepared to teach a few different grades, since plans change
- Hurricanes are a possibility; rain is guaranteed
- Sleep in mosquito nets and use bug spray to cut down on the bug bites
- Be prepared for critters in your house: cockroaches, geckos, iguanas, bats, and frogs
- Don't travel alone
- There are no supply teachers, so if you get sick you still have to work
- Don't give your passport to anyone
- Luggage can be lost and stolen (I experienced both) so make sure that you have a few things in your carry-on and that you spread out supplies in your luggage

WHERE IS MIRIAM NOW?

I am living in Brantford and have been teaching mostly Grades 2 and 3 for the Grand Erie District School Board. This year I am experiencing another adventure: teaching a special-education behavior class.

I eventually received the money I was owed by the school in St. Vincent. People often ask if I miss teaching there; the truth is that I do, and I wouldn't trade any of my experiences. I learned and grew a great deal. St. Vincent made a big impact on my life and I know that someday, I will return to the tiny island.

Chapter 6

Teaching in Kuwait

Neil Fairbairn

Look Out Real World (Mid-January)

Having come back to Nipissing University for my second term of teachers college, I knew that I had to start thinking about the future and where I would like to teach. I was pretty sure that I did not want to teach in Canada. I had taught some English-as-a-second-language (ESL) classes in Kyongju, South Korea, and had done my practicum in Lehwoh, Cameroon. I knew of the rewards of teaching internationally. I had gone to a presentation on international teaching and found out that there was a Web site (http://www.tieonline.com) that could help you find a job abroad. I paid the 40 American dollars then looked up schools at which I could potentially teach.

While my classmates were trying to set up interviews with schools in the Ottawa-Carleton District School Board, I was looking for a job in Cambodia. While friends were researching jobs in the Toronto area, I was researching jobs in the Middle East. I sent out my résumé all over the world to schools that needed a math teacher. My university in North Bay periodically put job placements on the message board, which I used to my advantage. One such posting was for a job with the Japan Exchange and Teaching Programme. Another was for a teaching job in Kuwait. Japan interested me because I had loved working in Korea. I job in Kuwait was less alluring, simply because my knowledge of Kuwait was limited to the unappealing news I saw on television. In the end I applied for both jobs. After all, what could it hurt?

Later that week, I received an e-mail back from the Kuwaiti school. After talking to one of my Middle Eastern friends, I decided that I should at least consider the request for an interview. I realized that I had received very little training in job-interview skills and that the practice would be good for me, even if I were not terribly interested in the school. I prepared a portfolio for myself and purchased a book on how to carry out an interview.

IT WAS ONLY FOR THE SAKE OF PRACTICE (EARLY FEBRUARY)

The following Friday I headed to Toronto with a friend of mine, and on Saturday I woke up early to get to my interview on time. A person once told me that I should check out the news before going for any interview, so I watched the BBC that morning, only to find out that a spaceship with the first Greek astronaut on board had blown up. This unfortunate situation proved useful for me, since the first question that my interviewer asked me was if I had seen what had just happened.

I arrived 30 minutes early for my appointment and spent the time eating in the lobby and going through my portfolio one last time. Five minutes before the scheduled time, I headed up to the top floor of the hotel, wiped the sweat off my hands, took a final deep breath, and knocked on the door. The gentleman in charge was just finishing another interview, so it allowed me a couple of minutes to continue wiping the sweat from my hands onto my pants and to practice my breathing exercises.

The door to the room opened and out came a 40 year old carrying a black leather briefcase who wished me the best of luck. Immediately

I began to think about the fact that I was a first-year teacher competing with experienced travelers and teachers, and yet I was not overly worried since I truly did not want the job and was only here for the interview experience (or so I told myself). Being prepared for the first question, regarding the spaceship, helped me relax. The interviewer then asked if we could watch the news, and right away I felt that this interview would not be as stressful as I had presumed. After a couple of minutes of watching the report, he began to talk about the school and then showed me a PowerPoint presentation of A'Takamul International School and Kuwait that I found captivating. I was asked a couple of questions but nothing that was too difficult to answer, and then the interview was essentially complete. I wanted to show him my portfolio and did, but I felt afterward that had I not brought it, it would not have been the end of the world. He did ask me one question that my readings had told me to prepare for, and that was whether I had any questions for him. I asked a question about safety and the school's procedures in the event that violence erupted in the country. We chatted a little more, then we shook hands and the interview was over. Every part of me felt that I had landed the job.

I talked with numerous people who knew a little about the Middle East to try to find out whether I should accept the job should it be offered to me. I checked my e-mail every day to see if any other schools besides the one in Kuwait had replied to me, but no other e-mails arrived. Then on Saturday, February 12, I received a phone call offering me the job. I tried to delay my answer, but he said that he needed to know as soon as possible, so I asked for 24 hours in which to think it over.

That night I did a lot of research on Kuwait and looked up the conversion of the Kuwaiti dinar (KD) to the Canadian dollar. At the time it was C$5.15 to 1 KD. I called one of my Middle Eastern friends and asked him if I should take the job and he said that I would be crazy not to. I questioned him about the tension between the United States and Iraq, and he convinced me that it would not affect me and that it would probably be over by the time I got to Kuwait. He was somewhat right in these predictions. The next day I called the gentleman who had interviewed me and I accepted the job. He informed me that I would be receiving a package in the mail with my contract and other information. He also said he would put me in contact with a teacher from Kuwait. I thanked him once again, hung up the phone, cracked open a beer, and then informed all my friends that we had to go celebrate. As we were celebrating, somebody asked me what my parents thought of me going to Kuwait. I thought that it was a good question and supposed I should find out.

LEAVING ON A JET PLANE (AUGUST)

The month leading up to my departure was an exciting but nerve-racking one. The knowledge that I would be leaving for not just another country but another continent and that this particular area was not the most stable in the world was starting to sink in. I had found out that I would not be teaching mathematics at my school as I had hoped but rather social studies. The social studies that I would be teaching would not be Canadian social studies, which is what I prepared for during my bachelor of education studies, but would be African, Asian, and Middle Eastern history. This task made me a bit nervous, so I had to keep reminding myself that I would be teaching at the Grade 6 and 7 levels and that if I did a little research, I would be able to stay at least one step ahead of the students.

Throughout August, I spent a couple of hours each day getting books from the library on such topics as Egypt, China, the Middle East, Ghana, and South Africa. Each day I looked on the Internet for information about culture and geography. My whole family was getting involved. I went to the bookstore with my mom, a former teacher, and looked at the children's section for information that I needed. My dad was going through his collection of newspapers handing me articles on apartheid and Nelson Mandela. That month I did more reading than I had ever done in such a short time. If I found information that I liked, I would go to my summer workplace and photocopy a page or two. After a while, my employer told me that I had to stop this practice, as I was using a lot of paper and ink. I was trying to learn everything—all the material that my students would have to know and everything they would expect me to have extensive knowledge of—in just a month.

The school had informed me that before leaving for Kuwait, I needed to get a few things done so that I could teach there: an HIV test, medical check, hepatitis A and B vaccinations, police record check, copies of my degrees, and so on. Getting an HIV test for the first time in my life was a little daunting. Although I was almost sure that I was not HIV positive since I was not in a high-risk group, the thought of having to explain to my parents why I could not go to Kuwait due to HIV was a worrisome thought. Getting my hepatitis A and B shots meant that I had to take off time from work to visit the doctor during working hours. I received an assessment by the doctor, followed by two rounds of shots, all for the reasonable price of $300. A police check and a copy of my degree were simple enough to obtain but still came with a price tag, though it was very minimal. In the end, paying for these formalities was worthwhile, given that it was necessary for the job that would pay me a handsome sum, but at the time I was still a starving student and it was hard to give up the money.

A couple of weeks before leaving for Kuwait I was starting to become a little more sentimental, wanting to see friends that I had not seen in years. Never known to be a party animal, I spent my last few days in Ottawa getting together with friends and family, sharing a beer (something I would not be able to do in Kuwait), and having a good laugh with them. The week before departing, I started to go through my room, cleaning out every nook and cranny, deciding what to pack and what to leave behind. Photos from the past, report cards from long ago, letters that I had received over the years, books that had been given to me, presents from past Christmas holidays and birthdays all had to be scrutinized. Soon enough all my possessions were delegated to boxes with labels written across them and then stored away. The room that I had lived in all of my life was now bare and empty, and it was almost time for me to leave. I would have one last dinner with my family, a final call to friends, and a final sleep (or at least an attempt at one) in my own bed.

In the morning it would be time to leave the world that I knew and head to a place of unknowns.

HOME SWEET HOME (LATE AUGUST)

While flying from Ottawa to Germany, I had trouble sitting down. I felt like the character Red in the movie *Shawshank Redemption*, as he sat on the bus, not being able to control his excitement over finally being a free man. Every time I spoke to someone, I mentioned that I was going to Kuwait, acting like it was not a big deal, although my heart was beating frantically. At the German airport, I began to realize I was not alone in this journey. While waiting for the plane to Kuwait, I met a couple of Canadians who were also going to Kuwait to teach for the first time. Eventually, more and more expatriates were joining our circle of teachers, some experienced and some new to the international teaching experience. Instantly I felt a lot more confident that what I was doing was not so crazy. Teachers who had been teaching in Kuwait already told me what to expect and made me feel more at ease about the whole situation. We got on the plane together and headed to what I would soon be calling my home.

On the way to Kuwait we flew over Iraq, and from the sky I could see the burning of oil, something that was new to me at the time; I also got to view the beginnings of the desert, another first for me. As we came closer to the Kuwaiti airport, the plane flew parallel to the coast so that we could see the Kuwait Towers. I could hardly contain my excitement.

After a 36-hour journey, I felt our plane touch down at its final resting spot. Not knowing what to do, I followed the crowd, went through customs, got my baggage, went through a security check, and then the door opened to what one of my friends would later call "a sea of white." To my left and right were men wearing their traditional clothing, called a *dishdasha*, which covered their bodies from head to toe in white. I was greeted by my superintendent and a lady who was wearing the traditional Arab clothing; I later found out that this woman was the principal of my school. She greeted me with a Louisiana accent and then handed me her cell phone so that I could call my parents back in Canada. I was introduced to my roommate and the other people with whom I would working and eventually be calling family. We were all extremely tired and were eager to get on the bus that the school provided so that we could get to our apartments and head to bed. Before the bus took off, a teacher (who was not on my plane) came walking with a slight limp to our bus and hopped on. The teacher, Lori, had taught in Kuwait before but was new to the school. During the bus ride she told us of all the great opportunities in Kuwait. She explained about parties that we could go to and sports teams we could join. She immediately made it known that if any of us needed help, she would be there. I liked Lori from the first moment that I met her.

The first week was a frantic one, as we were taken to new places every day. First it was a day at the Hilton, where the school unapologetically made us pay 5 KD (about $25 at the time) for breakfast. Then it was off to the Friday market, which was just like a big garage sale, where we could buy inexpensive items for our house. For lunch we were taken to a traditional Kuwaiti restaurant where we could smoke some *sheesha*, which, due to my lack of experience smoking, made my face go green. At last we were taken to the school where my first teaching job would be. Given what was said in the interview, I had expected to see a lot more resources (AV equipment, textbooks, classrooms that were already set up, etc.), but as I was still trying to find my comfort zone, I was not that concerned about the school.

The students had not arrived yet, and we spent the first week getting everything prepared. Rooms had to be decorated, chairs and tables had to be brought into the classrooms and set up, and there were meetings with heads of the departments. But before we began these tasks, the principal had one job for all the teachers. Our school had recently purchased 200 social–science textbooks, but according to the Kuwaiti Ministry of Information, they were not up to par. The ministry had issues with such things as Israel being on the maps and the Arabian Gulf being called the Persian Gulf. The ministry also did not like the idea of having pictures of the resurrection of Jesus or any mention of the holocaust. I asked a co-worker, who was Kuwaiti, how the ministry could defend wiping out the holocaust. He explained that while Kuwaitis accept that the holocaust happened, they do not believe it to be the only holocaust and therefore we should not call it *the* holocaust but rather *a* holocaust. I think I learned something that day, including how my upbringing in a Western school had influenced me and my way of thinking, and not always necessarily for the better. So my first day in school was spent with all the teachers using black markers to go through page after page of textbooks, deleting Israel, the Persian Gulf, and other material potentially offensive to the Kuwaiti people. I personally thought the students would be more interested in reading the material after it was blacked out and would immediately try to find out what was written underneath, so the whole situation was rather comical to me. Some teachers complained about having to do this task during their preparation time, but I found it to be a great bonding experience.

The first week the students arrived I was feeling a little anxious but excited. As the students streamed in, I got a glimpse of who I would be teaching. One of the first images that I remember was of them drinking from a water fountain in which they used their hand as a scoop and proceeded to throw the water on the ground. They had no concern that teachers were watching, as this was a normal activity and yet another sign I was not in Canada.

During the first 6 weeks, I had to take at least a day off each week, because new staff members had to go to different places for additional blood tests, finger printing, and paperwork. Each time we went to get something done, we managed to stop off and have lunch at a local restaurant. For a first-year teacher, I was working less than I had ever imagined and certainly less than my friends who were teachers back home. As there was always someone complaining about someone else being late, spending all that time with first–year co-workers led to some tension in our group; but just as you would in the first year in a school dormitory, we bonded with each other.

ARE WE ON HOLIDAY YET?

Teaching in Kuwait can be a challenge at the best of times, but one thing that keeps you going is the fact that a holiday is always around the corner. In a typical Kuwaiti school year, the average number of teacher–student contact days is about 169. Compare this number with other places in the world and you realize that there are definite benefits to teaching in Kuwait. Not only do you get the odd Christian holiday, like Christmas, but you also get the Muslim holidays, like Ramadan and Eid, as well as the Kuwaiti holidays like Liberation Day. We became so used to the many holidays that by March, when we did not have one weekday off, we began to think that we were being overworked. The funny thing is, by the end of March, the students were finally getting into a routine and remembering to bring their pencils and books. I even mentioned from time to time that maybe if we did not have so many holidays, we would not have as many classroom–management issues. Generally, I was told to hush up and enjoy the holidays. It was not long until April rolled around and we were back on holiday and the students had forgotten much of what they learned in March.

"Ramadan is the month during which the Quran was revealed, providing guidance for the people, clear teachings, and the statute book. Those of you who witness this month shall fast therein" (Quran 2:185). In theory, people are not supposed to eat, drink, smoke, have sex, or do anything else that indulges the body during the hours when the sun is out during the month of Ramadan. For this reason schools in Kuwait are open at different hours, letting the kids get home early to rest and prepare for the food they will eat after sunset.

The school forbids teachers, even if they are not Muslim, to eat or drink in front of the students. Teachers are tucked away in a separate room with the windows covered up so that they can have their morning coffee. Once they leave this room there is no mention of food, and what you witness in the hallways resembles something that could be seen in Michael Jackson's *Thriller* video. Students and fellow Muslim teachers are like zombies, having gotten up before sunrise to eat and not being allowed to touch food till sunset. Students slump in their seats and wait for the sun's rays to disappear. At night, the Muslims first eat some dates, then head out to their local mosque (there was one on nearly every corner it seemed), and finally come back for a huge family meal. So I students are eating at irregular times, sleeping very little, and starving throughout the day. Still they are expected to do their schoolwork and study for their tests. At the end of Ramadan, we get a weeklong holiday. For some Muslims it is a time to head to Mecca, but for non-Muslims it is an excellent time to visit the countries that surround Kuwait. There are two more long vacations during the school year: we get a 3–week vacation in January and we get another week off in April. During these holidays, I visited places such as India, Turkey, and Iran. Being situated in the Middle East allows you to travel to places that wouldn't be considered travel destinations by most Canadians, and from that opportunity you can learn so much.

The friendliness and generosity of the Iranian people make you wonder how they could be considered part of the so-called axis of evil; yet Kuwait is considered a Western ally. Also, from my travels, I noticed many similarities between Indians and Kuwaitis, but you would be hard pressed to convince the Kuwaitis that any similarities exist.

Not only are the holidays at different times in a Muslim country, but the weekends are on different days. While I was teaching in Kuwait, the weekend was Thursday and Friday, because Friday is a holy day, as designated by the Quran [Koran]. I did not ever get used to this idea, and I often told my students that a project was due on Friday when I actually meant Wednesday or that we would be doing a lab on Thursday when everybody nowle be at home. The number of holidays changed 2 years after I left Kuwait because they found students were missing too many business days in comparison with the Western world. Fridays will always be sacred, as that is the Muslim day of prayer, but in 2007, Kuwait changed its official weekend from Thursday and Friday to Friday and Saturday with Friday remaining as the Holy Day. Perhaps this change would have helped alleviate some of my mix-ups.

Christmas Shopping Will Never Be the Same

Although I am not an avid shopper, I still liked to go shopping once in awhile in Kuwait. Whether it was walking in the scorching sun in their huge outdoor markets or strolling in the air-conditioned malls checking out the latest fashion, shopping in Kuwait was always an experience.

Wherever you go in Kuwait, boys and girls, who are not supposed to be mingling with each other, are checking out the opposite sex, especially when shopping. The teenagers are playing a game, which is fascinating to an outsider such as me, in which they are trying to meet people of the opposite sex without anyone noticing. Technology has helped them gain the advantage in this dangerous game, as they can now text each other using their mobile phones, but some boys still like to use the traditional method of throwing their phone numbers into the young ladies' cars.

The girls, on the other hand, have a difficult task, as they want to show off their beauty but are in a country and culture where it is not acceptable to show your figure. With some girls you can see every curve of the body, even though they are fully covered; some others wear high-heeled shoes that give them an added 4 inches. In every mall, you find groups of girls wearing the brightest of clothes and elaborate make up. Groups of boys, who are wearing tight-fitting jeans and enough gel to make their hair stand on end, are scouting these women. The teenagers use sophisticated fashion design to try to entice the opposite sex, yet they still have to pretend that they are not interested. It's a game that all Kuwaitis must know is going on, but none seem willing to admit.

For a more traditional shopping experience, the Friday market and the Iranian market make for a fascinating day out. Most of the people that you find at the markets are older Kuwaitis, and all of them have their own maid or worker to help carry their goods. It would not be unusual to be in over 40° weather and see one of the Indian workers, wearing a bright orange outfit, carrying a sofa over his head. As you walk down the rows upon rows of tables, Indians and Pakistanis are shouting as loud as they can, trying to entice you to buy their goods. Although most merchandise that is being sold at these markets is not worth the dirt that it sits on, you sometimes find a priceless item or at least something that you have always wanted. If anything, the markets are great places to buy inexpensive Halloween costumes.

HAPPY NEW YEAR, A LIFE WITHOUT ALCOHOL

When I first met Lori at the airport, I noticed there was something different about her. No, it was not love at first sight; it was the way she walked that caught my eye. She had a bit of a limp, which I did not think much of at the time, but later on I realized the true meaning of this limp and would find myself with a similar limp. When living in a strong Muslim country, certain things make life very different: five times a day you can hear the call for prayer, women are a lot more covered up, pork product is always out of stock, and alcohol is never available. To last an entire school year without alcohol is something I never contemplated before coming to Kuwait, but after I had arrived, this possibility became an important factor in my life.

The first week in Kuwait, many teachers were having house parties, welcoming all the old teachers back and getting to know the new teachers. Back home I would usually come prepared for a party by bringing an alcoholic beverage, but in Kuwait I did not have this option. Other teachers, however, did not have this problem. At the parties, I witnessed people dancing around with a glass of wine in one hand and a beer in another. People were stumbling over their words as they poured hard liquor into their Cokes. Immediately I began to question where they got this alcohol and how I could get my hands on some of it.

Most expatriates, even some that did not drink, seemed to have their own special method of securing alcohol. Whether it was by making their own at home, buying it through the American embassy, or smuggling it across the border, everyone had a scheme. At parties you would constantly hear people telling stories of how they got caught by immigration trying to bring alcohol into the country or debating how to make the best beer (whether to melt the sugar before adding it to the mixture; whether to add 10 L or 12 L of water). Some people have contacts and get invited to the American Embassy, where alcohol can be purchased during certain hours; unfortunately, the Canadian Embassy is not so generous.

As I got to know Lori a little more, we talked about her different methods of smuggling alcohol over the border. Like most expatriates, Lori came from a country where alcohol was legal. So when she visited home, she would put alcohol into a bladder (a very durable plastic bag) and pack it nicely into her suitcase. Since the bladder can be rolled up, it is not detected as a bottle by the airport scanners, and security misses it completely.

Another ingenious way Lori smuggled alcohol over the border was by holding the bottles on her shins, rolling up long socks (we have found that rugby socks work the best) to the knees, and then wearing the baggiest pants that can be found. Although it is a bit painful and it is difficult to walk in a normal fashion, we have yet to be questioned by security at the airport. Granted, every time we go through, our hearts beat a little more quickly, but so far we have yet to be stopped. Even if we were to be caught, as some of our friends have been, the security officials would simply take the alcohol away (perhaps to drink at a later date, but that is just speculation). Before long, I too was walking out of the airports with a bit of a limp, but afterward I was able to share a drink with my fellow teachers.

A Coach's Nightmare but One That I Will Always Treasure

As most teachers know, the classroom is not the only place where you have contact with your students. In the hallways I was always shaking the students' hands or talking with the students about their weekends. Every second day at lunchtime, I monitored the students and was able to chat with them, and periodically our school had after-school activities that involved the students and teachers. Having all this contact with the students was great, but having heard that coaching allows you to really get to know them at a different level, I decided to give it a whirl. As at most schools outside of North America, soccer (or football, as it is known here) is the sport that the students play most frequently. After football, the prevalence of sports in Kuwait drops significantly. Unlike back home, where hockey, basketball, and American football are the most loved sports, in Kuwait these sports are simply a novelty. It was in this atmosphere that I thought I could share my knowledge of basketball by coaching the under-13 basketball team.

Most Kuwaitis are very well off, and the students at our school tend to have numerous maids, drivers, and other workers employed by their families. I students seldom have to walk to school, wash their own toilets, or do any other activities that are so familiar to many Westerners. Book bags are carried by the maids up to the front of the school, doors are opened for the students by their drivers, and even their homework is sometimes completed for them by their servants. Because of this lack of activity, the students become lethargic, uncoordinated, and, as I later found out, totally useless in organized sports.

Every coach has a little dream somewhere in the back of his or her head that he can lead his team to victory. After one practice, my goal was to teach my students how to run for 5 minutes without having a heart attack. Before my first practice, the head of the athletic department, Mr. Ryan, informed me not to be too hard on the students or they would simply quit within the first week. My aspirations of being the next Coach Carter were dashed by the wayside. Mr. Ryan, having learned from experience, informed me that we did not have a great selection of athletic students and advised me to focus more on having fun than on winning. With that advice, I began my first practice with the boys.

We started by just shooting the ball around so that I could get a basic idea of their abilities. After about 5 minutes and having seen the most fascinating shot selections, I decided to work on dribbling. For the next 3 weeks the students worked on the most basic of skills: dribbling, shooting, passing, and footwork. When we reached the point where I thought they could survive a simple practice game, I split the team into two halves and we had a go. Instantly the students forgot all rules, and a friendly game became a bad version of Red Rover as my players were clotheslining each other every time the person they were defending came near them. Double dribbles, traveling, and fouls were the norm, and I had not even tried to teach three in the key or backcourt violations. The day before our first big game, I still was not sure whether our boys could finish the game without all of them being fouled out.

At the end of the season our team went zero and six, yet it turned out to be a very successful season. My players showed up for every game, and although we never came close to winning, we improved all the time. In our final game we were losing in the second half by more than 20 points. We were playing on an outdoor court, with little protection around us. Although the sun was directly above us, there was a cool breeze from the north. I knew the direction because the surrounding mosques are always pointing in the same direction, toward Mecca. We had just been scored on and we were taking the ball up the court. Since the other team decided to play zone defense, it gave us the opportunity to carry the ball up the court with little to no pressure from the opposition. Suddenly the wind picked up, and sand from our soccer pitch started pelting us all over. Coaches were covering their eyes, the scorekeepers were ducking for cover, and my players were turning their backs toward the sand, all except for one player.

My point guard did not hesitate for a second and was still dribbling the ball up the court when the wind picked up. Like I had taught my players from day one, my point guard did a great chest pass to one of his teammates. Unfortunately, this teammate was hiding from the sand and therefore never saw this lightning pass (slight exaggeration) coming directly at his head. After getting dinged in the head by the ball, the boy fell to the ground. Hearing moans from this boy at first, I thought that he might have been hurt, but then I realized that the boy was actually laughing. Soon my point guard began to laugh hysterically, and then both teams began rolling around the court laughing at the situation. It was not long until the opposing coach, the referee, and I joined in this laughter. After the game I could overhear the students talking about the great pass or the shot that they almost made. I felt glad that I could be part of these moments in their lives. I still look back on this game and chuckle to myself thinking, "Only in Kuwait."

What's That Last Name, or Should I Say Wasta That Last Name?

Wasta is something very similar to the Indian caste system. Kuwaitis believe that some people are more important than others, and they apply this belief on a day-to-day basis. If the population were ranked and the classes formed into a pyramid shape, the ones with the least amount of wasta would be on the bottom, because they make up the largest portion of the population in the country. These people are not allowed to vote or enter courts; they do the most labor-intensive work; and even though some have lived here all their lives, they are not allowed to call themselves Kuwaitis. Most of these people originate from such places as India, Sri Lanka, the Philippines, Indonesia, or other East Asian countries. They are treated as second-class citizens even though they keep the country running.

Daily you read in the local Kuwaiti newspapers about women from these countries who have been taken to the desert and raped by multiple Kuwaiti men. The women go to the police for help, but their pleas generally fall on deaf ears since the police have little time for the people on the bottom of the pyramid. As is seen in this excerpt from a 2001 report by Human Rights Watch, other countries are starting to notice the Kuwaitis slavelike trade:

> Despite repeated government promises to amend labor laws and to crack down on the illegal trade in work visas, more than one million foreign workers faced serious restrictions on their ability to organize and bargain collectively, and had few legal remedies against abuses by employers. Female domestic workers, who were excluded from the labor law, were particularly vulnerable to physical and sexual abuse by employers. In March, India announced that it had stopped issuing immigration clearances to Indian nationals wishing to work as domestics in Kuwait because of abuses there. (¶ 3)

At the top of this pyramid is the royal family. When one of them does something illegal, such as driving a four-wheel–drive quad with no permit and hitting a person on the beach, it is not he who has to go to jail or pay a fine, but rather the person he hits, who also has to apologize. Schools that are supposed to have high standards will accept students based on the family's last name, which can make for an interesting class. If the child fails at the end of the year, the teacher is to blame, and the student who failed will be onto the next grade simply because of his or her last name.

From a teaching perspective, this practice makes it hard to teach equality and fairness in the classroom because the students see that these principles do not apply anywhere else in their lives. One may ask how a country such as Kuwait can survive, given the way that it is run. The answer is simple: it has oil. Kuwait has reserves of about 96 billion barrels, which is equivalent to about 10% of the world reserves. Petroleum accounts for nearly half of the GDP, 95% of the export revenues, and 80% of the government's income (Central Intelligence Agency, 2006).

As a side note, during my second year at A'Takamul, a student who was 6 or 7 years old came up to me and started talking about the tsunami. She said that one of her maids was from Sri Lanka and was crying when she heard on the news that her hometown was hit by this act of God. This girl's maid later found out that some of her family members had died in the catastrophe. This little girl continued her story by saying her parents decided that the best course of action was to send the maid back to her own country, hire a new maid, and not allow the new maid to watch television. Of course, this family does not represent all Kuwaitis, but the fact that a little girl could view such behavior as normal demonstrates how, in my experience, many Kuwaitis are taught to treat foreign workers differently.

It is easy to talk about the negative aspects of Kuwait, but I also must note that there were many Kuwaitis whom I came to like and respect. They were concerned not with their last names but rather with their culture and traditions of welcoming one and all into their homes. Lori and I were fortunate enough to meet special people who, without knowing us, invited us into their homes to share their food, their culture, and their families. How often do we welcome newcomers into our homes in

Western society? What I have come to love about teaching overseas is that you have the opportunity to see different aspects of a culture, and often you walk away a better person, one who is more knowledgeable, respectful, and open to differences in our world.

CO-WORKERS, FRIENDS, NEIGHBORS, AND LOVERS, SOMETIMES ALL AT ONCE

Teaching internationally is not just a teaching experience but also a life experience. You leave your home, family, and familiar lifestyle and take a chance on a whole new situation. For a first-year teacher, the thought of starting a new career is daunting enough without having to be in a new country all alone. But it is precisely this challenge that makes teaching internationally so rewarding. You leave your safe surroundings and head to an unknown place, and you have to force yourself to make the best of it. Since other teachers who are coming to your school and your country also realize the challenges of international teaching, they all do their best to make it as pleasurable as can be for other teachers. It is funny how someone from Canada has to leave for another country, such as Kuwait, to meet other Canadians, but sometimes this is the case.

Getting on the bus in Ottawa, I am rarely greeted by people I do not know, and when walking down the street, people never make a point of talking to me. But in an international setting you tend to be a little bolder and feel comfortable going up to another expatriate and asking how they are doing. Some people say that once you get in the international teaching profession, the world becomes a little smaller; I believe this change in outlook occurs because expatriates search out other expatriates when they are in another country. Parties are always happening, and the vast majority of partygoers are expatriates who have similar life aspirations. All of the people at the parties realize the difficulties of coming to a new country alone, and so it's easier to join in the conversations and be accepted as a friend. While doing my practicum in Ottawa, it seemed that every teacher had his or her own life and went home to a family at the end of the day. But when you're teaching in an international setting, your co-workers are your friends, your family away from home, and often your roommates. Housing is set up so that all your co-workers' houses are within walking distance of your home. Buses are supplied so that you can travel together to and from work, and parties usually have many of your co-workers attending. Spending this amount of time with your co-workers can lead to some frustration, but it can also lead to great friendships that can last a lifetime.

My first month in Kuwait, I had no phone, no driver's license, and very little knowledge of the country. Our school arranged for a bus to pick us up every morning to take us to work and then bring us back at the end of the day. We had a lot of strong personalities on our bus, and so we were always in for an interesting ride, especially when one of the teachers was late to get to the bus and we had to wait a whole 30 seconds. Whenever people would say that we should just leave him or her, others would argue to be patient. Sometimes while we rode on the bus, no one would say a word; other times, people would not stop talking. With constant complaints about the school, the housing, or fellow co-workers, the negativity would sometimes become overwhelming.

We were not just with each other 5 days a week on the bus. On weekends we would go grocery shopping together, and we would sometimes have the bus take us to Kuwaiti tourist sites. We jumped at the first chance to get a driver's license, and then we immediately set out to buy or rent cars. The funny thing was that after all of us had gotten our cars, the people that we spent most of our time with tended to be the people who had been on the bus. Given a little space, we grew to appreciate each other and enjoy each other's company. Later in the year, we would laugh about our times together on the bus.

Dating a co-worker is always a dicey issue, no matter where you live, but being in Kuwait made it that much more of a challenge. Lori and I started becoming interested in each other in late March or early April when each of us made the other one a birthday cake, and it was not long before we realized that there was a definite spark between us. The first couple of months we were determined to keep our relationship very quiet and not tell everyone at school, but soon people could see right through us. We were surprised that the first person to notice was our strong-minded Muslim principal, who was actually quite open to us dating. She began to make sly jokes and was ruining our cover. Soon all the staff members found out that we were dating, but by then we realized that the relationship would last, and we were not so concerned. We still had to deal with the fact that we were in a Muslim country, so holding hands or showing too much affection was not acceptable, but still it is amazing how much love you can communicate by a wink of the eye. Both Lori and I had already told the school that we were planning to come back to Kuwait for at least another year, so we began planning our summer and our future together. Having a special friend in Kuwait can make all the hard times seem more bearable and the good times that much better. No longer would I have to take trips by myself and ask strangers to take photos of me. I now had a partner in life; who knew I would find her in Kuwait?

Driving Through the Rearview Mirror

There were some days when literally my only goal in Kuwait was to get out alive. After experiencing some of the most frightening driving of my life, I believe this to be a worthy goal. Kuwait has a well-organized road system where the main arteries of the roads all run parallel or perpendicular to each other and cover most of Kuwait. The roads are moderately well maintained and have signs in both English and Arabic, although there are times when I wonder if the Arabic signs are saying different things than the English signs.

Stopping and yielding generally seem to be considered optional by most Kuwaitis, and the speed limit is rarely enforced or followed. "Road accidents in the State of Kuwait are the third cause of death and injury and is the number one cause of death among youths" (http://www.undp-kuwait.org). Drivers zigzag their way through the lanes at speeds of over 150 km per hour, often coming within inches of each other. The drivers are aggressive, and that, combined with the fact that they have little driver training, leads to very dangerous situations. Every day we would see a car turned upside down, some 15 m off the road, and would find ourselves trying to guess how this physically could have happened.

GOOD-BYES

Billy Joel once said in his hit song, *Say Goodbye to Hollywood*, "Life is a series of hellos and good-byes, I guess it is time for me to say good-bye again." This statement is very true when it comes to international teaching. Every year ends on a bit of a sad note, as inevitably some teachers decide to leave to go back home or to another country. Every year, e-mail addresses are exchanged and promises are made to keep in touch. People who are leaving are busy trying to sell off the items they do not want to take to their new destination, while others are simply busying themselves enough with the usual last chores that need to be completed. At school, the students' work is being removed from the walls, and the classroom textbooks are being stored away for another summer.

As students finish their last exams, they come up to the classrooms to wish us a great summer and to say a final good-bye to those teachers who are leaving forever, something that the students of international schools have gotten used to. Final exams are marked and last report cards are finished as teachers, feeling the wear and tear from the year, get ready for a long and much-needed vacation. The year seems to go by so quickly and the final weeks go even faster. Because schools fly their teachers out the day after school ends, you sometimes forget to say a proper goodbye to those who have made a difference in your life. Looking back at all the good times and bad times that I experienced in my first year as an international teacher, I can honestly say that I plan to do this for a long time, despite the struggles of hellos and good-byes.

MOVING FORWARD

Life here has been full of fun and activities. In my second year of teaching, I have gained a lot more confidence in my teaching abilities and have gained the respect of my students and co-workers as I teach mathematics, social studies, science, and outdoor education. The year started off with me proposing to Lori and continued with us planning for the future together. Some highlights include being able to take my students to Malaysia on a school trip and coaching the under-13 basketball team once again. Lori and I have decided not to return to Kuwait next year but instead to move on to Bangladesh for our next teaching experience.

Neil's Tips for Traveling Teachers

- Don't worry about bringing your entire house. You can get just about anything in Kuwait. The Sultan Center, one of the biggest grocery/retail stores in the country, carries everything from Old El Paso taco mix to chocolate chips (for you baking fanatics). You may find that shopping for the usual Western foods is a little more expensive, but we generally paid the price in order to get the comforts of home when we were missing them
- Bring loose, cool clothing, as it can climb to 50 °C in the summer. Women can, for the most part, wear capris and a T-shirt. I have seen some get away with shorts and a tank top, but that sort of clothing is generally frowned upon. Of course you can wear whatever you like in your own home. Make sure you check with your school about the dress code before you come, as our school was strict about making sure that women's bottoms were covered by whatever top they were wearing. Finding long tops may prove challenging in Western countries, where short shirts are generally preferred, but you usually can find these tops in Kuwait or get them made relatively cheaply, so don't worry about buying too many beforehand. Men can wear shorts and T-shirts; but don't expect to be able to take off your shirt in public
- One thing Lori wishes she had known beforehand was how many formal balls she would attend. Most organizations tend to host one each year, and Lori says she dressed up more in Kuwait for balls then she ever would have at home. If you have a few fancy dresses, it might be a good idea to bring one or two, as you will most likely have a chance to wear them should you so choose
- One of our greatest sanity savers was our hotel gym membership. A lot of the fancier hotels offer gym memberships, which also allow you access to their pool and beach. These are great places to be able to walk around in a bikini and not worry about what others are thinking. The gym is also a good place for an air-conditioned workout, as you will not want to run outside for most of the year
- In regard to shopping and food, I often call Kuwait a mini-America, as they have just about everything you can get at home—Starbucks, TGI Friday's, H&M, and a lot of designer stores
- I would recommend that you bring any medications that you need from home, although one thing countries in Asia seem to be known for is

cheap birth-control pills, so I wouldn't worry about stocking up for the year beforehand
- DVDs and CDs can be purchased very easily and cheaply, so unless you have a favorite eclectic movie or your CD collection is a little old and not very mainstream, I wouldn't worry too much about bringing these items
- If you are Muslim, you will definitely find your religious needs answered. For Catholics there are a couple of churches, but I am not sure how the other religions are represented
- Your social life is what you make it. If you are interested in meeting other people, then get involved. Lori joined the Kuwaiti women's rugby team and said that it made her entire experience more enjoyable. The friends she made while traveling around the Gulf playing rugby are still friends today. Others that I know joined darts leagues or played netball. There are a lot of things to get involved with; you just have to put yourself out there. Kuwait can be a very easy place to live should you choose to live like an expat—just don't forget there's an amazing culture waiting to be experienced as well! Enjoy!

Where Is Neil Now?

After 2 years living in Kuwait, Neil and Lori were married. They left 2 days after their wedding on a trip to Bangladesh to teach in their first International Baccalaureate school. During their time in Bangladesh, Lori and Neil experienced many highs and lows, including witnessing the force of Hurricane Sidr, living amongst cockroaches and ants, meeting some amazing people, and working with a local school that teaches students who live on the streets. But when they look back on their time in Bangladesh, what they will remember most is the birth of their first son, Dylan. Lori and Neil taught in Bangladesh for 3 years. They have since moved home to Canada and are dealing with all of the challenges that reverse culture shock bring. They hope their international-teaching days are just postponed, not over—Dylan has many countries yet to see!

References

Central Intelligence Agency. (2006). *The World Factbook.* Retrieved April 12, 2006, from https://www.cia.gov/library/publications/the-world-factbook/index.html

Human Rights Watch. (2001). *World Report 2001.* Retrieved April 16, 2006, from http://www.hrw.org/wr2k1/mideast/kuwait.html

CHAPTER 7

TEACHING IN THE UNITED KINGDOM

Kathryn Hillis

Who wouldn't want to live in a place where flights can cost as little as 1 cent, where places to stay are found on almost every corner, where there are people from almost every country of the world, where traveling around one of the most vital cities in the world can be done for C$5.90 a day? London, England, is where I was able to do all these things while I taught on weekdays and traveled any other time I wanted. I lived in East London in the county of Essex. The London Underground (or Tube, as it is known to us) stopped 20 paces from my doorstep and took 25 minutes to get into the heart of the city. If you are looking for an interesting place to begin your teaching career, London fits the bill. Teaching in the London area has provided me with many positive and negative experiences and has greatly deepened my understanding of teaching and living in another country.

When I first began the process of finding a job in England, it did not prove to be difficult. A quick search on Google yielded many different recruitment companies from which to choose. I had a friend who already had obtained a job in Essex through a company called TimePlan. TimePlan came to my university to recruit teachers for locations throughout the world. At the time, I had no interest in teaching overseas but later realized that doing so would be a wonderful opportunity. About a month after applying, I had a face-to-face interview with a representative of TimePlan and was soon offered the opportunity to work in a program called guaranteed work agreement (GWA). This program is offered solely by TimePlan and, in my opinion, is ideal for teachers who are in England to travel and teach. The program guarantees work 8 days out of 10 and is what Canadians would call supply work; in this situation, you do not hold a contract with any particular school but work for the recruitment agency itself. If I had accepted the position with them, I would have received a call every evening (or most often in the early morning) from TimePlan telling me where to go for work the next day. Most schools will keep you on to help with the planning, preparation, and assessment period or for certain specified days of the week if they like you. Schools also have the right to ask TimePlan never to send you back. After the mid-February break, it is more difficult to secure day-to-day work, and sometimes you may find yourself being paid to work 8 days even though you only worked 6 or 7. The downside of is this arrangement is that you will not know in advance whether your day is free, and the upside is that you can take days off whenever you like without calling in sick and you may get paid for more days than you work. At the beginning of the year, four of my friends were on GWA; only one now remains (by choice). The other three have secured full-time positions in schools where they did GWA work throughout the year.

When I received the offer to work on the GWA, I thought about it but quickly rejected the idea. My reason for rejecting it was simple: I wanted my own classroom. I began applying to different recruitment agencies on the Internet, and after four phone interviews, I secured two offers for positions in secondary schools in Essex. The position I chose was in the school closest to my friends. I am somewhat of an independent sort, but the thought of living far away from every person I knew was frightening. I secured a place through an agency called Uteach Recruitment based in Coatbridge, North Lanarkshire, Scotland (near Glasgow). I found them to be very friendly and professional, and they helped me secure a perfect position in a Catholic secondary school in the Borough of Barking and Dagenham—the same borough as my friend, Liam. Liam and I decided we should live together to help one another through the tough times as first-year teachers and moved into a house that was a 20-minute drive from our schools.

We both began teaching school 4 days after our arrival at our new place, but the experiences Liam and I were to encounter would prove to be very different. I was hired by the school to provide maternity-leave cover for the year. The teacher I was to replace was not due to leave until after the break in October, so I was assigned to be in her classroom to help out any time I was not needed to cover other lessons throughout the day. The secondary schools in the borough do not often call in supply teachers; rather, they have staff cover the lessons of other staff during their preparatory time. My job until October was to cover lessons of staff that were away sick, out on Inset (educational growing), or on school trips. I was happy to be this person for the first month of school, as I could learn words and customs that were foreign for me, see different aspects of the school, meet other teachers, and meet all the students in the school quickly. By October though, the novelty was wearing off and I found myself growing increasingly unhappy. I knew before I arrived that I wanted my own class, and this experience just confirmed it for me. I grew tired of covering lessons created by others, teaching French and science, and not having anything to mark or do during my off time, but with some difficulty I stuck it out until the end of the month. After the break in October, I was finally given my own religious-education classroom, and I felt great. I had some difficulty the first few weeks because the students had known me as a cover teacher who did not stand at the front and teach (more giving work to do for the lesson). I took the first few days to lay down my ground rules, and the students responded well.

The schools in England are all organized in the same way. Reception is the youngest grade level; primary school begins with reception. Then students complete Year 1 to Year 6, at the end of which they sit for Standardized Attainment Tests (SATs) in English, math, and science. Secondary school begins in Year 7 and ends in Year 11. In Year 9 they sit for SATs in English, math, and science. Mandatory education finishes in Year 11 with completion of the General Certificate of Secondary Education (GCSE) examinations, usually in 10-11 subjects. Pupils can then apply to enter Years 12 and 13, which are the gateway into university (this is called the college level or A level). An A level is required in order to go to any university in the United Kingdom. The students are not able to be held back a year; every student moves on, although which class they are placed in the next year is based on their test results.

At times I would find myself agreeing with this system, while at other times I disagreed. I found that some students did not have the drive to complete homework or assignments as readily as they would in Canada. I believe this difference is due to the fact that the tests have no bearing on what happens to them the next year, and the same can be said of homework and assignments. There are no finals to study for, and, as a result, many students tend to put in the most effort at the end of Year 9 and Year 11, which can mean that much of the remaining time seems wasted.

When I first arrived, the military-like treatment of the students in my secondary school was surprising to me. After speaking with Liam about his school, I realized that I was one of the lucky ones. Since my school is the only Catholic school in the borough, the students are selected based on Catholicity. Students must have a signed letter from their parish priest stating that they are a regular, participatory member of the congregation. There are 180 students accepted each year to begin Year 7 and more than 400 applicants. All of the other students must go to the secondary school in their school boundaries. Liam's school is one of these other schools. The positive aspect about my school is that when students misbehave in an extreme way and are to be expelled, it is simple enough to have them removed. The ability to remove difficult students from the school is an encouraging point about working in a Catholic school in England.

My experience in teaching in this part of England is that it is nothing like teaching in Canada. The school I work in would be considered an incredibly challenging school (in regard to teaching) in Ontario. So, if you are looking for a challenge, this is the place to be. Please don't misunderstand me: I believe teaching is teaching, and if you are in the profession to help students learn things about themselves and to achieve their goals, then it does not matter where you teach. But if you are in the profession to help only students who are highly motivated and who are already committed to being successful, then Essex may not be the place for you. As a younger teacher, if you treat the students with respect, they will respond to you, but they will initially try to take advantage of you. As I was young and from another country, the students did try to take advantage of my lack of knowledge when it came to the language. I recommend you try to learn quickly the slang and lingo of where you live. I have learned that the local slang here in Dagenham has been dubbed Dageneeze. Here, if a student says, "Is it?" in response to you teaching him a new fact, that means, "Really?" When a student says he had a *lady gidiver* stolen, it means a five-pound note (or a fiver). Do not say *garbage* or *trash* unless you want the class to erupt in fits of laughter or have students copying your accent—the word they use is *rubbish*. The worst mistake I made was in saying *khaki pants*. First of all, in England, pants are what you wear underneath your clothing (your underwear). Second, khaki, the color, is pronounced *cock-y* because if you pronounce it *cack-y*, they will immediately associate the meaning of the word *cack* with a bowel movement. Put these two meanings together and we get, "shitty underpants" rather than khaki pants! This use proved to be very entertaining for the staff as well as the students.

The town in which I live struggles with gangs and resultant gang violence. Currently, there is a major crackdown on gang violence, the possession of weapons (mostly knives), wearing of gang colors, and, most recently, wearing hats, scarves, and hoodies in public. There are often fights at my school, but at the school down the street, Liam personally breaks up students fighting at least once a day and sometimes up to three times a day. The issue with regard to students and violence in this community is serious; it sometimes appears that the city is doing little about it, but what I have realized since being here is that the city is actually doing the best it can. There are programs throughout the city that put police officers in the community. These police officers will charge parents if students are not in school during school hours—whether the reason is gang related or not. There are officers in most schools trying to keep the peace amongst the students, and the teachers are all aware of which students are most likely to cause trouble. Although violence seems to occur in school a lot, parents and teachers usually are better off with the students being *in school* causing trouble rather than out on the street. This realization has allowed teachers to handle situations more carefully and be more creative with punishments.

Though violence is a common occurrence, the regular everyday management of the classroom is very positive and proactive. In my school, the teachers are subject based, with multiple teachers in each area as well as the expected administration. The head teacher (like the principal) is at the top of the list, and, depending on the size of the school, is closely followed by (usually) two deputy head teachers (like the vice principal). There are a few people in senior administration positions who are not generally known throughout the student population, and then there are a few in these positions who are regularly seen and heard from throughout the day. The head of year is a position taken on by a member of staff who is planning to move toward administration in later years. The head of each year instills fear in his or her year group and is responsible for management of that group. The military tactics I mentioned earlier tend to be employed by the people in these positions. If I ever have a problem with a student in my class, I am asked not to send the student into the corridor (due to the chaos that would cause). My first point of contact is my head of department. I am very lucky in this area because my head of department is a man who is loved by all the staff and feared by all the students, and usually the mere threat of sending a student to him is enough, but when it is not, off they go. When my head of department is not available or when a student is being especially difficult, my second point of contact is the head of year. The heads of year have classes just like any other teacher and do not receive any extra time off, but they are very happy to take students into their rooms for the duration of the lesson. This not only gives the head of year the upper hand because the student must sit and fear his or her punishment, but it also allows classroom teachers to get on with the lesson without further disruption.

The heads of year and heads of department are not the only people supporting classroom teachers on a daily basis. The final backup comes from a useful source: other classroom teachers. I find that other teachers are always willing to take a student who is acting out of sorts into their class.

Most classroom teachers are responsible for 30 students in much the same way that a Canadian homeroom teacher would be responsible. Their system calls these homeroom classes *forms*. In Year 7, there could be six forms and, in my Catholic school, the forms are named after saints. For example, J-O-S-E-P-H would mean that 7J would report to one teacher before and after school for registration (attendance) while 7P would report to another teacher. Each form keeps the same form group, usually throughout their stay at the school. An exception is made if a form is particularly naughty one year and needs sorting out (more discipline). This would mean that the form teacher would then be a more senior member or staff or, most likely, a head of department.

The extracurricular involvement in England is very similar to that which one would see in a Canadian system. Most of the sports-related activities are coached by members of the physical-education department, while other groups are led by volunteer staff members. When I was in my early years of postsecondary-school education in Canada and tried to imagine myself as a teacher, my goal was to be the same kind of coach that positively influenced my life throughout my high school years. When I arrived here, I realized how difficult that would be. The sports that are so prevalent and popular in Canadian culture are not necessarily the same as the ones recognized in the United Kingdom. The main sports played by males are soccer (from here on called *football*, as it is in the United Kingdom) and rugby, while the female equivalent is netball. It was not a surprise to me that football is so popular here, in large part due to the well-known World Cup, but their passion for the sport was still a bit shocking. Their passion exceeds my earlier fervor for all things related to hockey, basketball or American football. When it comes to the female sport of netball, I have no words. I had never heard of netball before coming here. I have played basketball in one form or another since I was 8, and when I came here and was told that girls do not play basketball because it is a boy's sport, I was shocked and appalled. The same reaction was directed toward me when my students realized I was not kidding when I said that I had never heard of netball. I began holding a basketball session every Wednesday morning starting in October, and the number of players gradually decreased. The love of the game is not yet what I had anticipated and my heart is saddened slightly, but I digress.

There are regular after-school clubs here such as Homework Club and Art Club, just as there are in Canada. The need for teachers to volunteer to run these clubs is also the same, and if one is inclined toward a specific activity and asks early, the school is more than willing to get on board. Just like in Canada, if a teacher is interested in helping students outside regular school hours, the schools are usually more than willing to consent.

Overall, teaching in the United Kingdom has been a positive learning experience. At the moment, I am still trying to decide what to do next year. I can stay here, move to another place, or go home to Canada. It is a very difficult decision to make because after 8 months of teaching, I am getting used to being here and it would be hard to leave. I do not believe I have finished traveling (which was the driving force behind my coming to London), but I miss my family and friends. I have made many new friends from all over the world and feel that no matter where I end up, I will always be able to visit someone I met during my time in the United Kingdom. Teaching in London has been a challenge, but the rewards are numerous. I think that no matter where you end up teaching, the students will be somewhat similar. There may be different degrees of behavioral issues, but those issues are to be expected, as kids will be kids. As long you educate yourself with regard to your destination before you leave Canada, you will be able to adapt to any new surroundings. The world is not as big as it seems, especially in the United Kingdom, where you can travel to so many different countries in the span of a few hours.

Kathryn's Tips for Traveling Teachers

What to Bring

- Plug adapter
- Leave hair straighteners at home; buy a £30 one here and it works better than a $150 one from home
- Addresses of friends and relatives
- Phone cards
- Mobile phone with SIM card (or just buy one when you get here)

Questions to Ask

- When do you get paid for the first time?
- How often will you get paid?
- Are you working for a company? Do you have to stay with that company for at least a year or can you transfer to be paid by the borough (school)?
- If you are having financial difficulties, will your company help you out (by holding on taking your rent or loaning you money)?
- How much is rent?
- How close is your place to public transportation?
- What are the teacher's responsibilities (in your school)?
- What classes are you teaching? (Many of my colleagues had classes given to them unexpectedly, and they found themselves teaching classes they had never even heard of)
- Does the company you work for host social events to make it easier to meet others in the same situation as yourself?

What to Expect

- You will need to listen very closely to people (especially students); some accents are stronger than others and you will have to work hard to understand what is being said
- You will need to change your vocabulary slightly to match the place in which you live—slang is strong in some areas
- Curriculum is different from that used in Canada in minor ways, and marking is different in major ways; learn the marking scheme early—it will make your life easier throughout the year

Teaching in the United Kingdom

- Expect to ask questions and need help with school-related issues (behavior, policies, marking, etc.)

Important Paperwork

- Working visa (whether it is a 2-year working visa, a holiday visa, a 5-year ancestry visa, etc.); this takes awhile to get and involves a lot of paperwork, so look and apply early
- Copies of your passport; leave at least one copy at home in Canada and have a few on you when you go over. Whenever you travel anywhere, take at least one copy and leave one at home in the United Kingdom

Financial Considerations

- Make sure you have enough money in your bank account to last you for at least 6 weeks! Often you will not be paid for 4 weeks, but companies are known to make errors once in awhile and you may have to wait longer
- If you work directly for the borough, you will be paid monthly—this is the best way to go if you can swing it; otherwise be prepared to be paid biweekly or weekly
- Try your best not to compare the prices. Remember that you are being paid in pounds, not dollars, so comparing the prices will make you think that you are paying way more than you should for things (although alcohol and fast food seems cheap)
- There is a company in the United Kingdom called My Key Pay, which pays special attention to your financial earnings and the amount that is deducted for tax. Try to join a company like this one so you can keep the money that should not come off your pay in the first place. Claim everything you possibly can and your paychecks will be heavier

If I Had to Do It Again, I Would...

- Not live in the housing supplied by the company (such as TimePlan). Although it is a great way to meet new people, you also can meet people at school. Live somewhere you are comfortable and with the number of people you want. I lived with seven other people and had to share a room for the first 4 months.

- Actually read the Web site I found about the curriculum in the United Kingdom. It would have made the change a lot easier to bear
- Make sure the school I was going to was what I wanted (look up articles on them, check out marks, research administration)
- Check out the quality of the area in which I was to be living
- Try to speak to another teacher who was living and teaching in the area
- Find a company that fit my needs (TimePlan finds places for you to live, picks you up from the airport when you arrive, and, upon arrival, gives you a mobile phone to keep)

WHERE IS KATHRYN NOW?

I took the 6-week summer holiday and went home to Canada. Almost immediately after arriving home, I decided that London, England, was where I wanted to spend the next year of my life. I returned to Essex in September to work as a supply teacher for TimePlan (the company Liam worked for last year). They found me accommodations with five other Canadian women teaching in the area. I still see all of my old friends and continue to make new friends from around the world. I travel as much as I can and just spent a wonderful holiday on the island of Gran Canaria with 29° weather in February. Liam has also returned but he has moved to the south of England to live with some family and teach. He has met many wonderful friends and comes to London to visit me often. I am heading home (for good…I think!) in April to volunteer and look for a teaching job in Canada. I will miss all the new friends I've made, but I can always come back—or go to another part of the world. The past 2 years have allowed me to make friends from all over, so I'll always have a place to stay!

CHAPTER 8

TEACHING IN THAILAND

Erin Hoover

As I was sitting on the plane from Tokyo, Japan, to Bangkok, Thailand, there were many things going through my head. I was very excited to finally be fulfilling a dream of teaching internationally as well as teaching in Thailand. I really had no idea what lay ahead of me. I had done some reading on Thailand and of course knew people who knew people who had traveled through Southeast Asia or taught in Thailand. I heard many stories, some positive and some negative. I found my new teaching position through the Internet after many, many hours of searching and sending out my curriculum vitae. I knew that my school was small and was in some sort of compound-type area for foreigners. The name of my school was Rose International School (RIS).[*] I had been hired to teach in the child center at a level they call C1 (children aged 2 years) and to teach music to primary and high school students. The school was run by an American woman who was in the process of developing

---

[*] The name of the school has been changed.

a new curriculum. I was asked to help write a music curriculum for the school.

RIS was considered a private international school, and it had been open for 6 years. I had arrived to teach for the last session of their summer school program, before the regular school year began in August. I had been hoping that this would give me time to adjust to another culture, as the summer sessions are only half day, and I could ease my way into things.

I had no idea what my living accommodations would be like or which area I would be in (I knew it was not in the city.) All of these things were very exciting for me to ponder during my flight to the other side of the world.

When I arrived at the Bangkok International Airport, there was a woman from my school who was waiting for me. We retrieved my things, were picked up by the school van, and were driven to my new apartment. I was pleasantly surprised that my new condo was very upscale. The small community that was now my home was like a mini-America. I wasn't sure if that was a good thing or a bad thing. I knew that living there wasn't going to make venturing out into the real Thailand very easy at first.

When I arrived at school the next day, I was very hot, extremely anxious, and very excited. All of the Thai staff that I had met so far had been very helpful with their smiling, polite conduct. My classroom was small, but I only had eight students in my class. I moved in right away, rearranged things, and got comfortable. My kids were very receptive to me and understood enough English for us to communicate with each other and for them to learn. Having my afternoons free gave me a chance to work on a music curriculum and plan for the school year ahead. I worked hard researching other curricula and seeing what resources were available for me at the school.

When August 8 arrived, it was time for teacher orientation. At this time there was no school schedule, and I was informed that I would now be teaching the C2 level class (children aged 3 years) instead of C1 and would teach music only to the high school students. I thought this change was interesting. I am quite easy to get along with, and some might say too flexible. Having no other choice, I smiled and said, "All right then." I was very disappointed that I wouldn't be able to teach primary music, as it was my major subject area and the area that had originally ignited my passion for teaching. My first lesson about teaching in Thailand was that one must be very flexible and open to many changes.

As the school year began, there were a few more things that required me to be flexible. The first one was the music curriculum, which I worked quite hard to create for this special school. Nobody informed me that in the high school program, all the courses for which students will receive a credit have to be approved by a high school affiliate in the United States. Furthermore, the high school students attending RIS were mostly English-as-a-second-language students, students with attention-deficit disorder, students who had behavioral problems, or students who were having a very hard time making it through the tough International Baccalaureate diploma curriculum that many of the other international schools in Thailand offered. In addition, these students were going to be told on their first day of school that they were required to take three new specialist courses in order to stay at RIS, music being one of them. "Great," I thought, "these kids are going to love me!"

It was very difficult dealing with the closed-mindedness of the owner of RIS. The school director dictated everything that happened within the school, even the way in which the teachers set up their classrooms. She needed to be a part of every decision made, from the child center to the high school. Nobody ever knew whether she had any of the proper credentials for making decisions on every level of education within her school. Due to many teachers disagreeing with her philosophy on how to run the school, there was a big teacher turnover at the end of my first year. Teachers became tired of always waiting for approval on things like report cards, class trips, and anything dealing with the budget. Even though there were two co-directors, everything always came down to what she thought was right and what she wanted.

I was very surprised, however, to learn that every class in the child center as well as primary grades had a teaching assistant. Can you imagine?

I now had someone in my classroom to take my students to the toilet, clean up all craft messes, photocopy things for me, retrieve supplies from the storeroom, and help with preparing activities. Unbelievable—and I only had 10 students in my class! After practice teaching in Canada and working all night to prepare lessons, I now had been provided with an assistant to help with all of those small things that take up so much time. It took me quite awhile to get used to giving her things to do. I insisted on doing most things myself until, slowly, I was able to delegate some things to her.

The Thai people are very, very generous. In general, they always have smiling faces, always ask about your health, and ask if there is anything they can do for you. If you walk by a Thai person on the street, rich or poor, and you a smile, you always seem to receive a smile in return. This politeness is a part of Thai culture and behavior. Another cultural aspect that you will notice if you teach in Thailand is the obvious hierarchy that exists. I have witnessed many occasions of higher administration officials treating the Thai staff with disrespect and basically treating them like servants. The pay rate for Thai staff is very low, and they sometimes are yelled at in front of others and are told they are stupid. This kind of treatment is not always so obvious, but the general attitude is definitely always present. I also noticed that most Thai staff seem to separate themselves from the foreign staff. I'm sure that it has something to do with language, but it still makes me wonder why they seemed to put us on a pedestal. Every Thai person with whom I have had a conversation would love to come to North America and thinks very highly of the Western culture; but my reaction is to think to myself, if they only knew how lucky they were to have certain aspects of this easygoing, laid-back way of life.

The Thai culture has great respect for elders and family members. It's actually quite difficult to teach a family unit to young Thai children because everyone is their sister or their brother, even if that person is actually an aunt or a close family friend. You witness respect being shown from a very young age, when the children are taught to make a small bow, with their hands in a prayer position close to the forehead.

This is called a *wai*, and it is very rude not to wai someone who is older than you. They will, in return, wai you back. The Western culture is easing its way into Bangkok, and things that used to be considered very rude (such as showing your shoulders) are becoming more and more acceptable.

There are certain cultural understandings that teachers need to be aware of in order to avoid showing disrespect. They include patting children on the head (the head is thought of as the place the soul resides), pointing with your feet or pointing your feet toward a Buddha image or a well-respected person (the feet are low, and to show someone the most bottom part of your body is thought to be extremely rude), and elevating your feet up on your desk. The clothes that you wear to school must be very professional with no open-toe shoes, exposed shoulders, short skirts, or low tops. I found it difficult to keep all of these things in mind when interacting with students. A parent actually mentioned that they saw me pointing to something with my foot while speaking with the director of my school and thought that I should be made aware of this cultural faux pas.

When teaching in Thailand, teachers need to understand how parents will be involved and be aware of their expectations regarding education. Thai education is heavily geared toward homework and worksheets. Most parents do not speak to the teachers very often, and you might not see them more than four times a year. The families of children in international schools tend to have a lot of money, as tuition is very expensive, and many students are dropped off and picked up by their grandparents, maids, or drivers. Depending on the type of curriculum offered by the international school, parents may also need to be educated on the current teaching methods and curriculum.

Thai parents are very protective of their children. Most children up to the age of 10 years sleep with their parents. Thai people do not like the sun because it makes skin dark, and to be dark is to be of the lower class and ugly. Obviously these upper-class Thai parents would not want their children becoming dark. There are many whitening creams and powders that are intended to make skin whiter. I find it very ironic that Western people just want suntans and get as dark as they can on their vacations, and Thai people usually swim in their clothes to protect themselves from the sun. The first time one of my students came to school with white stuff on her face and arms, I was wondering why someone didn't rub it in for her. Some parents even go as far as bleaching their child's skin.

The students will also come to school with a handkerchief around the neck if they are slightly ill, because parents think that this practice will protect their child from further illness. You will also be told not to give them cold water if they are sick or have a fever; they must only have warm water. It is very hot in Thailand, on average 30–38 °C. Can you imagine wanting a glass of warm water after you just had recess? Maybe that will be me in another year!

Teaching in Thailand has been an enormous learning experience for me. For the most part, things are positive. But it all depends on your attitude, how much patience you have, and how flexible you are willing to be. International teachers experience a different way of life in Thailand. Most things happen slowly and people are not in a hurry for anything. The reason could be the heat, or it could be the smiling faces and the "mai pen rai" (meaning *never mind* or *don't worry*) that you hear quite often coming from the mouths of Thai people. Now that I have had this teaching experience and know that there are international schools in virtually every country in the world, I don't know if I can go back to teaching in Canada. Once you gain some international experience, you can choose your next destination. As with anywhere in the world, some schools are better than others. Some challenges remain the same regardless of location: politics, parental issues, and the busyness of life as a teacher. I feel very lucky to have taught in Thailand and to have discovered the international-school circuit at this point in my teaching career. International schools often have more funding than public schools in Canada and the United States and can provide different opportunities for students and teachers.

I love Thailand. After my initial 1-year contract ended, I decided to sign on for another 2 years at a trilingual international school that offers English, Chinese, and Thai. If I finally decide it is time to leave

Thailand, the decision will have been a difficult one. The only thing that will make it easier for me is knowing that I can continue to travel, embrace new cultures, meet new people, and experience the excitement all over again.

Erin's Tips for Traveling Teachers

When I began my teaching adventure in Thailand, I was ready for the journey and for whatever challenges lay ahead of me. Make sure that you are ready for the exciting adventure of living in a new country. You may not enjoy yourself during all new experiences, but keep an open mind! You may sometimes find it hard to appreciate the cultural differences you will encounter, but remember that all experiences, personal and cultural, will influence who you are and help to determine who you will become.

What to Bring

- All of us have different needs with regard to the things and resources that we bring with us from place to place. Many international schools in Thailand offer some sort of relocation allowance, but if you are going to work in a local school, this funding might not be available. If it is offered, then you don't have to be so selective in deciding what to bring. If you like to have your personal things with you, then bring them to help make your new living space comfortable
- You should contact some of the teachers who are currently working at the school to ask them for suggestions. If you are working in or close to Bangkok, you can get everything that you need at a slightly higher cost than at home. This includes clothes, food, medicines, and accessories. Depending on your size, it may be difficult to find clothes that fit you properly, so make sure that you bring some comfortable clothes for teaching. Even though it's very hot, many schools and buildings are kept very cool, so layers are good
- As areas in Bangkok and Thailand are fairly spread out, it's good to know where the school is located in regard to Bangkok, the airport, the city where you will be living, and your housing accommodations. If you are planning on teaching in southern Thailand, find out about the political situation first. You may need to follow some recommended safety precautions
- As there are many different types of places and areas to live, housing is important. You will want to know if the school will provide accommodations or if they will provide you with the monthly accommodation

allowance. Is the accommodation close to other teachers at the school? Is it close to public transport? Do you have to pay the water and electricity bills? (My water bill was always very low, but the electricity bill was high if the air conditioning was running constantly)
- Ask whether your salary is fixed to the U.S. dollar, as fluctuations in the exchange rate can affect your monthly wage. Ask whether you receive a relocation allowance and whether you will receive the money before or after you relocate
- Ask about insurance for health and travel
- Ask about the teacher resources that are available—not just books, but supplies as well. Are there resources to support the curriculum and your teachings? Ask for a copy of the curriculum that you will be expected to teach so you can get an idea of resources that you might want to bring with you
- To get an idea about the location of your school and home, ask about the travel time to and from certain destinations (e.g., from your home to the school, airport, bus terminal, or Skytrain). There is a lot of traffic in Bangkok, and at times this can cause a trip that should take 25 minutes to actually last an hour or more
- Ask about the school dress code, as sometimes the information in the teacher handbook doesn't coincide with what people actually wear while teaching
- You might also come up with other questions after you read through the teacher handbook, so ask if a copy can be e-mailed to you

What to Expect

Expect the unexpected! If you have never traveled to Thailand or Asia before, then you might be surprised by the different things that you will experience throughout your journey. The Thai people are amazingly respectful, kind, and helpful. The pace of life is very slow, and sometimes it can take a long time to get things sorted, confirmed, or planned—and that's OK! As Westerners, we're so used to a faster pace of life that it can get frustrating. Try not to let yourself become frustrated. Just go with the flow, as they say. It is hot in Thailand, but you will acclimatize and get used to the different seasons eventually. Everyone always says that there are three seasons in Thailand—hot, hotter, and hottest! Bring clothes for work and pleasure that you will be comfortable wearing in the heat.

Important Paperwork

Make sure that you get this information from the school before you arrive. You should receive an information package that will provide you with information regarding the required paperwork. Bring originals and copies of your diplomas and transcripts (even if they don't ask) because you will need them in order to receive your work permit. Leave a copy of all of your documents with someone before you leave the country and scan them into the computer so that if something happens and you lose them, you'll have a copy on your computer and a copy at home.

Financial Considerations

Make sure you know how much money you might need to have with you when you first arrive in Thailand and when you will be getting your first paycheck. If you leave money in your bank at home, you can easily withdraw money using the ATM, but it will cost you. You want to make sure that you can cover all of your financial obligations at home while you are away. If you have a student loan with the government, you can request a year at a lower interest rate. Also, if you are planning on sending money back to your bank at home, see how much this service will cost at that bank, as you'll also be charged by your bank in Thailand. Money orders are cheaper to send via Speedpost if you have someone you trust to deposit the money for you. Last, look into Canadian taxes and how you will go about filing them when you are overseas. Depending on how long you are planning to be away, there are several options for you to consider.

If I Had to Do It Again, I Would...

If I could do it all over again, I wouldn't change anything, as everything I experienced has made me who I am today and delivered me to where I am right now, and I can think of no better place to be!

 Once I entered the world of international teaching, I knew that I couldn't leave it and be faced with standardized testing, large class sizes, and limited resources. I recommend new teachers look into many different international schools and the packages they offer, as there are some schools that offer extremely good packages if you have the experience.

WHERE IS ERIN NOW?

After completing her 1-year contract with the Rose International School in Thailand, Erin moved to a larger international school on the other side of Bangkok, where she remained for 2 more years. At this school Erin discovered a curriculum about which she began to feel very passionate: the International Baccalaureate Primary Years Program (IBPYP). Over the course of her 2-year stay there, Erin had the opportunity to develop professionally. She participated in and conducted workshops, had the opportunity to take on administrative duties in the capacity of early years IBPYP coordinator, and learned from her knowledgeable colleagues while working alongside them. When her 2-year contract was complete, Erin decided to move on. She chose to remain in Southeast Asia, as there were many opportunities in teaching and administration. Erin took a position at an international school in Hong Kong, where she was promoted again to IBPYP coordinator. Erin also became an IBPYP workshop leader within the Asia Pacific area, where she traveled to different Asian countries to conduct workshops. She has taken a small break from the classroom in her role of vice principal and IBPYP coordinator. She will soon move to a teaching position at an authorized IBPYP school in Tokyo, Japan. Erin is a strong believer in the notion that you will never know unless you try. If you try teaching internationally and discover that working overseas is not for you, then at least you have gained experience both professionally and personally that would not have been possible otherwise, and these experiences will remain with you forever.

CHAPTER 9

TEACHING IN THAILAND

Amelia Swanson

The following is based on my personal experiences and perceptions. This commentary is not intended to speak universally nor does it speak for other teachers or expatriates at Lertlah School International Program.

THINGS ARE NOT WHAT THEY SEEM

"What have I done?" These were my thoughts as I boarded the flight for the final leg of my journey. I had left behind my family, my friends, and the man I thought I was going to spend the rest of my life with all to pursue my dream of teaching and living in a foreign country. In a matter of weeks, I had found a teaching job, signed a 1-year contract, received the required vaccinations, and moved my entire life across the world. I chose to walk away from familiar surroundings and a network of support and go to a country where I could not speak the language and I didn't know anyone.

I left Ontario on July 11 for my first teaching job. I had graduated 6 weeks earlier and was set to embark on an educational adventure halfway around the globe. My destination: Thailand, the country of exotic beauty, intriguing culture, and thousands of years of history and tradition. I was to become a part of it for 1 year; a blink of the eye in the context of its existence. And yet, that short span of time would alter my perceptions of teaching, learning, and myself more than I ever could have imagined. My travel and work-abroad dreams were finally becoming a reality; the prospect was terrifying, exhilarating, and irresistible all at the same time.

As the plane finally touched down in the country that was to become my new home, I accepted the inevitable adventure that surely awaited me. Turning back was not an option. Fortunately, the school was prepared for my arrival, and I was greeted by a small group of teachers, both foreign and Thai, holding a sign with big bold letters that said, "AMELIA SWANSON—LERTLAH SCHOOL." The relief that accompanied seeing those words was enormous. I would not be left at the airport forced to navigate my way through this strange new world of cultural and communication barriers.

As I walked toward the group, I could not anticipate how the next 365 days would challenge me beyond anything else I had ever experienced.

Introductions were completed, suitcases were unloaded, and I began my journey into Bangkok. I had been warned about the severe heat; and yet, I could never have been prepared for the wet blanket of humidity that hit me as I exited the airport. It was 3 a.m.; how would I survive the heat of the midday sun? (As it turned out, I never really adjusted. I simply learned to accept that sweat was ever present and that baby powder really was a necessity.)

I was offered the front seat of the school van so that I could take in the sights. Even at that hour, there was much to be seen! Within 10 minutes of leaving the airport, we passed a car completely engulfed by flames in the middle of the highway, but there were no police officers, ambulances, or even a fire truck. Welcome to Bangkok, where one's senses are never dulled! I may have been awake for over 30 hours, but sleep was a distant thought. Who could close their eyes with so much to see: trucks filled with groups of people sleeping in the cabs, packs of dogs roaming the streets, Christmas lights, vendors on every corner—did this city ever experience a quiet moment? I quickly realized this was the land of smiles and never-ending action.

And so I began my journey of exploration and growth as teacher, student, and foreigner in Thailand.

JULY 14 DIARY EXCERPT

"Sleep is impossible. My internal clock is completely out of synch and I cannot fathom lying in bed when there is an entire world to be explored right under my balcony. The three hours I did manage to find ended abruptly as I wakened to Bon Jovi's song, *Living on a Prayer*, blaring from the street below. I never imagined that I would travel half way around the world to be met with Bon Jovi music. Is this the exotic life I had anticipated? Where is the Thai music?"

I remember standing on my balcony staring with fascination at the sights on the street below: Thai children running barefoot chasing a soccer ball, dogs barking, row upon row of metal roofing and homes doubling as store fronts. Adrenalin flowed with this onslaught of stimulation, and I headed straight to the streets of my new neighborhood.

The first couple of days were an explosion of sensations: new (and often foul) smells, intense heat, spicy flavors, exhaust from vehicles, incessantly honking horns, and above all else, sights that enticed me from every direction. I never knew where to look: at the orange-robed monks, elephants walking down the busy streets, pink buses, roosters on the sidewalks, limbless beggars on the bridges, endless rows of market stalls—I needed another pair of eyes! But nothing could compare with my discovery that elephants lived in my backyard in the field across from my apartment building. Even after a year, I never tired of watching my backyard friends. I truly was a long way from North Bay!

No matter how many situations I learned to master, it was often difficult to adjust to my surroundings, and I quickly realized I would forever be a *farang*, or foreigner, according to Thai people. One could live in Thailand for 20 years, speak the language fluently, and even marry into a Thai family and yet remain forever an outsider in this place. As a 6-foot-tall white woman, I truly experienced what it was like to be a zoo animal; people hanging out of buses to get a better look, pointing, cameras clicking (I still wonder how often my picture was taken by strangers). My first weeks were a real challenge in this respect, as I was completely unused to the constant attention I received every time I set foot out of my apartment building. I discovered that being viewed as a celebrity can be highly intrusive. Blending in with the local people was not an option. My height was definitely a disadvantage when it came to public transportation; I am certain the day I had my hair sucked into the fan while riding the bus is still a great story for those lucky enough to witness the event! The ability to laugh at oneself is truly essential when trying to navigate through a foreign country, which is a humbling experience indeed.

Adjustment to life in Thailand was challenging, but my sense of adventure helped me embrace the struggle—most of the time. On an immediate level, the maniacal pace of Bangkok was overwhelming. It took me 3 weeks to feel confident enough to travel around the city on my own. I lived on the edge of Bangkok, at the city limits. The neighborhood was completely Thai, and the only other foreigners were my colleagues from Lertlah. I remember eating phad Thai every day for the first 2 weeks until I learned how to pronounce another dish. Living in this neighborhood was preferable to living downtown, however, where many of my colleagues congregated. The pace was less frenetic and there were not many Western amenities, malls, or movie theaters; nor was there much contact with the numerous expats living in the city. I was able to tolerate only one trip per weekend into the city core, as it was always an intense experience. My apartment doubled as my refuge after a day in downtown Bangkok, where there was 35° heat, 100% humidity, noise pollution, air pollution, and crowded streets. I could only handle so much.

August 23 Diary Entry

"...even grocery shopping is intense. There is great fascination with what foreigners purchase and one's shopping cart is the source of great intrigue and observation. Not to mention dance music blaring throughout the store and an entourage of Thai women selling hair products and washing hair in the fish sticks aisle..."

I entered Lertlah School International Program only 48 hours after stepping off the plane, and I felt I was in a dream. The newness of the city combined with the newness of the school, staff, and hundreds of energetic Thai children often led me to ask if I was really there or simply dreaming in my familiar bed in Canada. (As soon as my alarm would go off every morning, I would walk over to my map of the world—scanning for cockroaches on the floor first—and look at Thailand and think, "I can't believe I am really here!")

My position at the school was as an elementary Physical Education (PE) teacher—the first female PE teacher the school had experienced. The female Thai teachers were horrified that I actually enjoyed teaching sports, running around outside sweating, and displaying a great deal of boisterous energy. Apparently, I was looked at in wonder and perhaps as less feminine for behaving in such a stereotypically male manner. I had to battle to make PE a priority, as it was always the first period eliminated if an assembly was called. I was up against deeply ingrained ideas of male and female behavior. For instance, one of my female Grade 6 students was not allowed to participate in the lunch-hour basketball league I had organized, because her mother deemed it inappropriate behavior for girls. I tried to convince her otherwise but to no avail; swimming, tennis, and running were considered female activities, not basketball. That expectation was very tough to comply with, as this student was not only the best athlete in the school, but she adored participating in athletics.

This idea of behavioral expectations based on gender was a constant source of frustration for me. My personal experience and socialization in Canada certainly contributed to my struggle with this aspect of Thai culture. I often found it difficult to shelve my own ideas and accept the Thai way of thinking. I had never experienced anything like this conflict, and it took many months of reflection after leaving Thailand to understand that life in a foreign country is far easier when one stops trying to impose one's own philosophy and ideals.

Although I was able to adjust to daily life fairly well in a Thai city (travel, food, shopping, etc.), the cultural adjustment was often far more difficult. Prior to my arrival in Thailand, I had expected culture shock to be one all-encompassing moment of surprise and overwhelming astonishment. I also believed it would dissipate after my initial moments in a foreign land. So how can I explain the many days in which I felt frustration, confusion, and anger? These emotions were a result of the near-constant culture shock I experienced. I felt I was playing a game in which the rules were always changing and were never explained to me. It really was not until I had returned to Canada that I was able to identify the ways I had resisted cultural acclimatization.

AUGUST 4 E-MAIL TO PARENTS AND FRIENDS

"Well, this experience has opened my eyes up to the frustrations of teaching in another country. The Thai administration is a bit of a nightmare and the way this school runs, or doesn't is quite surprising. The idea of a community within the school does not seem to exist. Students spend nine hours a day at school and eight of them are in the class learning. Recess does not exist and, therefore, six and seven year old children are expected to sit in their desks for eight hour days. I have even witnessed one Thai teacher tying a child to his desk – the student was six years old. Any surprise they want to get up and run around? I set the child free. Ridiculous."

The school was the first in the country to offer a bilingual immersion program. The owners of the school, four siblings, modeled the syllabus for the school's operational direction after the provincial curriculum in Manitoba. After touring Canadian public schools that offered French immersion, the Ajans (directors) realized this would be a great success in Thailand. The idea was to have a Thai teacher and a foreign teacher paired up for each subject: one would teach with an emphasis on language acquisition and the other with a focus on knowledge and content. In theory this sounded great, but in actuality, only 3 of the 50 Thai teachers spoke English. This was a minor detail according to the school directors but a challenging situation for me. My teaching partner was a man, and not only did I have a major communication barrier to overcome, but I also had to deal with the insult he felt he had been delivered when he was replaced by a foreign *female* teacher. This situation cannot be trivialized. Kroo Tung (Teacher Tung) lost his job as the teacher of PE to a woman, and he was not provided with another teaching position—he became the head of the audiovisual department, not nearly as prestigious. The result was that he rarely, unless forced by the supervisor, attended my class as my assistant. This outcome was understandable in the context of a cultural slight, but it definitely made my job that much more challenging when trying to teach 35 six-year-olds who spoke minimal English.

In a groundbreaking role such as mine, it was not only my reticent teaching partner and the language barrier with the students that contributed to my frustration. I also had to contend with a Thai supervisor who resented my popularity with the students. As this is a culture that for the most part does not believe in confrontation but instead subscribes to the notion of saving face, she displayed her dislike toward me in various ways. For instance, I had to have a meeting with my Canadian supervisor, his supervisor, and finally, the director of the school regarding my choice of attire. My fashion crime: wearing shorts. Women in Thailand do not wear shorts, and anything above the knee is considered disgraceful. I decided that I would find a compromise to wearing a thick, polyester track suit in 37° heat: I instead wore long, baggy, NBA basketball-style shorts that fell below my knee. This decision landed me in a series of meetings with my Canadian supervisor, who desperately explained why this was appropriate in a PE class. I eventually won this battle, and the Thai supervisor lost face as she was unsuccessful in her insistence that I teach in the track suit. For the record, this track suit would have been very suitable in an unheated gym in Northern Ontario in January. Needless to say, we never became close friends. This was only one instance in which my desire to be comfortable in PE class placed me in an awkward situation. I did not intend for the supervisor to lose face, and even now I wonder whether I did the right thing.

My position as the PE teacher also meant that I was to be involved in Sports Day, which is a day of competition among the students at Lertlah School. Again, my experiences in schools and education impacted my reaction to Sports Day and challenged my notions of activity and contest within a school environment. My understanding of such an event was clearly incompatible with that of the Thai teachers and with the longstanding traditions at Lertlah. Essentially, the lead-up to the day involved 3 months of daily cheering practice, where the students would sit in the gym (naturally canceling my scheduled gym classes) and learn the words to the songs. Everything was in Thai, but I was provided with a translation of the words. I recall something along the lines of "You look like a monkey and you are a terrible team." I had provided my own cheers that I believed were appropriate for such an event with 7–12 year olds, but they were not used. The school had a student population of almost 800 students, and only the top 50 were eligible to compete. The elite athletes played sports, and the others sat on the sidelines and learned to cheer. This reality was only the beginning of my frustration regarding this event. Sports Day also consisted of the most attractive students being chosen to join the elite cheering squads. They wore highly inappropriate costumes more fitting for the Dallas Cowboys Cheerleaders and tons of makeup and were taught dance moves that would normally be seen in questionable establishments. While the athletically and aesthetically gifted students competed, the less talented and less attractive students played the part of supportive classmates. I had been warned by my Canadian colleagues that I would dislike Sports Day intensely, and this statement was becoming truer by the day. I witnessed a team of 10 year olds being humiliated on the basketball court as an older and stronger group of students completely outplayed them. Increasingly offensive to me was the reaction of the Thai teachers and coaches, who only laughed and taunted the weaker team and encouraged the older players to further run up the score. It was at this point that I faced my nemesis once again: culture shock. Anger, disbelief, and disappointment in the behavior of those around me reminded me that life in a foreign country was always full of struggles. I also felt great sadness for all of the students who were prevented from participating in a school event that I viewed as an opportunity for schoolwide fun and exercise. This was yet another example of my notions—entrenched by my upbringing—conflicting with the environment in which I was living and working.

Another difficulty I faced was in the disparity of the working conditions of foreign teachers versus Thai teachers. I was paid six times the salary of a Thai teacher, but I worked 5 days a week, while they worked 6 days; my days were only 8 hours in length versus their 10–12-hour days; and all supervisory duties, extra tutoring, and work outside the immediate classroom were always assigned to the Thai teachers. The foreign teachers contributed where we could, but the level of expectation was entirely different for us. Somehow we were deemed to be above having to contribute to the daily duties that enable a school to function. Many of us challenged this notion (although a few happily accepted the lenient expectations), but rarely were we included in the functioning of the school. This way of operating allowed the school to function according to Thai direction while sidelining our influence on classroom knowledge; they did, however, take advantage of our ability to elevate the status of the school with our white faces and North American education. We were celebrated for our language and image but definitely discouraged from challenging Thai tradition, culture, educational direction, and school operation. This situation was a direct philosophical test of my ideas regarding the role of a teacher in a school. I believe that my job there should have involved much more than the dissemination of information. It should have included acting as a role model beyond the classroom, while interacting with the students in less formal settings. Therefore, I was prevented from performing my job to the best of my understanding. It seemed my good intentions were in conflict once again with Thai culture and school expectations.

Just when I believed I was adjusting to the Thai way of doing things, I would quickly be confronted with a new situation. One of the events that impacted me most as a teacher was the legendary phenomenon known as the school talent show. Again, my preconceived notions of what a school talent show should entail were not in sync with the Thai expectations or the expectations at Lertlah. Foreign teachers paired up to teach their students a song and dance routine to Raffi; Sharon, Lois and Bram; or Fred Penner—all acceptable by Western standards for young children on stage. Meanwhile, many of the Thai teachers insisted on dressing up their students like pop stars: tons of makeup, tight costumes, and dance moves in no way suitable for students of this age. I witnessed 8 year olds dancing with classmates of the opposite sex while mimicking movements of adults in sleazy videos. It was incredibly difficult to adapt to this part of the school curriculum, and my own opinions and experiences battled against this display of school talent. Not all of the performances were distasteful: Thai dance performed in its cultural elegance and beauty was definitely a treat to witness, and many of the students truly displayed their artistic talents. But once again, I faced a situation I could not understand.

This lack of understanding carried beyond the classroom and into life outside school. I traveled to the local library one Saturday afternoon armed with my passport, visa, school contract, and mail with my Bangkok address in an effort to obtain a library card and, thus, use the library. I proudly marched up to the librarian and informed her that I was looking to sign up for a library card. She simply stared at me with a lack of comprehension. I pulled out my paperwork and proceeded to explain as best I could why I was there. She quickly understood what I was asking for but was completely shocked that I would even suggest such a transaction. She said, "Oh, no, the books do not leave the library; you read them here." I stared back and asked if this policy applied to Thai nationals as well? "Of course," she said. "You come here and read the books but they never leave the building." I will never forget the next 10 seconds in which we stared at each in other in equal disbelief. She was just as horrified that I would suggest books be signed out as I was that they could never leave. That moment certainly summed up a majority of my time and experiences in Thailand. We were communicating but not understanding the message.

One of the most successful and rewarding experiences was my participation in a schoolwide fundraiser for Klong Toey: the poorest section of Bangkok. Klong Toey was rife with drugs, prostitution, and extreme poverty. A group of Canadian teachers had taken it upon themselves to hold a fundraiser for a variety of charitable causes once a year, and this year Klong Toey was the target. We sent home a letter to the parents of our students outlining the purpose of this fundraiser and the resources to be donated. As the students' families were very wealthy, we knew that this effort would be a success. During a 4-week period we managed to collect three truckloads of food, toys, clothing, and educational resources to be sent to Klong Toey. These donations were distributed by our contact who lived and worked in the area. The students demonstrated an understanding of the need to reach out to the less fortunate, and they felt immensely proud of their achievements—and rightly so! I believe we also demonstrated to the Thai teachers and students the ability to work together and accomplish great works in the community—essential lessons in a school setting.

One of my personal successes in the classroom involved a Grade 1 conversational English class that I taught. Given that the children were only 4 and 5 years old and that the class followed an 8-hour day in regular studies, their attention span was often minimal. I had to work very hard to find methods of teaching that were useful and exciting for these young Thai students who spoke very little English. I often discussed with my colleagues successful strategies and incorporated them into my lessons. For instance, I used a hands-on approach whenever possible: eating food when teaching English words for flavor and texture or using a cut-out human skeleton with removable body parts for a pin-the-tail-on-the-donkey-style game. The gains these students made in our 45-minute after-school sessions were quite remarkable. I quickly learned that the taste of success is a fundamental motivator not only for students but also for teachers.

I was not ever able to reconcile my understanding of how to resolve conflicts with the methods used in Thai culture, try as I might; and I often conducted myself according to my philosophy. For example, I struggled with the concept of saving face and its importance in Thai society. I had one student who was becoming increasingly unruly in the classroom. The behavior resulted in a meeting with the principal, the mother of the child, and me. I remember the astonishment I felt when I gently explained to the mother how her son's behavior was affecting the classroom climate and she burst into tears at the news. She proceeded to apologize many times over, as she had clearly been shamed and had lost face when told of her son's behavior. She bowed many times in humiliation and blamed herself entirely as an inadequate parent who had endured the worst kind of embarrassment: a meeting with the teacher and the principal. As educators are held in very high esteem in Thailand, the significance of this meeting was enormous. I recall feeling incredibly sorrow stricken for this woman, and I wanted to erase the entire episode. The principal and I tried to ease her mind by explaining that this difficulty was certainly not the end of the world, but to no avail—the blow had been dealt. This event emphasized the deep-seated cultural significance of saving face, even when confronting a difficult situation in which a beneficial solution could be achieved!

The notion of following the chain of command was also challenging, and I recall the first time I circumvented it in the name of expediency and safety. I had been teaching a Grade 6 PE class, and we were playing basketball on the only court. I had previously commented on the unsafe surface, as it was sheer smooth cement and the students, as well as myself, were often slipping. It was only a matter of time before someone was injured. One minute the students were playing basketball, and the next I had someone on the floor with a broken wrist. I managed to make one student understand that the school nurse was needed as well as a trip to the hospital. After the student was driven to emergency, I proceeded to write up the event and then made my way to the director's office. Unfortunately, my sense of urgency in preventing any further accidents deterred me from behaving according to Thai rules, and I completely ignored the chain of command. I bypassed my Canadian supervisor, the Thai PE coordinator, and the curriculum coordinator. This oversight was not intentional, as I was in a state of distress after what I had witnessed, but it did not matter why I did what I did—the sin had been committed. Fortunately I had a good relationship with the director, and, when I went to see her (much to the dismay of her secretary), she agreed to speak with me. I was emphatic in my argument that a new gym floor was needed, and within 3 weeks the job was completed. I was told by my colleague, one of the Thai teachers, that I had lost face in the eyes of the Thai supervisors, as I had neglected to speak with them and had proceeded straight to the director. I recall rationalizing my decision in the name of safety, and yet I knew that I had committed a faux pas. This was the quandary in which I often found myself: trying to balance my philosophy of people and proper conduct with the Thai concept. It was never an easy feat. Reconciling my ideals and behavior with those practiced in Thailand was definitely the biggest challenge, and I am not certain I was ever successful.

Culture shock could not have been encapsulated any more clearly than in the popular Thai phrase *mai pen rai*, meaning never mind. This phrase was used in almost every situation: a mispronunciation of the Thai language, forgetfulness of an appointment, misunderstandings, accidents causing injury, death— it was the multipurpose answer to any awkward situation. I was absolutely stunned that a serious accident involving pain or death could be simply erased with the wave of a hand and a simple uttering of "mai pen lai." How could one say "never mind" and ignore a serious situation? I believe that in Thailand, this attitude is essential when one wants to save face and keep emotions hidden; but coming from a culture that does not value that philosophy in quite the same way, I had trouble accepting this approach. Again, I learned that physically fitting in while staying in a foreign country is the easy part. Finding a way to fit in mentally and philosophically is the true challenge. I learned to become much more adept at incorporating this mai-pen-lai philosophy into my daily life, but I had to draw the line in certain situations.

My experiences in this world definitely screamed that some things were worth a strong reaction, and I could not change that mind-set.

The social problems in Thai society were incredibly eye-opening and the most difficult to comprehend. The problems that Thailand faced are similar to those in other countries—including Canada—but they appeared to me to be far more apparent and extreme. I found the country to be full of contradictions. For instance, prostitution was rampant and illegal, and the problem was compounded by police officers often not enforcing the law. I witnessed several prostitutes in bars and on the street who were free to conduct their business in plain view of the police, who looked the other way. Children were often sold into prostitution as many families, particularly those from rural areas, were unable to care for them. These children would work as prostitutes while sending money home to their families, and the families could rarely afford to buy them out of the trade. Some people lived in abject poverty, in corrugated-metal huts under train tracks and along the river banks, and bathed in the polluted river; but next door, a huge mansion would be protected by a security fence and a guard. Prostitution was an integral part of the Thai economy, and the buying and selling of boys and girls occurred everywhere. (And yet I was not allowed to show my knees while wearing shorts in a PE class!) The extremes of wealth and poverty were unlike anything I had witnessed in Canada, and they forced me to reflect upon the good fortune of my life. It was the prevalence of people being bought and sold that was truly the most heart wrenching.

Within all of this struggle and challenge lies an experience that I would not trade for anything in the world. My ideas, philosophies, and personality were questioned on a daily basis, and I often found myself forced to confront my perceptions and ideals and dissect my preconceived notions regarding people, culture, and education. I learned to understand culture shock and how its broad reach affected nearly every facet of my life. I met beautiful and kind Thai people who demonstrated a way of existence so very different from my own. I learned from this amazing Thai culture that life as I have understood it should always be open to change, and that my way of doing things is most definitely not the only way. I spent a year in the land of paradise and frustration, and it opened my mind to a new way of thinking and a new approach to people. I am a better person for my experience teaching in a foreign country: my ideas are broader, my patience runs deeper, my quest for new experiences is unquenchable, and my appreciation for familiarity is unfathomable. My growth as an educator and as a person surpassed anything I would have learned in my first year as a teacher had I taught in my home country amidst stable and well-known surroundings. I accepted the challenge to leave familiarity and step into the uncharted waters of international teaching. It was the best decision I ever made, and I will never regret it.

Amelia's Tips for Traveling Teachers

Thailand: Things They Didn't Tell Me

If I could do it all again and relive that year in Thailand, I would—in a heartbeat! Of course, hindsight is an amazing thing, and I would make a few adjustments. In terms of expectations, I found reading about the cultural, social, and political fabric of the country to be extremely helpful, but reading can only prepare you so much for immersion in a foreign land. What would I change if I did it again?

- I would look more closely at the cost of living versus teaching wage and how to balance those two factors with bills to be paid at home. Thailand is an incredibly inexpensive country, but you need to be sure that you are making enough money to be able to make payments to credit cards, student loans, etc.
- I would increase scrutiny of employers and schools. I wish I had been better prepared to teach in a school that was run like a business. I also wish I had researched my employers by asking teachers (current and past) about their experiences while working for the school
- I would ask more widespread questions of staff instead of only speaking with the one person who was recommended to talk with new teachers as per the request of the school administration. Hearing about a variety of experiences definitely creates a more accurate picture of life abroad
- I would find out in advance how the tax system works; you need this information before arriving in a foreign country so that you can file your taxes in Canada properly
- I would find out what resources were available at the school. Availability of curriculum resources was one of the biggest challenges I faced. The school had limited materials for the teachers, and we had to learn to be incredibly creative and build teaching supplies from scratch. Make sure the school is equipped with what you need to teach your subject; it is definitely an added stress for a first-year teacher if you find yourself without adequate resources
- I would research the climate of the school. I found that the expectations for foreign teachers were incredibly different from those for Thai nationals. We were expected to teach our subjects but not take part in building school culture and unity. These different expectations made it very

difficult to voice our opinions amongst staff and administration, and we were often relegated to the sidelines

Most important, I found that attempting to familiarize myself with the religious traditions, cultural expectations, and societal values of the country was an exciting part of preparing for my adventure in Thailand. The more knowledge one has entering a strange situation, the less daunting it can be. Although I would have appreciated more information about the school, learning and adjusting to life in Thailand were two of the most rewarding aspects of teaching abroad.

Where Is Amelia Now?

Amelia is currently working as a senior adviser for the minister of community safety and correctional services in Toronto, Ontario. Prior to this posting, Amelia worked for the Minister of Natural Resources and the Ontario Liberal Party as a political organizer.

She did try her hand at teaching after her experience in Thailand, and her last overseas assignment led her to Medellín, Colombia, where she taught Grade 9 history. Although Amelia is not currently involved in education, her experiences in the field have prepared her for the fast-paced and exciting world of politics and government.

CHAPTER 10

TEACHING IN SOUTH KOREA

Nathanael Johnson

South Korea is a unique country and much different than its surrounding neighbors. Before embarking on my journey, I thoroughly researched the culture, living conditions, and educational system in Korea. Despite this research, I found that I had many unanswered questions and also some misconceptions that needed to be cleared up after I arrived in Korea. I am hoping I shed light here on every aspect of teaching English as a second language (ESL) in South Korea, especially with regard to hagwons (extracurricular English academies, pronounced *hog-wons*). I want to emphasize that despite trying to be as unbiased and informative as possible, everything I have written here has, inevitably, been influenced by my own research, personal experiences, and things that others have told me about South Korea. But I have also found that much of a person's experience while living in a foreign country is determined by the individual's attitude. One must be willing to try new things, learn and live with respect for the country's culture, and grow personally in order to have a successful experience abroad.

Why Korea?

After exploring teaching options in Europe, Australia, and northern Canada, I came to the conclusion that I wanted to spend a year in Asia. Not only was it a part of the world that I had not yet seen, but it also would provide me the opportunity to live and participate in a culture completely different from my own. I felt that this experience would provide me with different perspectives on both teaching and life. I also felt that it was important to have these experiences under my belt as a future geography teacher.

In Canada, I am qualified to teach geography, physical education, and health education. However, after investigating the various teaching opportunities, it quickly became evident that teaching ESL was the easiest way for an inexperienced teacher to begin working abroad. International schools, the other main option, usually required at least 2 years of teaching experience and often looked for previous international experience as well.

ESL in Korea Versus Japan

Two of the top destinations for ESL teachers in Asia are Japan and South Korea. During my own search for an overseas position, these two countries seemed equally desirable. I made quite a few lists of pros and cons regarding the job opportunities in both countries, but I found the deciding factors to be the salary and the level of support for the teachers.

The jobs I examined in both countries had approximately the same salary. However, Japan's cost of living appeared to be much higher than Korea's. Japan also appeared to be a more refined culture with higher expectations in regard to things such as dress code. Korea, on the other hand, is often referred to as a frontier, which implies that it is less posh than Japan. Japan's architecture, well-documented culture, and serenity were attractive, but much of Japan is also saturated with Western culture. As someone who was looking for immersion in a completely different culture, this similarity was a deterrent for me. Korea's inward-looking and self-preserving attitudes, which include discouraging the importing of foreign products, have earned it the nickname The Hermit Kingdom. But this environment seemed to me to provide more of an opportunity to experience the desired level of immersion.

Truthfully, as someone planning to work in an unfamiliar place for at least a year, what really mattered to me the most was the support network I would have at my individual school. The programs and agencies that I corresponded with about teaching in Japan could not guarantee where I would be living, how many English speakers would be in the school or community, how close I would be to my manager in case of emergency, whether or not this manager spoke English, or even if I would have to pay my own rent. In contrast, the academy I talked to in Korea guaranteed all of these things and also had an established network of more than 60 foreign employees within the city. It comforted me to know that if I experienced any emergencies or problems that I couldn't resolve on my own (due to language or cultural differences), I would have people who could guide me or offer suggestions.

A Brief Lesson on the Geography and History of Korea

Korea is a mountainous peninsula located on the northeast coast of China. It consists of two parts: the Democratic People's Republic of Korea (North Korea), which is Communist and borders China; and the Republic of Korea (South Korea), which is democratic and lies just west of Japan.

This location, along with a long and turbulent history, has fostered dynamic relations between South Korea and its surrounding countries. It is best to research these complex relations independently for a true understanding of them. However, I will try to give a brief summary of my understanding of the South Korean political climate.

Throughout history, Korea has been invaded thousands of times by numerous countries and mostly by the Mongolians and Chinese. During the 1200s and 1300s, Korea reluctantly agreed to become a colony of China. During this period, Koreans adopted many Chinese traditions that are still evident in their culture: part of the Korean language was derived from Chinese, martial arts and games often have Chinese roots, the influence of Chinese food is present in some Korean dishes, many Chinese holidays are observed in Korea, and Chinese calligraphy and language are still valued and taught in academies. From my experience, most Koreans think highly of China, often citing it as the future world power. However, a small amount of resentment still exists towards China. This is mainly because China insists on claiming Korea's historical accomplishments for itself (since Korea was a part of ancient China).

During the Russo-Japanese War in 1904 and 1905, Japanese forces moved onto the Korean continent and in 1910 began a brutal occupation of Korea. During this time, the Japanese tried to uproot Korean culture and replace it with Japanese culture. They also exploited Korea's natural resources. Many Koreans still hold much resentment toward the Japanese for this occupation. Although some are more open minded, many of the Korean students I teach speak of Japanese people with a surprising amount of disdain. The governments of the two countries do cooperate, but they still dispute issues such as the ownership of minor islands.

After the Japanese surrendered during World War II, the peninsula was divided into two independent countries. The Communist Soviet Union was given control of the northern half of Korea, while the capitalist United States was given control of the southern part. This situation can be compared to the divisions that happened in Berlin, Germany. Two separate countries formed, and heavy restrictions were put on crossing the border. Some families were separated and never saw each other again. In addition, the North Korean army, which desired reunification with the South, invaded South Korea in 1950 to begin the Korean War. Communist volunteers supported the North, while American and United Nations forces backed the South. During the 3 years of war, thousands of people on both sides were killed. The eventual result of the war was the declaration of a demilitarized zone along the border between North and South Korea.

This situation has left South Koreans with mixed feelings about their northern counterparts. Some people feel that the North Koreans are family and are being oppressed by a corrupt government. People who hold this attitude look upon North Korea with sympathy and hope or believe that reunification of the North and South will happen as it did in Germany. Others feel that North Koreans are tyrants and killers. People who hold this belief usually hope that North Korea will be invaded and reformed by the United States or other countries. In either case, South Korea continually acts as a middleman during talks between the Americans and North Koreans.

South Korea's attitude toward Americans is similarly divided. Currently, South Korea has a stable democratic government and a strong economy. Some attribute this stability to their strong ties with the United States and see great economic potential in continuing this partnership. The United States has also managed many army bases around South Korea since World War II. Many South Koreans fear that if the United States pulls its troops out of the country, then they will be vulnerable to an attack from North Korea. In contrast, others feel that Korea should protect itself and that Americans are only there to control and exploit Korea. Some Koreans resent that many U.S. Army bases occupy coveted urban land. American soldiers have also gained a reputation, deserved or not, for causing trouble in local bars and taking advantage of Korean women. Foreigners who are romantically involved with Koreans receive some ridicule from other Koreans, who occasionally confront these interracial couples; however, confrontations have more to do with trying to keep Korean bloodlines pure than with the foreigners themselves. In addition, Americans have also become the targets of those who feel that American culture is saturating Korean culture. Despite these negative undercurrents, the prevailing Korean view toward Americans is positive. As a Canadian living in a major urban center, I found Korea to be a safe and very hospitable place for Westerners to live.

MY EXPECTATIONS

Korea, the Land of the Morning Calm, is a tiny peninsula on the edge of a vast continent known for its exotic materials, spices, and philosophies.

Leading up to my departure from Canada, I was fully expecting to find a landscape and architecture filled with ancient tiled roofs, elegant paintings, and dragons. I imagined the people to have a quiet and orderly dignity and the atmosphere to be serene. As is often the case, my expectations were mostly wrong.

My 13-hour flight from Chicago to Seoul on Korean Air initially fed into my preconceptions. The flight attendants were very reserved, pleasant, and helpful. The tourism advertisements were filled with Buddhist shrines and traditional Korean clothing.

My arrival at Daegu airport from Seoul was accompanied by a rude awakening. The mountainous landscape was dominated by generic concrete apartment buildings. The streets were wide and congested with traffic. The mountains surrounding the city were lush, but there seemed to be a lack of trees within the city. I was disappointed to see that there was no prominent botanical gardens or dragon-influenced architecture. I later found that rural Korea is filled with rice fields, farms, and forests; mountains do contain traditional Korean architecture and aesthetically pleasing shrines; and there are also many beautiful beaches, gardens, and islands to explore and parks that contain some wildlife. However, none of these things was immediately noticeable during my first experiences in urban Korea.

As I was exiting the plane, Korean people arriving back from their travels pushed past me and cut in front of me in line. Even elderly people were intent on not letting me get ahead of them. I had expected people to have the mind-set of a Buddhist monk. Instead, they came across as abrupt. After initially taking offense at the injustice of people pushing ahead of me, I quickly realized that this was done without malice. I later learned that due to the historical oppression placed upon the country, many Koreans hold a mentality of self-preservation.

THE KOREAN MENTALITY

The Korean mentality is unique. It has helped South Korea to transform itself from a poor and impoverished country, following the Korean War, into a strong economic power. The way many Koreans think and act is also the thing that confuses and frustrates foreigners the most.

The first thing that a Westerner will probably notice about Korea is the different attitude toward personal space. Many Koreans do not observe or respect personal space as much as Westerners do. It is a common experience to be waiting at a crosswalk (or in a line) and have someone come stand beside you, shoulder to shoulder. Likewise, it is difficult to walk downtown in an urban area without someone bumping into you. Accidental physical contact is seldom accompanied by an apology. People are not trying to be rude; this behavior is simply the understood etiquette for pedestrians.

Another thing that I have found to be both shocking and refreshing about Koreans is their bluntness. If there is anything unusual about a teacher's appearance, the students will be sure to make note of it. This remark is usually made in a good-hearted manner. Personal questions also are not taboo in Korea, and people will ask and answer them without reservation.

Along with their openness, Koreans are usually very helpful. Looking confused at a bus stop or in a department store is an open invitation for someone to offer you help. Everywhere I traveled in Korea, I was approached by people who either wanted to aid me or welcome me to the country. Someone suggested to me that maybe Koreans were more helpful because foreigners are much easier to distinguish in Korea than they are in Western countries. Therefore, it is much easier to assume that the person doesn't know what they are doing. Occasionally this openness and hospitality has fostered the development of a friendship. It has been a delight to get to know many Koreans. They are extremely loyal and warm individuals.

One thing that many Koreans especially appreciate is when a foreigner takes the time to learn some of their language and culture. Learning simple, polite phrases such as hello, good-bye, and thank you is not expected, but attempting to speak even the most basic form of Korean language or demonstrate proper etiquette can go a long way in gaining respect from co-workers, students, and parents.

The thing that is most confusing about the Land of the Morning Calm and is the largest paradox in the Korean mentality is the presence of a social hierarchy, even though Korea is said to be an egalitarian society. This hierarchy exists in every part of the culture and is influenced by age, social group, employment level, and position in a family. Giving respect to those who are older than you or higher up on the employment or family tree than you is demanded.

And yet, despite the importance of hierarchy, equality is also very important to the South Korean way of life. Koreans want to be equal with everyone else. Throughout his book *Korea Unmasked*, Won-bok Rhie suggests that Koreans view equality as a personal burden (2002). They feel that it is their responsibility to make sure they do not fall behind others or allow themselves to be last. If someone in a social group or neighborhood does something to better himself or his family, the other members of that group feel it is their responsibility to similarly improve their personal standards. If their neighbors acquire a new television, they may feel that it is their responsibility to also acquire a new television. If someone in their social group begins attending a club, Koreans often feel obligated to join the same organization.

By competitively maintaining the status quo, Koreans often develop a strong feeling of camaraderie within their social group. These bonds begin developing in childhood and carry over into adult life. The bonds are so strong that they can become the main determinant in the hiring of a new employee. If the prospective employee attended the same school or after-school club as the employer, the chances of being hired may be greatly increased. This is especially true with university alumni. In Korea, where you went to university is often more important than your degree. Prestige seems to be valued more than quality of education. Attitudes such as this have created a polarization of the country's higher education system. The competition to get into the most prestigious universities is fierce. Entrance into university in Korea is based on the Korean University Entrance Examination.

Everyone eligible for the entrance examination writes it simultaneously at designated exam writing centers across the country. There is no opportunity to rewrite the exam or write it on another day. For weeks leading up to this test, parents of exam writers demand silence from their other children and from their neighbors. This behavior is aimed at helping maximize the studying ability of exam writers. On the day of the exam, most Koreans will go to work late in order to keep the roads clear so that the students who are writing the exams can get to the writing centers without any problems. In addition, schools are shut down and entire areas are closed to traffic to prevent noise while students write. Every year, students who are under great stress devise and execute elaborate high-tech cheating schemes during the exam (sometimes with the help of their parents). Unfortunately, the anxiety created by this annual event also accounts for a high number of suicides among high school students. The pressure to succeed on this test, coupled with the pressure to not fall behind their peers, has helped to fuel the rise of extracurricular institutions.

In order to give their children the best opportunity to succeed at this entrance exam, parents enroll their children in extracurricular academies. If someone in a neighborhood begins sending their child to an after-school English program, others feel pressured to follow suit. Likewise, enrollment in a math, science, or sports academy will set off a chain reaction of other families enrolling. As a consequence, it is common for a student to participate in multiple extracurricular academics.

EDUCATION IN KOREA

Koreans take education very seriously. Following the Korean War, South Korea was destitute. The country had to work its way up, and within just a few decades, South Korea's economy flourished. People were the resource that made this feat possible. Education was and is seen as the key to the Republic of Korea's success as a nation. This history is still prevalent in the Korean psyche. The importance of being accepted to a good university further illustrates this view of education.

Standardized tests are the primary evaluation tool at every level of the educational system. As a consequence, the entire system is focused on teaching the material that will appear either on the quarterly exams or on the university entrance exam. Students spend their years before university memorizing information. Although many may lack life skills, Korean children are some of the most book-smart children in the world (Rhie, 2002). Almost all of the elementary and middle school students that I have taught in Korea know exactly which profession they will enter (e.g., doctor, dentist, judge) and how they will achieve their goal. Unfortunately, once Koreans complete the university entrance exam, most are burned out and unmotivated to learn during their time in university. University campuses in North America are often viewed as places where students perpetually party, but in Korea the party atmosphere is even more of a problem.

Unfortunately, the Korean approach to language acquisition mirrors their approach to education. Students in my academy are expected to memorize an average of 50 English words, definitions, and sentences every week. More emphasis is put on pronunciation and on dictionary definitions than on understanding what the word really means or how to use it correctly. The rationale for this emphasis is that students should be exposed to as many different words as possible to provide the students with the best opportunity to recognize all of the words that they will be exposed to in an English-speaking country. Then, with the aid of a dictionary, they can process the meaning and pronounce their reply correctly. It is assumed that from these building blocks, students can develop their understanding of English through experience. Thus, many foreign teachers are encouraged to teach style over substance in their classrooms.

The result is a society of people who can say and use many English words but often have no idea what they mean. This problem is reflected not only in the grammatically incorrect and contextually ambiguous English slogans used by Korean companies but also in people's spoken English. Students pick up words from easily accessible English music, television, and movies, and they occasionally repeat these words in class without knowledge of the context or meaning. This method of language acquisition supports the effectiveness of the system, but it also illustrates one of its downfalls. Here is an unfortunate example: one of my students was once explaining his reasons for wanting to visit Africa; this kind and well-mannered elementary student exclaimed that he wanted to see black individuals, whom he had never seen before, but he referred to these people by using a derogatory term that is considered highly offensive to most native English speakers (the n-word). Although the student used a new word in the correct form, it inevitably led to a discussion about the inappropriateness and dangers of using such a word. Similar situations involving other forms of inappropriate and profane language have also occurred in my classroom. Consequently, I have made it a point to incorporate understanding of words into my class.

Korean parents insist that their children attend school and academies no matter what the circumstance. Students frequently come to class exhausted from their late-night homework session the night before. Falling asleep in class is a common occurrence. Students also come to class after traumatic experiences. On two occasions I have personally witnessed this situation. The first instance occurred when a student informed me that his friend had been hit and killed by a car before school that day. The second one occurred when a student told me that he was not feeling well because before class he had learned that his mother had an incurable form of cancer. Both of these situations left me speechless. Although I felt that the topic should be discussed, I was not prepared to explore it. I was afraid that the language barrier could generate misunderstandings. So I simply provided my assurance, privately offered to let them take a washroom break at their own leisure, and tenderly continued on with the lesson. It should be noted that most schools and academies do not employ counselors or child psychologists. The burden of this responsibility rests on the shoulders of the teacher.

Hagwon Organization

There are a few different explanations for the demand for English academies in Korea. First, they help students to excel in the English curriculum that is presented in their schools. Second, they prepare the students to do well on the Korean University Entrance Examination. In addition, Korean men with good English ability are given desirable posts on American army bases during their mandatory 2 years of military service. Knowing English also increases the ability of Koreans to penetrate the international business world.

Private learning institutions are a major form of business in Korea. In 2000 Koreans spent around 5.5 billion U.S. dollars on extracurricular studies (Rhie, 2002). Hagwons are run like businesses. In the business world, the customer is always right. Likewise, parents dictate the direction of the school. The wonderful thing about this setup is that parents are involved with their children's education. They attend the open houses, check the students' homework, discipline their children if they behave badly in class, and contact the teachers and managers regarding any concerns that they have. They also demand a lot from the academy. Complaints and suggestions made by parents frequently lead to amendments to the running of the school and to the content of the curriculum.

Being a business, academies must also try to retain their clients while increasing their enrollment. Student often advance to a higher level based on their length of stay in a level rather than on their ability, in order to keep the parents satisfied. Students have also been known to prematurely level up based on the amount of money their parents contribute to the hagwon. Due to these occurrences, students with a wide range of abilities may be present in any given class.

The hierarchy in a hagwon reflects that of Korean society. Students show respect to their teachers and rarely challenge or question them. Likewise, teachers may find managers unwilling to bend on the rules because they do not want to deviate from the instructions passed down from the owner. Keeping all of this in mind, teachers are also expected to be completely submissive to management and to never question their decisions. Coming from a society that values the concept of the individual, standing up for your own rights, and challenging authority, this expectation can be difficult for some Westerners. Managers are usually open to listening to comments or concerns from Westerners but often do not act on them due to the pressure from their superiors to maintain the status quo. When a teacher approaches a manager about an issue, it is extremely important for the teacher to be respectful, constructive, and nonthreatening. Otherwise, a suggestion can be mistaken for a personal attack on a manager's competency. In Korea it is vital never to cause anyone, especially a superior, to lose face. A person should always be provided with the opportunity to correct any mistakes and to maintain dignity. A failure to provide this opportunity could foster a negative work environment for the offending teacher.

Hagwon Setup and Expectations

I am working at MoonKkang English School. MoonKkang is a well-known and respected company that presently has 22 academies throughout Korea and is continually expanding. There are 17 academies in Daegu alone that employ more than 60 people from Canada, Australia, England, and the United States.

The upper management of the company consists of the owner, a Korean teacher manager, and two foreign teacher managers, both of whom are from Canada. All of the members of the upper management are fluent in English. The foreign teacher managers are responsible for coordinating vacations and ensuring that the needs of the foreigners are taken care of. They also observe and evaluate foreign teachers and promote professional development.

Each school is headed by a branch manager and contains between two and six foreign teachers accompanied by an equivalent number of Korean teachers. Students are separated into groups of 8–15 per class according to English ability and age. I work with the advanced-level elementary and middle school students. I teach four classes from 5:10 p.m. to 9:30 p.m. Monday through Friday and from 2:20 p.m. to 6:50 p.m. on Saturdays. There is either a 5- or 10-minute break between each of the hour-long classes. I am also expected to be at work 30 minutes before I teach. Most academies in Korea have longer working hours on weekdays but aren't open on Saturdays.

Every month I am provided with a package of material to teach each class, and I am expected to adapt this material to make it appropriate for each class. At the end of every other month I am expected to provide the manager with a simple letter grade (A, B, or C), along with a short comment, for each student. I also have one open class every 2 months, during which parents are invited to observe and provide feedback about my class.

One thing I have appreciated about my school is that the foreign teacher manager observes my class quarterly, providing me with three informal evaluations and one formal evaluation. In addition, our school also holds bimonthly professional-development meetings for all of the company's foreign teachers. These meetings encourage teachers to develop new teaching and management methods. They also allow teachers to share comments, concerns, and ideas with each other. This opportunity has helped spur my improvement as a teacher.

VALUES OF HAGWONS

From my first day of training at my academy, two rules were emphasized. The first is that students were only to speak English in class. The belief is that if students are forced to communicate in English, they will eventually rely less on their native language, thereby accelerating their English ability. Despite the students' awareness of this rule and its rationale, you can imagine how difficult it is to uphold. Not only do students have the tendency to want to interact with each other in their own language, but they also try and help each other out in class in Korean. I have realized that although it is important never to ignore the use of Korean in my class, a small amount of leniency is needed when students are trying to help each other.

The second rule that is emphasized in most academies is that the teacher must always stand and the students must always sit up in class. Enthusiasm is valued as one of the most important qualities an ESL teacher can possess. Without it, the students will easily become distracted and bored. According to my branch manager, a teacher who is standing up and moving around is considered to be an enthusiastic teacher, whereas a teacher who sits for the majority of class is considered to be an unmotivated teacher. Although this may be a good general rule, it is not always true. While trying to promote conversations and debates in class, I feel as though my tall figure can be an intimidating presence when I am standing over my students. It can be difficult to express your ideas when you feel intimidated; this is especially true when you are trying to express them in a language with which you are not fully confident. I explained this concept to my manager, and he reluctantly agreed to allow me to sit during a conversation-based activity in class.

Periodically, I get the impression that how I look is more important than the content of my lesson. This situation happens in North America as well, but it is magnified in Korea. On a few occasions I have taught open classes, in which my students' parents observe the class. The feedback I receive from the parents always revolves around how I moved about the classroom, my teaching attire, the students' posture, and the opportunity their child was given to talk. I found some of these suggestions helpful, but I found it odd that the focus was placed on the appearance of the teacher and class. I initially attributed these comments to the fact that most of the students' parents could not speak English themselves; however, the feedback I receive from my Korean superiors often reflects the values that the parents exhibited. In response to these values, I have developed my ability to constantly move around the classroom. Despite this positive outcome, it is still difficult to feel valued as a teacher when you perceive that you are being evaluated based solely on your physical appearance.

CLASSROOM DYNAMICS

The dynamics of an ESL class in Korea are quite different from those of traditional classrooms in Canada. The average class contains approximately 10 students, most of whom have only recently begun to grasp the English language. In addition, the expectations and workloads of foreign teachers are lower than I expected, especially when compared to those of traditional teachers in Western cultures. The same cannot be said of my Korean counterparts, who work tirelessly phoning parents and planning lessons.

Teaching in a small classroom environment that has frequent student turnover has allowed me to witness the influence that each individual student has on the collective class. One girl had been in one of my Monday classes for several months. She and her friend always seemed very lethargic and disinterested during class. It was a constant struggle to motivate them to learn. I tried everything from talking to them in private and giving them personal goals to contacting their parents for suggestions. Only minor gains were made. Consequently, it was difficult to maintain a positive atmosphere in this class of 10 students. Then, one day, she was moved into one of my Tuesday classes. In her new class, she was a completely different student. She put forth an effort in every session and began to excel at English. The atmosphere of the Tuesday class benefited from her presence. In addition, the girl's friend soon stopped attending my Monday class. After her departure, the atmosphere of that class improved greatly. It soon became one of the more delightful classes I taught.

One issue that does arise from an ever-evolving classroom is a lack of continuity. Most traditional classrooms develop some cohesiveness throughout the course of a semester or school year. However, with a monthly departure of old students and arrival of new students, there is a need to constantly reestablish the tone of a class. Teachers and students seem to be perpetually trying to get a feeling for each other. At the beginning of each month, the rules must be put in place and the teacher must determine which students work well together. Due to the impact that one student can have on a small classroom, activities that worked well one month may not work the next. One constructive aspect of this experience is that it has given me the opportunity to continually deal with changing dynamics in my classroom. This experience has allowed me to become much more confident in establishing a positive classroom environment.

TEACHING HABITS

As with all first-year teachers, I discovered myself developing both positive and negative habits as I progressed through the year. I have found that although my students are fairly advanced in English, there is still a small language barrier. During my first few weeks of teaching, my students could not always understand me. This problem forced me to cultivate a slower and more deliberate pace in my classes. I quickly developed my questions and instructions to make them more concise and direct. In order to give my students the best opportunity to learn, I began to rephrase the things that I said. I was also able to refine some of my learning accommodations to help promote a better classroom environment.

Unfortunately, teaching ESL also promoted habits that could be detrimental to teaching in a North American classroom. The biggest problem has been the decrease in my language skills. In order to help compensate for the language barrier between my students and me, I began to intuitively speak English like an ESL student instead of speaking correctly. I would pronounce words the way I had heard Koreans pronounce them, and I would use phrases that were familiar to Koreans but were not part of North American dialect. After catching myself, I began to monitor my speech and correct my linguistics so that they reflected standard English.

In addition to my language deterioration, I also found that I missed out on planning my own lessons and units from scratch. Without the opportunity to develop curriculum and take ownership of it, my motivation and ability to prepare lessons began to decline. I felt that I had reduced influence over the direction of the curriculum, and I discovered that influencing curriculum was one of the things I valued about teaching. It wasn't until I began to examine and rework the curriculum that I rediscovered my passion for teaching.

One taboo in North America that is commonplace in Korea is physical contact with students. In Korea it is normal for an elementary student to run up and hug a teacher. It is also normal for a teacher to give a student an encouraging or comforting pat on the back or touch on the shoulder. This type of behavior is viewed as both acceptable and positive. However, this conduct is often viewed as unacceptable in a North American classroom. Therefore, I will have to make a conscious effort to refrain from these actions when I return to Canada.

CLASSROOM MANAGEMENT AND LEARNING ACCOMMODATIONS

Corporal punishment is the main form of management in both Korean homes and schools. It is common for a teacher to hit students in class (to which the students are expected to respond, "Thank you for the punishment!"). Having students hold up their arms for long periods of time or sit in uncomfortable positions is also normal. Some hagwons have been known to encourage their teachers to also use these punishments. I have found, however, that most classroom issues can be addressed by using management strategies common to North America.

I rely heavily on nonverbal feedback to help direct my teaching. From observing students' reactions, I can usually decipher whether or not they understand what I am saying. One of the first things that I noticed in both my elementary and middle school ESL classes was that the students often did not react to what I was saying. They did not nod or make a confused look. Instead, many students seemed to simply sit in their chairs with a blank look on their face. Similarly, after asking the class if they understood, I still received little reaction. This was very difficult for me. Not having access to instant feedback made me feel self-conscious about my teaching style. It wasn't until I asked each student individually that I learned whether or not that person understood the concept I was trying to convey. To deal with this issue, I decided to implement a thumbs-up policy in my class. If I asked, "Do you understand?" the students were expected to give me either a thumbs-up sign for *yes*, a thumbs-down sign for *no*, or a thumb-to-the-side sign for *I need clarification*. This worked quite well for the first month, after which it became a bit tiresome. The next method I implemented involved asking simple questions for clarification (i.e., "What should you do when this happens?"). This method proved to be much more effective than the thumbs-up method. As I continued to study about and experience Korea, I slowly learned to recognize the subtleties of Korean mannerisms. Although I still utilize clarifying questions, I find that I can now obtain more feedback by observing students' reactions. Likewise, as some of the students have become comfortable with me, they have opened up and respond more often to what I say. To further promote communication, during each class I emphasize that students should put up their hand to ask about anything they don't understand.

Many Korean elementary school children are competitive. Asking a question in class usually prompts a loud contest to see who can yell out the correct answer first. Although this enthusiasm is refreshing, a loud classroom atmosphere can be intimidating for quieter students. One or two students can easily dominate a small class with this type of learning environment. In order to provide everyone with an equal opportunity to participate, I had to quickly establish and enforce a policy of requiring students to raise their hands before answering.

In addition, elementary students are quick to indicate that they are finished with an activity by yelling, "Teacher! Finished!" At first I was not sure why students were so intent on making this announcement for even the simplest task. I soon understood that this behavior was their way of showing superiority over other students. Unfortunately, it also intimidated the slower students in class and promoted speed over quality in their work. In order to curb this behavior, I demanded that students not yell out but rather perform a silent action when they were finished. An example would be to have them put down their pencils or put their hands on their heads. After each activity I also began to ask each student to share a sample of his or her work with the class. This helped encourage students to put more effort into their work.

Although I found both of these accommodations increased the level of participation from my quieter students, they were difficult to maintain from class to class. It took awhile for me to realize that the students couldn't remember the specific rules for my class, because they attended many different schools and private institutions and had to follow a different protocol in each class. To improve compliance with my rules, I only had to remind them of the protocol in my class. By prefacing a series of questions with my expectations (e.g., "Put up your hand if you have an answer"), I was able to help them remember and follow the class guidelines.

The last thing that some teachers might find odd about elementary students is their refusal to interact on any level with the opposite sex. Although this behavior does occur in North American classrooms, it is much more extreme in Korea. From an early age, many Korean children are encouraged to interact only with children of the same sex. During their elementary and early middle school years, it is culturally inappropriate for a student to work with a student of the opposite sex. In order to respect this cultural difference and still have my lessons work properly, I have been forced to continually adapt my lessons. Allowing for groups that vary in size and having backup plans for times when only one boy or girl may be present in class are crucial to the success of an activity. In addition, I have found that making larger groups with at least two boys and two girls can also work.

The middle school classes I teach are much different from the elementary classes. Like many adolescents in North America, Korean middle school students are often hesitant and self-conscious about their ability. As a consequence, they don't like using English in front of a group of their peers or talking to their English teacher. In order to promote more speaking in these classes, I have learned to include more group work, which allows students to speak and help each other in smaller groups. It also minimizes the times that they have to speak to me and provides me with the opportunity to circulate and monitor their ability.

I have also worked on decreasing the effect of the language barrier in my classes. In addition to employing the more obvious methods of slowing the pace of my speech, simplifying my questions and language, and increasing my repetition of ideas and questions, I have also implemented a few different techniques. The first is to constantly encourage students to raise their hands if they don't understand. Reinforcement of this invitation is vital because some Korean children don't want to ask questions because they worry that it will make them appear incompetent. If they don't ask questions, it can be difficult to gauge their understanding of both the English language and North American culture. By inviting them to help determine when to move on with the lesson, I am better able to promote a more complete understanding of English.

Another technique that has improved my ESL teaching is the use of examples. After asking a question, I often found my students struggling to understand the context of the question and what was expected of them. By providing examples or asking further questions, I was able to reinforce the context or to model an answer for them. Sometimes suggesting an incorrect answer was the best way to get them started. If I asked, "What is a form of transportation that uses an engine?" I would follow it up by saying, "Does a horse and buggy use an engine?"

One of the biggest challenges of ESL teaching is preparing the students to learn English. I do not have a homeroom and instead move between classrooms. This makes it more difficult to set up instructions or activities before class, such as bell work. I had to develop other methods instead. The most successful of these methods has been giving the students a review activity to complete at the beginning of class. After a short verbal reminder of the previous lesson, I give them a small assignment that is to be completed quietly during roll call. Providing this activity performs two functions. First, it keeps the class occupied while I interact with each student individually. Second, it allows the students to work through something on their own and to warm up their English skills. Providing the students with a time to prepare their minds for English class has visibly increased the amount of participation in my classes.

STRUGGLES OF TEACHING OVERSEAS

The biggest and most obvious struggle that people have when they move to Korea is the language barrier. Although bigger cities do have a larger percentage of people who can speak English, the majority of Koreans still do not know English. During my first month in Korea, I felt very limited as to what I could do and where I could go. With some coaching from fellow teachers, I was soon able to ask a taxi to take me home. This ability allowed me to feel safer and more confident in exploring the city. If I got lost, I could just tell a taxi to take me home. Next I learned how to say hello and thank you. This lesson was followed by learning how to order things and express different values of money. A person can get along quite well once these few phrases have been tackled.

Once I had a basic grasp of the spoken language, I decided it was time to learn the Korean alphabet. Although the symbols appear complex, they are actually very logically constructed. It takes an average of 2 hours to learn them and a couple days of practice to master them. Within 3 months in Korea, I had these few skills mastered and was able to travel alone confidently.

Homesickness often weighs heavily on people's minds when they are contemplating moving to a foreign land. Since coming to Korea, I have often heard people talk about the 1-month and 3-month blues. These terms refer to the toughest times for people during their stay. The consensus in the ESL community is that after you have been in Korea for a month, you start to evaluate why you came and whether you belong. A more intense version of this introspective evaluation is said to occur after 3 months. If you can make it through these periods, then the rest of your time in Korea should be much easier.

I personally experienced a mild case of the 3-month blues. I found I was unhappy about missing out on events that were happening in the lives of my friends and family in Canada. Above all else, being involved in the community helped me to deal with these feelings. Exploring the area and joining in activities like martial arts, yoga, sports clubs, Korean language classes, or foreigner associations can help you to better understand the culture. The hapkido martial arts class I attended made me feel like part of the community and provided me with a sense of belonging. It is in these classes that I learned the most about Korean history and culture and developed an appreciation for the Korean way of life. It is also where I developed my closest friendships with Koreans.

One thing that foreigners often misunderstand and are offended by is Korean bluntness. If one has a physical feature that differs from the norm, students will point it out. My students have often surprised me by their forthright fascination with my freckles, arm and leg hair, and prominent nose. Colleagues of mine have been approached in public with suggestions about how they could lose weight or become healthier. While Koreans view this as being friendly and helpful, foreigners can be deeply hurt by these comments. Needless to say, it can be difficult for a self-conscious person to live in Korea. Having a relaxed attitude toward life can make these experiences much less stressful and more amusing.

It should also be noted that Koreans are equally as quick to approach you with positive observations. I have been complimented numerous times about my height, my smile, my blue eyes, and my polite manners. Koreans of either gender are not afraid to compliment your personality or appearance. From these interactions, it is easy for me to understand how much others watch me while I am in public. Whenever I step out into public view, I am an ambassador not only for my country and my school but also for Westerners in general. I realize that if I do something inappropriate, then I could negatively influence people's view of English speakers. This awareness has prepared me for life as a teacher in a small town, where I will be equally noticed and monitored in public.

Another positive aspect of Korean bluntness is the honesty with which many Koreans view themselves. It is refreshing to hear so many people offer honest personal evaluations. Exaggeration does not seem to be as common a practice here as it is in North America. People seem more concerned with how they can improve themselves than with trying to elevate others' perceptions of them.

The business mentality of English academies promotes frequent and sporadic turnover of both students and teachers. Students advance in the program at different rates. Foreign teachers begin their 1-year contracts at different times throughout the year and consequently end them at different times. Korean teachers are constantly leaving to fill vacancies at other schools and are soon replaced. One of the rewards of teaching is building relationships with students and co-workers. These relationships create an environment where people can positively impact each other. The lack of continuity in a hagwon setting has forced me to learn to adapt to change. Unfortunately, it has also severed the development of some of my relationships.

While working in Korea, one must be concerned not only with learning differences in infrastructure and culture but also with maintaining one's personal health. I work 6 days per week and have few holidays. By the end of my first year I will have worked more than 300 days at my academy. Working this much could easily take a toll both on a person's physical health and stress level unless care is taken. The need to be healthy is especially true when teaching abroad, because a foreign teacher's immune system does not recognize many of the germs and viruses that the students bring to class with them. Developing a daily exercise routine and maintaining a nutritious diet is vital to the health of a teacher in a foreign land. Involvement in athletic clubs and classes has helped motivate me to exercise regularly. Preparing meals at home has allowed me to monitor my eating habits.

One thing that has made my stay much more enjoyable and fulfilling has been the support of fellow English teachers who are foreigners. I have found the ESL community to be very supportive. These teachers are constantly exchanging teaching stories, giving encouragement, and offering suggestions. Equally important, they are an invaluable source of information about where to eat, shop, work out, travel, and find employment.

Conclusion

Teaching ESL in South Korea has been a rewarding and enjoyable experience. Living as a minority in a different country and trying to understand a different culture has been challenging at times. Likewise, teaching ESL in a private academy proved to be much different from teaching in a traditional Western classroom. However, learning to overcome and adapt to these differences has helped me to develop as a person and an educator. With a positive attitude, teachers will find Korea to be a beautiful place with much to offer. It is also a place where teachers can develop and broaden their teaching ability, as well as learn new techniques that are used in different parts of the world. It is crucial, however, that a teacher find an academy or school that he or she feels comfortable with. By carefully researching and selecting a school, a teacher can better ensure a positive experience.

Nathanael's Tips for Traveling Teachers

Things You May Like About Korea

- Korea is a small country with an abundance of transportation networks. You can travel the country inexpensively and conveniently
- Seoul is a major transportation hub, so it is easy and inexpensive to travel to Japan, China, and Southeast Asia
- Cereal boxes have prizes that are practical, such as bowls, mugs, plastic containers, and so on. These prizes are taped to the outside of the boxes, so you don't have to dig through the cereal for them, and you know what you're getting
- English movies, music, and books easily can be found in most Korean towns
- Singing rooms (nori bong) are abundant in Korea. They are small rooms with couches and karaoke machines that usually run 24 hours a day. You rent them out for a period of time and can sing as many songs as you like
- DVD rooms (DVD bong) are rooms with surround sound, comfy couches, and a big-screen television. You can simply look though their vast DVD collections and choose which movie you want to watch. Like singing rooms, they often run 24 hours. If you are in a bind, DVD rooms are also a cheap place to get a few hours of sleep. Simply order a really long movie, turn down the volume, and enjoy the comfortable furniture.
- Bathhouses (or saunas) are also a place to relax. For 2,000 won, you can get into one of these luxurious bathing rooms, which are located throughout Korea. Usually containing a variety of hot and cold baths and showers, as well as barbers and masseuses, these facilities are divided into separate areas for men and women and are enjoyed while in the nude. However, unlike the North American bathhouses of the 1970s and '80s, Korean bathhouses are very family friendly. Often I've witnessed fathers scrub down their preadolescent and teenage sons, only to have their sons turn around and return the favor. After a long day or a hard game, co-workers and teammates will often go to a bathhouse together. Bathhouses also often have inexpensive overnight sleeping quarters in them and are a great place to sleep while traveling the country
- Tax is included in all the prices, and there is no tipping for service at a restaurant

Teaching in South Korea 207

- The postal system is much cheaper than in North America. This makes it very convenient to send packages home to your family or to mail some of your excess belongings home before you plan to leave Korea
- The starting fare for a taxi is 1,500 won (C$1.50), and the price doesn't increase with the amount of people
- It only costs around $6.00 to watch a movie at a state-of-the-art cinema. The cinemas also all have arranged seating, so you can book your seat well ahead of time and don't have to worry about pushing your way into the theater
- The Internet connection in Korea is one of the fastest in the world
- Korea, home to both LG and Samsung, is a world leader in cellular phone technology. In addition, unlike some places, in Korea it does not cost money to receive a call
- You can buy numerous types of flavored milk, including strawberry and coffee
- Korean-style restaurants provide numerous side dishes with unlimited refills
- Food that is ordered for delivery usually comes in metal bowls with metal cutlery. When finished, one simply places the dirty dishes outside the door, and the delivery person will pick them up by the next day
- Many couples wear matching clothes. From what I can gather, it is usually the woman who decides what they will wear
- Crosswalks have meters that inform you how much time is left for you to cross the street
- Most of the monthly utility costs come on one bill each month. You can pay these bills easily at ATM machines located at most banks
- There are street vendors year-round. You can purchase anything from handcrafted furniture to fruits and vegetables
- Many companies use random English phrases and words to market themselves. These phrases and words are often used out of context or simply don't have any meaning. Many clothing companies also put these slogans on their products. The people wearing these products often do not know the meaning of the slogans they are wearing, which can be very amusing. An 11-year-old student of mine once wore a pink shirt with the words *Hell's Angel* inscribed across the front with glitter. It was interesting seeing her reaction when I explained that the Hell's Angels were a notorious biker gang
- Korean has a large market for stationery and office supplies, so teaching supplies are very inexpensive and easy to find

- There are many kinds of of ice-cream bars and other packaged ice-cream goods. Most of them you can purchase for less than 500 won (C$0.50)
- Sweet pickles and packets of hot sauce are always included with pizza deliveries
- Spoons are a prominent utensil in Korea. If you are eating out and have trouble using chopsticks, there will usually be a spoon nearby
- There is an abundance of Korean superstitions, and it is amazing how seriously people take them. For example, my students will not allow rain to get on their heads because they believe this will make their hair fall out. Other superstitions include the following: If you write a person's name in red, that person will die; if you sleep with the fan on, you will suffocate in your sleep; if you shake your leg, you will lose all of your good fortune; you must avoid the number four, because it is associated with death

THINGS YOU MAY NOT LIKE ABOUT KOREA

- Corporal punishment is used in some schools and academies
- The money is quite large and might not fit in your North American wallet
- The largest form of currency is a 10,000-won bill (C$10). Therefore, if you are paid the average teacher salary (2 million won) in cash, you will have to carry around a thick bundle of cash
- You cannot withdraw money from an ATM machine between 11 p.m. and 7 a.m.
- Although there are many English programs available on television, they are mostly soap operas and reality shows
- The tariffs placed on foreign products make them both expensive and difficult to find
- Due to the language barrier, the English music played in public places sometimes contains content that would be deemed inappropriate by North American standards (e.g., gangsta rap in Wal-Mart)
- Ballads and pop music are the overwhelming music of choice
- Laundry dryers and dishwashing machines are rare
- Ovens are small and are usually not included in a bachelor apartment
- The tap water is usually not consumable
- Smoking is very popular among the men of Korea. It is difficult to find a restaurant that has a nonsmoking area

- Spitting on the sidewalk is common—especially by elderly men and women
- Almost all schoolyards and playgrounds have dirt playing surfaces. Grass that you can play on is rare and usually can only be used if you rent it
- Most of the English taught in Korea has the American spelling. In addition, the American pronunciation is emphasized. On occasion I have even been challenged for using the Queen's English in class
- Many of the students have a fixation with dung (feces). They will draw pictures of it, make jokes about it, and buy dung-themed stationery. There is even a popular cartoon character that uses dung as a hat
- In rural and more conservative cities that have not been visited by many foreigners, it is very common for a Westerner to be stared at for a prolonged period of time. In addition, random children will usually run up and yell, "Hello," or "Hi," or "Nice to meet you," to Caucasians. Although this can become annoying after a while, it is usually done in a good-spirited way
- Korean names are all three syllables long, with the family name appearing first. This makes many of the names sound similar and makes it more difficult to learn them
- If schoolwork is circled, it means that it is correct. This can be confusing if you are accustomed to grading things with circles around mistakes. Koreans use circles for correct answers, while check marks are used to indicate mistakes
- Cherry tomatoes are considered a fruit. They are served for dessert and are always present alongside pears, blueberries, and truffles on the top of cakes
- Parents occasionally encourage or force their children to undergo medical procedures that North Americans would consider unnecessary. I once asked a student why he had red scabs all over his face. He said that his parents had made him undergo a freckle-removal procedure the previous day
- Korea is famous for eating dog meat as a delicacy, although many Koreans I have met are opposed to it

What You Should Know Before Accepting a Job in Korea

Jobs teaching English are plentiful in South Korea. However, finding a secure job with a reputable school can be difficult. The first thing that one must understand before searching for a job in South Korea is that there are three main types of English-teaching jobs for foreign workers. Most foreigners are recruited to teach at hagwons (pronounced hog-wons), or English academies. Teaching English in public and private schools is also common. Finally, some foreigners accept jobs as English instructors at Korean universities.

REQUIREMENTS

In order to be an English teacher in Korea, you will need to meet a few standard requirements. First, you need to be from an English-speaking country. Second, English must be your native tongue. Finally, you must have a degree of any kind from a university (an English degree is not required). Foreigners with teaching degrees are highly coveted, but a teaching degree is often not a requirement. Likewise, special ESL courses may not be required and are often not even considered during the hiring process. However, if your résumé is short on teaching experience, then it might be a good idea to take an ESL instructional course. One last thing must be mentioned in regard to requirements: bias against Caucasians being hired to teach English still exists in Korea. Although this bias is diminishing, it may still have an impact on whether you are hired or not. If you encounter this problem, don't let it discourage you; there many places in Korea where employers are open-minded about who they hire.

WHERE TO FIND A JOB

The most common way of finding jobs in academies and schools is through a recruiter. Recruiters often advertise in newspapers, at career centers, and around university campuses throughout North America. Recruiters are also often paid by prospective employers to find teachers to fill job openings. This means that their main income derives from the commission that they make from hired teachers. Therefore, some recruiters may not look out for the best interests of the potential employees.

The second way of finding a teaching job is through direct contact with the school. You can often find contacts for schools through university career departments and through advertisements for specific schools. There are a few benefits to direct contact with a school. Direct contact removes the need for recruiters and their potential personal agendas. It also allows you to receive accurate and precise answers to your questions, and it allows you to personally judge the English-speaking ability of the people who will be supervising you during your time in Korea. This final point is especially important because your supervisors will be the people who can help you with setting up your living arrangements, help you if you have an emergency, and pay you every month! Needless to say, clear communication with the people running your school is vital for a healthy and successful experience in South Korea.

If you are interested in teaching at a hagwon, I would highly recommend MoonKkang English School (http://mkeslteaching.com/). They really take care of their foreign teachers, and I have had a fantastic experience with them. From what I have gathered so far, the few positions that are available are often offered to people who have previously taught English in Korea or who have connections with people in the university.

WHAT TO EXPECT IN AN INTERVIEW

I contacted the academy I work for through an e-mail I had for the personnel manager who was working in Korea. She was a fellow Canadian who had graduated from an Ontario Faculty of Education a few years earlier. After she looked at my résumé and the cover letter I had e-mailed to her, we arranged to do the interview at 9 p.m. EST (10 a.m. Korean time) on a Thursday. The interview was fairly casual and included the questions that we had for each other (most of which I have listed in the following sections). Although it didn't seem like it at the time, I think that she may have been evaluating my ability with English during our conversation. After the interview, she offered me the job and e-mailed me a contract.

QUESTIONS YOU MAY BE ASKED DURING AN INTERVIEW

- What will your role be as an ESL instructor?
- What are your classroom philosophies?
- What are your most difficult classroom challenges? How did you overcome them?
- What are your positive classroom experiences?

QUESTIONS YOU MIGHT ASK DURING AN INTERVIEW

- What is the salary and what are the benefits? (See the contract expectations in the next section)
- How many days a week will I work? What will my working hours be each day? Are their split shifts (i.e., work in the morning for a couple

of hours and then again at night)? All of these things vary greatly from school to school
- Will I be shared with other agencies? This is another common occurrence that can increase the difficulty and stress related to the job (see contract expectations in the next section for details)
- Who will my supervisor be? Does this person speak English? Is he or she easily accessible if I have any questions or emergencies?
- What type of training does the school provide? My school provided me with 3 days of training, including plenty of observations. However, I have heard that many schools expect their new teachers to teach during their first or second day in Korea
- What is the expected attire on an average day? My school expects clean and casual, while others in Korea expect a shirt and tie. This question will help you to determine what the work environment will be like, as well as what to pack
- What are the class sizes? This question is often overlooked, but you could have anywhere from 5 to 50 students in a class, depending on your school
- How many other foreign and English-speaking staff will I be in contact with? There are 50 foreigners who work in different divisions of my school, 4 of whom I work with directly. In addition, all of the Koreans that I work with are fluent in English. This is not always the case. In some schools, you may be the only foreigner or English speaker. You may not be prepared for this. For me, it was very important to have other foreigners and English speakers who I could befriend, socialize with, and turn to for advice or help
- Are there any people on the school's staff who will be there to help me in a time of need? My school has two Koreans whose job is to take care of foreign teachers. They helped me set up my Internet and phone service, acquire furniture, send things home, pay my bills, and do many other things that the language barrier made more difficult
- When will my departure from my home country occur? When will I begin my training? When will I begin teaching?
- How will the travel arrangements work? Will anyone be there to meet me at the airport or bus station?
- What type of accommodations will I be given? How far will they be from the school? Will I live near a bus or subway route? This information will help you to determine what mode of transportation you will need to use each day. Public transportation costs 500–2,000 won ($0.50–$2.00) for

a one-way ticket. Many teachers can walk to work in 10–20 minutes, while others are a short bus ride away. Some teachers also choose to buy a motorbike or scooter for about 500,000 won
- Is there computer and Internet access at the school? This information will help you determine whether you want to take a personal computer or laptop with you and if you need to set up Internet service at your residence in Korea
- If there is an urgent need to return to my home country (e.g., a wedding or funeral), will I be able to take a leave of absence and return home?
- If there is a major emergency, how difficult is it to break the contract and return home? What are the ramifications?
- How much money should I bring? Will I be able to get an advance if I need money before my first payday?

Contract Expectations

South Korea is full of English teachers who do not have a teaching degree, so qualified teachers are an asset. Most of the teaching contracts in Korea are for a period of 1 year (12 full months of teaching). Here are some standard benefits that both qualified and unqualified teachers should look for in a contract:

Salary
- 1.8–2.3 million (C$1,800–$2,300) won per month should be the starting base salary (depending on your level of education). A qualified teacher should expect to receive more than 2 million won per month
- The contract should also state the date that you will be paid on each month. There are some schools that do not specify this information, often leaving their teachers frustrated and unsure of when they will get paid
- Jobs at universities often have substantially lower pay (1.1 million won), but the job usually includes a couple months of vacation time each year

Taxes
- The contract should also state the amount of tax that will be deducted per month (taxes should add up to about 10% per month)
- Both Canada and the United States have an agreement with South Korea that allows their citizens to get a tax refund upon the completion of their time in Korea. Unfortunately, England and some other countries do not share this agreement

Severance and Holidays
- Expect a full month's severance pay upon the successful completion of your contract
- Expect all paid national holidays plus two 1-week vacations. This benefit often varies among contracts, but it is something you should look for

Other Standard Benefits
- Your round-trip airfare should be covered. Some schools make the flight arrangements and send the tickets to your door. Other schools will expect you to make your own arrangements and then will subsidize the price of your ticket when you arrive. Either way, if you fail to complete your contract, you should expect to pay the full price for the flights. In some cases schools will also have a clause that states that if you terminate your contract after completing half of it, you will only be liable for your ticket home
- A fully furnished bachelor apartment should be provided
- Your employer should offer 50–50 national medical coverage. The school should pay for half of your medical insurance, while the rest will be taken off of your monthly paycheck. Medical care in Korea is extremely inexpensive, so this coverage should be more than enough for your stay

IMPORTANT CONTRACTUAL DETAILS
- Specify no split shifts. Many schools will ask their teachers to work for 2 or 3 hours in the morning and 2 or 3 more hours at night. This can make for very long days and can be quite inconvenient
- Specify no sharing employees with other agencies. In order to get their money's worth, some schools also have agreements with other agencies. These usually state that if one school cannot find enough work for an employee, then the school will lend the employee out to another school

PAPERWORK

After you find the perfect situation for yourself and are hired on at a school, there will be a few things that the school will need you to send in. The following section details paperwork that I had to complete before I could begin teaching:

- Passport: This requirement is obvious, but you would be surprised to learn how many people procrastinate in either getting or updating their passport. During my first month in Korea, two teachers had to delay their flights to Korea and their contractual starting dates due to problems obtaining passports. Keep in mind also that you must have your passport before you can obtain your working visa. Complications can occur, so make sure you arrange to get your passport well in advance of your trip
- Original university transcripts and degrees: My academy required me to send these documents via courier. I was a little uncomfortable about having to send my original degrees through the mail, but they were required for arranging immigration. My school promptly returned them to me upon my arrival; however, I suggest sending a high-quality photocopy of your degrees instead
- Contract: Your school should send you an official contract either by mail or electronically. You will also need your contract to obtain a work visa
- Up-to-date résumé, cover letter, three passport-sized photographs, and a photocopy of your passport information page: These documents are also required for immigration. The photographs do not have to be official, and I found it was much cheaper to simply take a digital photo of myself and print it out on my computer
- E2 work visa: After you send all of the required information to your employer, they should obtain your E2 visa issuance from the local immigration office and send it to you. You must then either take (or mail) the issuance to the closest South Korean Embassy or Consulate along with your original passport for further approval
- Extra passport-sized photos: Your school should arrange for you to receive an alien registration card with the photos you previously sent. In the event that they do not make the arrangements, you will need to obtain this card at the local immigration office upon arriving in Korea. In order for the immigration office to be able to process this card, you must provide them with three current passport-sized photos. As previously mentioned, these do not have to be professional photos. It is also a good idea to bring four or five spare passport photos, in case you need them for something else

IMMUNIZATION

There are some vaccinations that are recommended before you arrive in South Korea. I tried searching for this information on the Internet but came up empty on more than one occasion. The best information and recommendations that I received came from my local travel clinic in Ontario, which offered a free consultation. The clinic also was able to provide me with the vaccinations. This service was covered by my parents' health plan, which I was still eligible for at the time. The clinic recommended vaccines for hepatitis A, hepatitis B, and typhoid. They also recommended that all Canadian booster shots be up to date.

Things That Are Good to Know Before Arriving

Monthly Expenses

- Electricity and plumbing: For a bachelor apartment, these bills should be 20,000–30,000 won (C$20–$30) on average. However, an apartment that uses oil will usually be much more expensive
- Cellular phone: Korea is one of the leaders in cell-phone technology, so almost everyone in Korea has a cell phone. The start-up cost (including the phone itself) should be 9,000–20,000 won, depending on your plan. I use a pay-as-you-go plan that costs me 10,000 won per month
- Home Internet and cable television: The setup cost for an Internet connection in an apartment should be about 15,000 won, while the monthly cost should be 30,000–50,000 won. Cable television costs 5,000 won per month
- Korean lessons: Lessons at the local YMCA run for 2 hours every Saturday. The cost for the 4-month course is 85,000 won
- Fitness club or gym membership: There are many fitness clubs in the urban areas of Korea. Membership at a gym ranges from 40,000 to 60,000 won per month or 100,000–150,000 for 3 months. This price includes all of the classes at the gym (step class, spin class, yoga, etc.)
- Hapkido or tae kwon do: ESL teachers often have some free time during the day and choose to join a martial arts class. The two most popular classes to join are hapkido and tae kwon do. Martial arts training typically runs for 1 hour a day, 5 days a week, and costs 80,000 won each month. With dedicated training it is common to be able to attain a martial-arts black belt in 1 year
- Food: The cost of food will depend on how much you like to cook for yourself and on the degree to which you enjoy Korean food. The average meal at a Korean restaurant will cost you 2,000–3,500 won, while Western

style meals are usually much more expensive. If one of your goals is to save money, then cooking for yourself is a better option. You can easily get by spending less than 150,000 won per month for food

Transportation
Driving in Korea occurs on the right-hand side of the road and can rattle the nerves of even the most seasoned driver. However, some foreigners still choose to drive. In order to drive a vehicle, one must have either an international driver's permit (IDP) or a Korean driver's license. An IDP can easily be attained from the nearest automotive association in North America (such as the Canadian Automobile Association), while a Korean driver's license costs 10,000 won and can be acquired without a driving test. Most people choose to drive motorbikes or scooters because then they don't need insurance or a license. The cost of a used motorbike is often around 500,000 won, while a scooter can be purchased for much less.

I would recommend using public transit, which is both efficient and inexpensive. Taxis are also very inexpensive (starting at 1,500 won) and provide another good option.

Banks
Bank accounts can easily be opened by taking your alien registration card into a branch. Most banks will have at least one employee who speaks English. Bank machines are both abundant and prominent in most towns and can be accessed from 7 a.m. to 11 p.m. with a debit card, which you will receive with the opening of an account. Service charges only apply if you withdraw money from a machine outside of the bank's hours of operation (600 won per withdrawal).

Wiring money to your account in North America can be easily accomplished from any branch. All you will need is your alien card, the pay stub from your work, and the information on the account to which you will be transferring money. Each wire costs about 17,000 won to send from Korea and an additional C$10–$20 to receive the money in your Canadian account. The maximum amount of money you can send home at one time is C$10,000. If you are planning on paying off loans on a monthly basis, it may be a good idea for you to attain a line of credit from your Canadian bank. By doing this, you can save up money in your Korean bank and send it home in lump sums (thereby reducing the amount of transfers). This will also afford you some flexibility and allow you to send money home when the currency exchange is advantageous.

Private Lessons
Although illegal, private English tutoring is common and well known in Korea and provides many English teachers with another form of income. The law enforcers usually turn a blind eye to the giving of private lessons if done in moderation (similar to breaking the speed limit in Canada). It must be said, however, that the penalty when caught is often a fine and deportation from the country. Getting a private tutoring job usually involves either being approached in public by a potential student or finding a client through a fellow teacher who already has connections. Private lessons are usually taught in the student's home and earn the teacher 30,000–60,000 won per hour for every student.

WHAT TO BRING

- Your passport; it is also wise to make a photocopy of it for yourself and someone back home in case of an emergency
- Your social insurance/security information
- A hard copy of important contact information: Although Korea has one of the fastest broadband speeds in the world and is packed with Internet cafes (called PC rooms), you never know when electronic information will malfunction on you
- An IDP if you plan to drive a vehicle during your stay
- Clothes for summer and winter: The summers are hot, often averaging more than 30 °C, and the winters average just below freezing, so you will need a coat and sweaters. The average Korean is much smaller and skinnier than the average North American, so finding clothes that fit can be difficult for some people. In addition, women may have difficulty finding underwear and bras that fit. Finally, there are many beaches along the coast of South Korea, so be sure to bring your bathing suit and sunscreen
- Shoes: During the summer, most Koreans and foreigners use slip-on shoes or sandals to walk around town. Plastic slippers can be easily purchased in Korea, but if you would like a pair of more comfortable slip-on shoes, bring them from home. In addition, anything larger than a U.S. size 10 men's shoe is difficult to find, so bring your own
- Your banking information from home: In order to wire money home, you will need your bank name, branch address, branch number, account number, and transit number
- Extra sheets and towels: There are no dryers in Korea, so you might want an extra set for wash days

- Your favorite brand of tea or coffee: North American brands can be both expensive and hard to find
- A Costco or Price Club card: The numbers of Costco and Wal-Mart stores in Korea are growing. Costco is the cheapest place to buy your favorite North American goods, such as coffee and frozen vegetables. North American memberships to these kinds of stores are valid in Korea, so make sure that you bring your cards if you have any
- A plug adapter for your computer or any other electrical device you bought in North America: Korea uses an Asian–style, 220-V plug (with two round prongs on the male end). Some apartments have power converters for North American voltage, but others do not. If you plan to bring a few things that require adapters, then a power strip with North American outlets may be very handy
- Medication: Korean doctors and pharmacists will probably be able to provide you with anything you need. Most pharmacists speak a little bit of English and will be able to provide you with a good substitute for your favorite brands if they do not have them. However, it can be difficult to find medication with codeine in it, so bring that with you if you need it. Also, you may want to bring decongestants, cold medicine, cough syrup, Gravol or Pepto Bismol, and Polysporin
- Deodorant: Koreans usually don't wear deodorant, so it is difficult to find. Although the increased access to Wal-Mart has made North American brands more readily available, the number of brands of deodorant is still limited and it tends to be expensive
- Toothpaste with fluoride: Toothpaste is readily available in Korea, but Korean toothpaste is very different tasting and does not have fluoride
- Shaving products: They are available, but the variety is limited
- A few good books to get you through the year: Again, English novels are available in Korea, but they can be expensive and hard to find
- Photos of your family and friends: These pictures are always nice to have when you begin to miss home. You can also use them to decorate the barren walls of your apartment and office
- Money to hold you over until your first payday: How much money you will need will depend on how quickly you will receive your first paycheck. I recommend bringing about C$700 for the first month
- Seven or eight passport photos for your alien registration card
- DVDs: English movies are shown in English with Korean subtitles, which is nice. However, you may want some of your favorite DVDs on hand in case you can't find them in Korea. Also remember that Asian

DVDs and DVD players use a different regional code than North American DVDs and DVD players. Therefore, a universal DVD player can come in very handy while overseas
- Music: Most of the music that gets airtime in Korea is either pop or pop ballads. So if you are not a huge fan of Korean pop music, it might be a good idea to bring some of your favorite music from home
- Linens: Western-style sheets and blankets are expensive. Korean quilts are quite inexpensive but can be a little hot during the midsummer nights
- Your favorite pillow: Korean pillows are very different from North American pillows, so if you need a certain type of pillow in order to have a good sleep, bring one from home
- A record of your car insurance from Canada: If you decide to buy a car in Korea, proof of Canadian insurance will make your insurance rates lower
- Your eyeglasses and contact lenses: These items are very inexpensive in Korea, so you may want to pick up a few pairs while you are here
- Your camera: I haven't seen too many scanners in Korea, so a digital camera is best if you plan on making a Web site or blog to share your experiences or if you plan on sending pictures home
- A Korean phrase book: This book will help you get around and learn a bit of the language. I recommend the Lonely Planet products, which are widely available in North America
- If you cannot fit all of these items in your suitcase, sending some things by surface mail (on a ship) is another good option. It will take between 2 and 3 months to get to Korea from North America, so plan ahead. In my experience, the only problem with this method is that Korean customs officials seem to open almost every package that enters the country. Usually they leave everything in the package, but be sure not to send anything that could be interpreted as illegal (i.e., something that looks like drug paraphernalia or an explosive device). It is very inexpensive to send packages home to North America, so don't worry about acquiring too many things while you're here

Further Reading

- http://mkeslteaching.com/: The MoonKkang English School Web site is an excellent, user-friendly resource for any ESL teacher

- http://www.eslcafe.com/: Dave's ESL Café is a world-famous resource for ESL teachers. With nearly 32,000 users and more than 1 million articles, this Web site is a great place to find out more about international ESL jobs. It includes lesson-plan ideas, message boards, discussion forums, and job postings for ESL jobs around the world. You can also often find reviews of employers, so you will know which companies to avoid and which to seek out
- http://www.efl-law.com/: This Web site provides extensive information on taxation, pension plans, and other concerns of English teachers in Korea and around the world
- *Korea Unmasked: In Search of the Country, the Society and the People*: This book is an extremely informative cartoon-style book that explains Korean history and culture in layman's terms (Rhie, 2002).

WHERE IS NATHANAEL NOW?

After teaching in Korea, Nathanael held teaching contracts at both Eenchokay Birchstick School in Pikangikum First Nations (a fly-in Ojibwe reserve in Northern Ontario) and at Haliburton Highlands Secondary School in his hometown of Haliburton, Ontario.

Nathanael is currently working full time at Medeba Adventure Learning Center, in West Guilford, Ontario, where he enjoys developing and promoting unique alternative educational experiences. He also takes pleasure in pursuing new adventures with his wife, Dawn.

Reference

Rhie, W. (2002). *Korea Unmasked: In Search of the Country, the Society and the People* (J. Un & L. Choi, Trans.). Seoul: Gimm-Young International.

CHAPTER 11

TEACHING IN CHINA

Carissa MacLennan

AUGUST 16

After almost 28 hours of travel, we arrived at our school at 10:30 p.m. to be met by the school's principal and some fellow Canadian teachers. What a fabulous group of people! The secondary panel is made up of mainly first-year teachers and retired teachers. I am eager to work with these people. One of the retired teachers has been hired strictly to help with curriculum planning and assessment for the first-year teachers, so there is an abundance of support. Everyone is so positive, energetic, interesting, and curious about the world.

Our apartments are brand new, fully furnished, and equipped with high-speed Internet. The first order of business was to go shopping in local markets to equip our apartments with the basic necessities, such as towels, sheets, dishes, and cleaning supplies. All of the teachers, including the principal, live in the same complex, which makes the living experience reminiscent of a first-year university residency.

The school is second to none, as no costs have been spared on the facilities. The basketball courts were imported from Poland, and the soccer fields and track came from France. The food is real Chinese food, not the kind found in North American Chinese restaurants. This difference, I am quickly discovering, will take some getting used to. The owner of the school is identified as one of the most affluent businessmen in China. From what I have gathered during public speeches and dinners, he seems to have a big heart. His decision to build this school, which offers The Ontario Curriculum to local Chinese students, was made based on his observations of the staff working for him in his national chain of stores. The owner perceives that problem solving and critical thinking are skills lacking in the Chinese educational system. His goal is to educate the next generation of Chinese to be competent in these skills. From what he states in his speeches, it seems he does not want to make a profit off the students. All profits made by the school will feed directly back into the school.

AUGUST 21

Being blond, I am a bit of an anomaly. I am frequently stopped by parents who put their babies in my arms and snap a photo. Apparently it is good luck to have a picture taken with a white foreigner. Who would have expected this reception, considering the long history with an empire that closed its doors to European invaders and ideals?

I am learning a fair bit of Mandarin, which surprises even me as it is such a difficult language. Each homonym of a word can have four tones. However, I have learned some key phrases. I was with two friends of mine the other night and we stumbled across a coffee shop. I was able to ask the hostess, "Yo-mayo-piju?" Translation: "Do you have beer?" I think I may manage just fine!

AUGUST 22

I went into town today and bought a stereo and a color printer for C$150. Although the prices are cheap, the process to make such purchases is extensive. When you choose a product, the salesperson will write you a receipt. You then take the receipt to the *till* where you fight your way through the line (there is no queuing in China) to pay. Once your receipt has been stamped, you return to the salesperson, present your stamped receipt, and receive your purchase. At first, the process seems redundant, but what else do you do with so much manpower in an overpopulated country?

The other great discovery we have made is the availability of cheap DVDs. You can purchase a DVD movie for less than $2.00. Yes, I am admitting to my engagement in what is considered an illegal activity in the realm of international intellectual-property-right crimes. However, it is difficult to avoid buying the DVDs, as the only English station we get on the television is BBC Asia. When watching BBC, there are intermittent blackouts during which the television screen literally blacks out and the sound cuts out. We have discovered that the government will cut the cable whenever BBC airs stories that do not look favorably on China. It is moments such as these that quickly remind me that I am in a Communist country.

Here is one more reflection: while at a local market today, a man tried to give me his baby girl. As often happens on a typical day out, a man pulled me aside from my wandering in the market and tried to put his beautiful baby girl in my arms. Having people ask to take a picture with me has become such a normal occurrence that I opened my arms to accept the child, waiting for the mother to pull out a camera and take a photo. As I was opening my arms, my Malaysian friend who speaks Mandarin intercepted and pulled me away. Apparently the man was going to put the girl in my arms and run away, leaving me with the child. I cannot shake the image of this father wanting to pass this precious and pure soul over to someone he assumed could provide a better life. I keep trying to tell myself that this was not a selfish act but a selfless one.

August 25

Yesterday we went to the Great Wall of China. However, we didn't go to the Beijing tourist attraction. We went to a remote section outside

Tianjin. The trip was fascinating and surreal. It took us 2 hours to ascend to the point where the wall ended. Much of the wall has been rebuilt within the last few decades, but in this location we were able to climb to parts of the wall that are 1,500 years old.

This is the secondary school's first year in operation. As such, the school is definitely a work in progress. Our textbooks have still not arrived, and the library currently has only Chinese books. I consider it a great learning experience as a first-year teacher to see the development of this aspect of an educational system and to be able to contribute to the planning. As I have said before, the school is incredible. Our classrooms are enormous, and we only teach 20 students per period. We have been told that each classroom will be equipped with a computer linked to a 57-inch television. We have seen a couple of models in the classrooms. We have also been told that anything is available at our request. I have ordered an overhead projector for my room and a data projector to supplement the equipment promised. If all unfolds as promised, I am not sure I will be able to go back and teach in Canada!

August 28

The students will arrive on Sunday, but the school is so far from being ready. Many of the things we were promised have yet to come to fruition. I will try to help visually summarize the extent of the supplies that were provided. I was handed a basket that contained a notepad for lesson plans, two pieces of chalk, two pens, and a brush for the blackboard. We are trying to be good humored about the situation, but it is starting to become stressful, especially for first-year teachers. Construction of the school appears to be rudimentary. With each bout of rain, rivers of plaster flow off the walls. Everything leaks. Despite the pleasing aesthetics of the buildings, it is becoming obvious that the construction was rushed and is seriously flawed.

We were also told today that many of our students may speak little to no English. With that news, I stopped my planning. I had been working on developing my unit and lesson plans for the Grade 9 geography course from The Ontario Curriculum. There is great concern that many of our students will not be able to function in a class that uses The Ontario Curriculum no matter what level of English as a foreign language (EFL) support we provide. I am left with some pre-assessment activities to conduct the first day to determine the English proficiency of my students.

As a good first-year teacher, I have done as much as I can to prepare my classroom. After scrambling to find the bare minimum of supplies, I was able to write an introductory letter to my parents and have it translated, create a homework Web site for students, create sign-out sheets, put together student portfolios, create an introductory display with pictures of me and my life, and start a classroom newsletter. Despite the lack of supplies, I am excited to get in the classroom to decorate and set up.

SEPTEMBER 2

Our students, who board at the school during the week, arrived on Sunday, and we had a full day of orientation. This was my first introduction to how things really work in China. As I already explained, by Saturday we still had the absolute bare minimum of supplies. Our classrooms were empty, with the exception of desks, chairs, and a blackboard. The school still had no textbooks, library books, posters, printer paper, markers, scissors, or tape. Knowing the language proficiency of our students, I thought these seemed like essentials for creating an EFL-friendly classroom. True to what I am quickly realizing is part of the business culture of China, a shipment of essential supplies arrived at 5:00 p.m. on Saturday, but these were only the bare essentials. We still had no textbooks or library books. Needless to say we all had a very late night on Saturday preparing our rooms for the students' arrival.

Monday was our first day of official classes. I have been assigned to teach the Ontario Grade 9 geography curriculum; however, with many students, there is a huge language barrier. Yesterday was like pulling teeth with the students. Today was better, and the students are beginning to open up and speak to the foreign teachers. I have some wonderful students who are very eager to learn more about the Western world. Many of the students are aiming to go to Harvard or the University of Toronto to study computer science.

We still have no geography textbooks, so most of my planning comes from the Internet and my head. I am having fun though—the students are starting to understand North American humor. Today, however, I still had moments when I was laughing at my own witty humor only to see a classroom of blank faces. The successes are small, but when my students get one of my jokes and faces light up with understanding, I consider it a great step toward overcoming language and cultural barriers.

For all you first-year teachers out there trying to remember your students' names, please think of me getting to know 75 students with Chinese names. Each attempt to pronounce a name brings a round of giggles. Here's one example: Hu Xiaoguang, which may not seem too bad; but in China, the first name is the family name so I am left trying to let Xiaoguang roll off my tongue.

SEPTEMBER 5

I received an e-mail this week from a friend teaching in Kuwait. It was interesting how so many of our experiences were similar. This teacher has had to literally black out portions of the text dealing with topics such as Israel and the holocaust from the history textbooks with which he was provided. This is very similar to what happens in China. We have been told that part of the reason our textbooks have not arrived at the school is that the government reads and censors all of the books that come through customs. A colleague bought a book on China in Beijing last week; the section on the protests of Tiananmen Square was covered with black marker. There seems to be such a large gap between what is practiced and what is preached in this country. On the surface, it appears that there is relative freedom of expression and press; however, each day something happens that reminds you that this is still very much a Communist country.

In order to try and bridge the language barrier, I find myself playing educational games with my students. Today I took my students outside to learn the cardinal directions (north, east, south, and west). After they did much running around and learning (I hope), they were provided a candy. They were elated. I find it so hard to believe that these students are ages 16–19.

September 17

When people tell you that flexibility is the most important aspect of working internationally, it is easy to brush off, telling yourself that flexibility will not be a problem. Well, I cannot stress its importance enough. If you are not flexible, it can ruin your experience.

The mood amongst the Ontario teachers is dismal due to the ongoing lack of resources, despite the grandiose promises upon our arrival. We still have no textbooks or atlases, so I am getting everything off the Internet and photocopying, which is something I can handle, but yesterday both photocopiers broke. My boss, an Ontario administrator who is not working in the classrooms, told me to wing it. I could handle this advice on a good day. However, I admit that this response was frustrating, as I feel like I have been winging it for the last 3 weeks. I expressed my frustration by stating, "If you expect me to teach Ontario curriculum content to EFL students with the quality that was promised to the parents paying for their child's education, I need books, an overhead projector, and a working photocopier." I think he has finally recognized the frustration of unsupported first-year teachers in a foreign culture. I have decided to resort to using my own pocketbook and purchase the supplies I would like on my own.

Apparently the Ontario teachers are not the only frustrated group involved with the school. Two days ago, a group of angry parents arrived at the school and literally stormed the gates. Apparently a boy at the school had been harassing some of the girls in the dorms. When the girls told their Chinese teacher, the teacher ignored their complaints and literally asked the girls to forget about the incident. The girls called their parents, and on Tuesday night there were 30 parents who rushed the front gates and started to scream and yell at the Chinese teachers. The parents proceeded to tell the school to fire all Chinese teachers and make it a Canadian school. Eventually the police arrived.

The parents of this school are quite wealthy. The class system is very evident here in the parents' perception and treatment of the Chinese teachers. It seems that their behavior is relatively normal, and the wealthy in China are able to bully their way in and out of almost any situation. However, the Ontario principal is not backing down and told the parents that if they were unsatisfied with the school, they could withdraw their child. It will be interesting to see where this goes.

Last night I came by the school with a colleague to visit with the students in study hall. As we were leaving, I caught two students smoking. Smoking is not allowed on campus. One of the students had a pack of cigarettes on him but would not hand them over for confiscation. We stopped a Chinese teacher to translate to ensure the student understood the choices he had and the potential consequences. However, the Chinese teacher refused to translate. It became evident he was afraid to discipline the student. This student has been a problem since the first day and has already been suspended. Eventually he gave up the cigarettes, and he will yet again be suspended. It is difficult though, as many parents feel it is the teachers' responsibility to parent their kids during the week. Even if a student has engaged in enough negative behaviors to be suspended, the parents will still defend the child and refuse to support the school.

September 27

We had the opening ceremonies for our school last weekend, and it was quite the show. I am amazed at how little money and energy have gone into the classrooms compared with how much goes into public ceremonies. I acted as master of ceremonies and had a translator. The agenda was changing moment to moment throughout the ceremony. It was all I could do to interrupt the rapid-fire Mandarin backstage, moments before taking the podium, to try and determine the latest change. I felt like a marionette being pulled by strings. It didn't take me long to realize I was on stage not for my public-speaking skills but rather for my very Western appearance, complete with blond hair. The ceremony went off without a hitch, to my surprise. I was glad to meet the parents of my students; they spoke very little English but were obviously happy to meet the foreign teachers of their children.

Each day is proving better than the last in terms of developing rapport with my students. I am finally able to introduce content from the Grade 9 geography curriculum into my lessons. The first few weeks have involved focusing on building the vocabulary required for my course. However, the sad reality is that very few students I teach will be awarded an Ontario credit for the course, as they will not be able to meet all the expectations due to both language and skill barriers. In the Chinese educational system, students are put into classes based on their exam scores. Senior 1, Class 1 is the brightest according to the exam results, and Senior 1, Class 5 is considered the lowest academically. Language was not taken into consideration when streaming the students. The result of this decision is a great range of language proficiency in each class I teach.

In order to accommodate the differences in language skills, I have begun an enrichment program with a couple of my students from each class who have a real thirst for knowledge and are able to think critically and analyze information, skills which have not been reinforced in their educational experiences to date. My goal is to guarantee these students a fair opportunity to receive the Ontario Grade 9 geography credit. When I told the chosen students of my plans, they were elated. They wanted to know exactly what they would be learning throughout the year so they could start studying the information on their own during the national holiday. I was favorably impressed. All of my other students will receive an Ontario EFL credit for completing the course, even though it is all geography content.

I still have no books, so I need to be as creative as possible in developing activities and providing resources. This challenge is proving difficult, as when teaching EFL students, you want to provide as many visuals as possible. The Internet has become my dear friend in my efforts to provide visuals. All of my handouts are made from scratch, which is time-consuming and exhausting; however, I also think that I am building skills in curriculum development that not many first-year teachers have.

The students are starting to loosen up and laugh in the classroom, and I am starting to recognize their unique personalities. A couple of the students are starting to seek my help when they do not understand the lesson or homework. Apparently it isn't appropriate in China to ask for help, as that is considered an insult to the teacher; it suggests that the teacher has not done a good job of instructing the students.

Another Canadian teacher and I are in the process of starting a student council. We have asked those students who are interested to write a letter explaining why they should be on the council. We have decided to not conduct elections, as the concept of democracy is very foreign to the students. We decided it would be best to avoid broaching this controversial topic with the parents, Chinese administration, and the owner of the school.

October 12

Yesterday marked the 1-month anniversary of my arrival here in China. It feels like I have been living here for much longer. I chalk this perception up to how much I am enjoying most of my moments here.

The school is receiving calls from parents praising the Canadian teachers. The days, however, are quite long for both the students and teachers. Students wake at 6:00 a.m. for exercises. Classes begin at 7:40 a.m. and run until 4:20 p.m. At this time, students go to their homeroom for extra help until dinner at 6:00 p.m. From 7:00 to 9:20 p.m. students are in study hall. Lights are out at 10:00 p.m. The days are structured from morning to night. The students are exhausted, and I am discovering that many of them are staying up in the dark to work by the light of their cell phones late into the night to complete their homework.

As I have already commented, our students come from very wealthy families. Some carry a sense of entitlement and show very little respect toward some of the Chinese teachers. I admit that I am surprised by these behaviors, as they contradict the North American stereotype of Chinese students. Many of the Chinese teachers seem afraid to discipline the students. The Canadian teachers have had to work very hard to implement structure and rules in our classrooms. Students talk over each other and the teacher, they sleep during class, cell phones ring and are answered, and students never bring materials to class and are often late. The students are quite respectful toward the Canadian teachers, so it has been relatively easy to provide positive reinforcement to curb undesirable behavior. However, being the only ones enforcing the schoolwide rules about cell phones, uniforms, and cheating can be exhausting for the Canadian teachers.

This week was busy, as we had Teacher Appreciation Day and Mid-Autumn Festival. We were showered with gifts from our students and the school put on a huge barbecue on Teacher Appreciation Day. I found it strange that there were large placards posted around the school saying "Teachers are Lovely, Respect your Teachers, Love your Teachers," despite the blatant disrespect by some of the students toward some teachers. The celebration came across as extremely superficial to me.

Thursday was Mid-Autumn Festival, which is a very important festival in the Chinese culture. People travel great lengths to be with family. Each homeroom put on a program or performance in the classroom. During the evening, the Canadian teachers traveled class to class to watch the programs and eat traditional foods. What really struck us was the presence of beer at the school for teachers. It is outside of my comfort zone to drink alcohol in front of students.

Life at school continues to be a struggle. Everything feels so chaotic, unorganized, and inefficient. Everything seems to be the exact opposite to what one is used to in Western culture. As an example, to make a photocopy, one must go and get paper from a woman who is rarely in her office. Once you track her down, you have to sign three different cards stating you have taken the paper. You then have to chase down the maintenance worker to get the power plug for the photocopier. Once you have taken a half hour to do these things, you head to the photocopy room, which is typically locked. We are not sure why the room is locked, as the only item in the room is a photocopier with no power cord. So you now must find the man with the key to unlock the room. Remember that we have a huge campus, and it is still 25° here during the daytime, so we are running around, sweating before our day has really begun.

OCTOBER 18

I am giving my students a test on Monday but am more worried about how their organizational skills are going to impact their performance than the language barrier. Friday was a catch-up period. I have created a sample binder to show the students what their notes should look like with all of the work completed in the binder. I have hinted numerous times that it would be a really good idea if they got their notes in order and made sure they had all of their notes complete. The test is open book. I am hoping this will kick some of the kids into gear who didn't bother to make sure they had all of the notes.

The process is frustrating, but I have to remind myself of how foreign my expectations are to the students. Keeping notes, having their own paper, and even owning a binder are not typical experiences of Chinese students. They are given a workbook and a textbook for each class. Teachers follow the workbooks for homework and assignments. There is no need for students to take extra notes or have a place to organize their extra notes. Everything is taken from and written into their textbooks and workbooks.

The students are beginning to open up about their lives on campus outside of the classroom. These students live together, eat together, travel from class to class together, and have study hall together. I am quickly discovering that teenagers are teenagers, regardless of geography. A student approached me and the other student-council adviser about the female student we had chosen as co-president. Apparently the female students of this school were not impressed with our decision. It is so hard to please everyone, especially when we cannot have an election.

The school is absolutely freezing now, and the heat won't be turned on until November 15. In addition to the cold weather outside and the lack of heat inside, we have the windows open because the Chinese like to keep doors and windows open for fresh air; however, the air is really anything but fresh, considering the air pollution. I have succumbed to wearing my winter coat all day and often wearing gloves while working on the computer. The Chinese are all wearing long underwear under their uniforms and work clothes. My goal this weekend is to find some long underwear!

OCTOBER 27

Report cards come out next week, and we have parent–teacher interviews the following week, so I have been getting my student portfolios up and running. I am not sure how the parent–teacher interviews will go. There isn't much formal parent–teacher interaction in the Chinese educational system. With most families only having one child, that child has much pressure on him or her to succeed, and many parents take a vested interest in their academic performance, if not their behavior. However, I am almost positive this will be the first time the Chinese parents have experienced the parent–teacher interview in this kind of formal forum. We have each been assigned a Chinese translator, as most of the parents do not speak English. Because our students' parents do not understand the goals of The Ontario Curriculum, I believe there will be many parents asking for explanations. The grades of my students, even those who are the best of the best in the Chinese system, are quite low. This fact does not surprise me, as these students are experiencing a whole new culture of learning as well as struggling with the language. However, I know that many of the parents are going to be angry and frustrated. I am not sure how well I will be able to communicate through a translator how very different the expectations in the Ontario educational system are from the traditional Chinese educational system and that despite the grade, their child is actually doing quite well.

Hey, I finally got the filing cabinet I asked for in August!

October 29

I have broached the idea of holding workshops for the female students with the principal. Sex education is lacking, to say the least. Some of the male students are quite aggressive, making very sexually charged comments when speaking with the female students. I have noticed that some of the younger female students are being taken in by this behavior. There are also many rumors circulating about the after-hours activities taking place in the student dormitories. I suggested we created some information sessions for the female students that are tactful and do not come from an explicit feminist viewpoint. The response was positive; however, we are all concerned about how to approach such an important topic while maintaining cultural sensitivity. We have been specifically asked not to discuss sex, religion, or politics with the students.

The student council had its first meeting on Monday, and the students brought proposals for having a Halloween party and for writing the school mission statement in the school newspaper. Today was the second council meeting, and the other teacher adviser and I were blown away with the tenacity of the students. They had written a Student Council Mandate and prepared a proposal for a Halloween party this Thursday. The latter seemed like a strange proposal, yet it was reflective of a very formal culture, and we want to support a student-driven organization. Unfortunately, there has been a kibosh put on the party. Our students write their Chinese exams next week, and as of right now, the Chinese principal is not impressed with their academic performance at the school. The student council is disappointed, as this was their first opportunity to do something they consider Western for the students. However, they are going to host a pizza and movie night for the students after their exams are finished.

Tomorrow I am playing volleyball on a teacher-student team. It is a house league at the school, but not a single one of the female students would sign up. I am risking absolute embarrassment due to my total and complete lack of volleyball skills in order to encourage the female students to partake in coed sports. We will see how big my cheering section is tomorrow; we have played up how comical my contribution to the team will be.

NOVEMBER 7

Things are moving well with the students. It is incredible how much their English has progressed in the 2 months they have been at this school. At the beginning of the year, I couldn't get them to say the name of their favorite food in English. Now they are yelling out answers in class and doing presentations on urban plans they have designed. It is time for report cards and midterm exams. The students wrote six Chinese exams in 3 days. They were exhausted, and half of my time monitoring the exams was spent shaking kids awake who had fallen asleep, pen still in hand.

Teaching in a boarding school is interesting and emotionally exhausting, as you are involved with all aspects of student life. Because we have some rich, spoiled kids, we have problems with fights and smoking in the dorms, typical teenage activities. I sheepishly admit that I did not expect this to be the behavior of the students I would be teaching. The school administration has suspended a couple of students. However, we discovered today that the parents have refused to pick their children up, so the students have just been hanging out in the dorms and playing basketball in the gym. Every day there is some new drama or crisis going on with the students and teachers. I feel like I'm watching a foreign soap opera: I know there is drama, but because of the cultural differences I can't really keep up as to how the drama unfolds.

NOVEMBER 9

Our school has a principal from the local area and another from Ontario on campus, but we also have a consultant from Ontario who advises the owner of the school. Apparently the school's owner asked the consultant to come in for a week to meet with the staff and discuss our concerns.

I have not yet openly expressed just how frustrating the last 2 months have been. The principal from Ontario who was assigned to work full time at the school has disappeared. Most days we do not know where he is. This leaves the teachers from Ontario without support. We still have none of the resources promised when we arrived at the school, meaning we have no textbooks, curriculum documents, or supplementary resources. Our frustration is aggravated even more by being expected to teach The Ontario Curriculum to students who do not speak English well enough to understand the content. In one of my classes, the average grade was 26%, and that was being generous. No one at the school is listening to the Ontario teachers as we express our frustrations, make pleas for support, and give recommendations; we have also stated that we believe a year needs to be devoted to build the language proficiency of the students before offering Ontario credits.

I admit that I am getting lonely. It is daunting to know that I have met all of the people I am going to meet for the next 10 months, especially as a single woman. Our community seems relatively isolated, and there are not many other foreigners in the region. All of the teachers get along, but it is hard to work and play with the same people every day and night. I am also finding it difficult to make friends with the local teachers, as many of them do not speak English. And, as much as I am trying, my Mandarin is weak. At this point I would like to stay another year but am not sure it would be the best choice for me in terms of my mental health.

November 10

I just found out that five boys from my top class, whom I have come to truly enjoy teaching, beat up another student from their class last week. I was so angry. I spoke with one of them today in class while we were in his monthly conference to discuss his progress in the class. We spoke about the stress of the exams last week and why he chose to join the other students in beating up the one student. I expressed my disappointment and explained how he needed to find another way to vent his frustrations and stress. I think he was more upset that he got caught than that he hurt another person.

I found out after speaking with the student that the reason for the gang-style attack was because the one who was assaulted was speaking out, quite loudly, about China. This student does not fit in. He is a little reclusive and spends much of his time playing video games. When this student does speak in class, he often expresses political ideologies that do not ring true to the Communist Party of China. It is moments such as these that further highlight the power the Chinese government has over the majority of people in the country.

I am extremely disappointed in each student who engaged in the physical assault, but such is the life of a teacher or parent. It is very different from my experience working in a group home in North America. You expect this sort of behavior in that setting, but you don't expect it here, and not from straight-A students.

Just as this issue was settling down, I found out that three girls in my class have been accused of holding down and beating their peer. I had to give a formal statement today. Apparently the police are involved, and this case could go to court. However, there are also rumors that this story is a sham to get money from the school through a lawsuit for medical expenses.

NOVEMBER 13

I had a meeting with the Canadian curriculum director on Wednesday. During the meeting I had to show him all of my materials: lesson plans, handouts, student portfolios, assessment rubrics, and so on. He said that I am an exemplary teacher. In all honesty, I think this can simply be attributed to being from a different generation of teachers. As a first-year teacher, I am trying to do it all by the book. Many teachers who have been in the trenches for a significant number of years have their own systems based on their training and experiences.

We are having a meeting on Monday, and he wants me to show all of the teachers what I am doing to plan, organize, and assess my students.

I am flattered, but I know this is going to make a lot of the other teachers really angry. The staff is already frustrated with the administration's ignorance of the situation in the classroom. This additional pressure is just going to add fuel to the fire. The administration does not seem to trust that the teachers are fulfilling their professional responsibilities. In Ontario, there are systems in place to evaluate, monitor, and provide support to all first-year teachers. However, dragging professionals who have been teaching for up to 30 years into a meeting to listen to a first-year teacher speak about her approach to planning is insulting and unprofessional, in my opinion.

NOVEMBER 24

I had a frustrating day as my students wrote a test for which apparently few students had studied. Only one student was able to complete the test without a translator dictionary. I will review the content tomorrow and have them rewrite the test on Wednesday.

Although there are many students who are just not putting in the effort, there are many factors working against their success. These students have too much to do in a day. With six classes a day, three of which are The Ontario Curriculum, they do not have the time they need to study and learn. Their language is also not at the level it should be to complete an Ontario credit with ease. These students likely spend three times longer on homework for their Ontario classes than an Ontario student would, and many of them are still failing. The shame of it is that if we just stepped back as educators and took the time to build skills such as research, problem solving, and independent learning and encouraged them to practice critical thinking and build their language proficiency, many of these students could be quite successful. No one seems to be hearing or seeing that truth—except the teachers in the classrooms.

I came home tonight to find water leaking under the tiles in the bathroom, so my floor is soaking wet. I guess I will have to wait another 3 days to get that fixed, and the workers have already been here seven times to fix my plumbing.

Tomorrow is another long day with meetings both after school and after dinner. These 14-hour school days are starting to take their toll.

NOVEMBER 26

I came out of the market tonight to find about 20 older Chinese women line dancing in the street to Chinese hip-hop. I sat and watched for awhile. Exercise comes in all forms at all ages here.

Most of the students aced their makeup test today. I am relieved to see that I am not wasting my time here! Small victories mean the world these days.

DECEMBER 1

It has definitely been an interesting month here. About a month ago, four boys were expelled for literally beating up another student in the school. This is just one of three violent incidents involving students that have occurred in the last 4 weeks. Two of the male students who were expelled on that Friday returned to school on Monday as if nothing had occurred. Despite the presence of the very young, petite guards who are hired to prevent incidents such as this, the students made it onto school property. The school administration made the decision to refuse to allow the students to take part in their classes.

The result of this decision was a large group of parents came to the school on Wednesday, and accompanying the parents were members of the military. The father of one of the students is in the Red Army Guards. Under his direction, four armed guards and a reporter came to the school. From this point on, all hell broke loose. The Army guards forced their way past our school guards and found the classroom the boy was supposed to be in. The Army guards brought the expelled student to the classroom and physically pushed themselves past the Canadian teacher. Once the student was seated in the class, they stood at the back of the classroom waiting for the Canadian teacher to continue instruction. When the administration and school morality officer came to confront the guards, death threats ensued. As Canadians, our first reaction was to call the police. However, the Chinese police have less authority than the military—no matter their actions.

After 18 hours of yelling and screaming between the owner of the school and the parents of the two boys, it was settled that the boys would not return to the school. However, the following Monday, one of the expelled students came back again. A few days have passed, and the student doesn't seem to be around anymore. People are saying that the parents finally agreed that they made enough of a fuss to save face but that the best decision was to remove the student from the school.

We also had a meeting last night with the owner of the school and found out that our Canadian principal quit. We were informed that the new principal would be the man who has been our curriculum director for the last 4 months. This was a big blow to us, as there seems to be a lot of disconnect between his philosophy of education and that of the teachers. We realize that this kind of situation could happen anywhere, but because we are in a foreign country where we are asked to work weekends and evenings and without proper policies in place regarding the structure of the educational system, it impacts all aspects of our life. As the new principal stated during the meeting, "You are either with me or against me." Although the principal who was dismissed did not have a strong presence in the school, we trusted him to defend the rights of the teachers. The reality is that our contracts are consistently being broken, and we feel that we have no one here to defend us.

So, it would be nice if we could comfort ourselves by thinking about Christmas break being only 2 weeks away, but at this point it looks like there won't be a break. Despite what is stated in our contracts, we may not receive time off since the school's owner is leaning toward not closing the school for the holidays. Needless to say, staff morale is down.

December 16

It has been a frustrating couple of days. The Canadian teachers are all in low spirits. We were just informed that a couple who were teaching at the school were let go. This loss was another big blow to the staff, as the teachers had provided vital professional support and were like surrogate parents and friends to all of the younger teachers here. There is no reason we can think of for their firing other than their openly disagreeing with a decision made by the new principal. I am not sure how comfortable I am working in a foreign country where I can be fired on the spot without warning. On a brighter note, we have been granted our Christmas break. We are all really looking forward to some time away.

January 7

We are in the midst of exams and report cards. It is hard to believe we are at the halfway point. Unfortunately, I caught one of my exemplary students cheating on her exam with her cell phone. The students text message answers to each other. That makes five students who I have caught cheating during these exams. The joke has become that I have eyes in the back of my head. I think that the students just haven't had to hide their cheating before. Some of the local teachers actually fall asleep at the back of the exam room instead of monitoring the students.

I am at the bottom of the slope on the roller-coaster ride that has become my China experience. I am not getting much word from friends and family at home. I feel like people are forgetting about me.

January 14

Today marks the first day of the Chinese New Year which lasts for a month—all of which we get off as holidays. I am leaving for the sunny beaches of Thailand!

Celebrations of any kind in China involve the constant setting off of fireworks, usually of the smoky and loud variety—no pretty explosions in the sky. As we tried to talk above the noise of the fireworks over dinner, someone commented that it felt like we were living in the midst of a war.

One of the Chinese teachers from my office was asked not to come back after the New Year. It is best for the students, as he has very poor classroom management skills, but it breaks our hearts as he has become very dear to us. His behavior reminded me of *Mr. Bean*. For example, yesterday we were sitting in a meeting and I looked over to see a huge ball of tissue hanging from his nose, and it remained there for the duration of the meeting. From the outside it would look like he was being funny; however, he does not really have a sense of humor. This teacher is a very serious and dedicated member of the China Communist Party. It is embarrassing to admit, but we wonder sometimes if he is spying on us. Whether we are in the office or not, he will come over to our desks and start rifling through our papers. When we are writing e-mails on the computer, he will come and read them over our shoulders. Realistically I don't think he is a spy, just a curious young teacher who, like many locals, does not share the Western value of privacy.

However, this was yet another incident that makes one reflect on the relative job security available in Canada. On the flip side though, it also makes one think about the teacher's federation. In Canada, this teacher would have been left to continue teaching, despite his struggle with the students.

I went to the bank yesterday to transfer money to my Canadian account. This took an hour and a half and a whole lot of trees. The amount of paperwork required here is unbelievable. There is also a lot of inconsistency with regard to services. I asked for American traveler's checks and the bank teller said they didn't have any. Yet, I had two friends go to the same bank, one the day before and one an hour after me, and they were both able to buy some traveler's checks. It makes me wonder if it just depends on the mood in which you catch your teller.

February 18

I am suffering postvacation blues, as is everyone in this very bitter cold period. However, it was great to see the students again, and we actually had a productive week. I feel like I am in the teaching flow or the students are in a learning flow or maybe a little bit of both. I was really expecting to have a difficult first week back with the students as we settled back into our routines, but they are all working hard. I am able to move at a much faster pace than the sluggish pace prior to the holidays. I felt like I was trying to wade through a pool full of mud before. I am sure their parents had a few things to say about their report cards. I did lose a student over the holiday. The students tell me he has gone to a Chinese school. Although I was disappointed, it might be best for him in the long run.

We are facing contract renewals at the school. Most of the teachers have not been asked to return. I have been asked to return, as has a couple from Ontario who are retired back home. All of my other colleagues have been told that they will not be needed next year, as the school has hired staff with more experience. We were all shocked. Needless to say there is a lot of anger and hostility brewing amongst staff. I have also heard that all the teachers who were hired at the international career fairs over the holidays are couples. I think this knowledge is going to make it tough for me to return, even though it seems wrong to be selfish at a time like this.

All the local staff and students find my tan from the holidays amusing, and I have been the topic of much discussion since being back. China suffers from something I call shadism, which is much like racism. People are classified and judged based on the color of their skin. If you have darker skin, you must work in the fields under the sun and so are a peasant. The lighter the skin, the better.

February 26

I met with the principal today, and he is offering me tons of professional learning opportunities at the administrative and curriculum levels for next year. He asked me to become an administrator of the new administration software the school has purchased. I would be trained on the system and then offer training to our staff and teachers. I am being offered many more professional growth opportunities here than I would anywhere else as a first-year teacher, but I have trouble feeling excited as I reflect on how I am benefiting from a very ad hoc system that has let so many other teachers down. The principal has also asked me to help organize and supervise a trip to take 25 of our top students to Canada in the summer for 2 weeks. I think that it would be incredible to see the students experiencing firsthand the many things I have taught them in the Canadian geography course.

MARCH 3

Time is not my friend these days. I have been spending many hours working on a couple of projects for the school. However, it has also been an eventful couple of weeks. Yesterday we had the grand opening of the ESL Cafe for the students. The school actually came through with some funds to set up a room with beanbag chairs, books, magazines, computers, games (Scrabble), and books on tape. Kids are welcome to come every day after school to practice their English. The event was supported by most of the teachers, Chinese and Canadian, in the school.

Student council has also been busy. The students are looking to contribute a Saturday or two at a school for the blind and to organize a fundraiser at the school for an orphanage. The two boys who are in charge of sports have also come up with basketball-related activities for boys only. When we asked the students to revise the program for the inclusion of female students, we were met with much resentment. However, it seems like some kind of deal has been made on creating an athletic after-school program that is inclusive.

We also finally received our textbooks! We have heard that the textbooks took so long making it from customs to our school because a bribe was expected. Apparently it was dutifully paid. Because the school fired the Canadian librarian, we cannot use the hundreds of supplementary books that she ordered, which also arrived, until an informal cataloging system is put in place. In the hopes of being able to actually use the books this year, I have been assigned/volunteered to inventory the books and develop a circulation system, which has turned out to be a huge task.

I am starting to question my decision to return next year. This principal is experiencing difficulty convincing the owner to raise our salaries, as was promised as a part of the contract negotiations. Due to the remoteness of the region and the understanding that it will be all couples working here next year, I am finding this environment a difficult one in which to live. At this point, I feel like I will be sacrificing much in my personal life to return and need a financial incentive. I can survive another year if I know I am saving money. I am also concerned about the direction the school is taking. We had a staff meeting this week during which the principal told us he did now know the future of the school. There are some concerns that the school will shut down and also some concerns over our relationship with the local Ministry of Education in offering dual diplomas. However, the principal held a meeting with the students in the evening, during which he laid out the plan for next year.

Tuesday morning, the teachers were faced with many questions from students on the new plan for the school. We could not answer any of these questions, as we had not been debriefed. When the principal was approached about the unprofessional manner in which teachers were informed (or not informed) of the school's plan and about the teachers being left to deal with the emotional strain this put on the students, he was quite abrupt. There seem to be a lot of different issues brewing behind the scenes, which is not comforting when contemplating contract renewals.

Yesterday the school invited professional photographers, members of the media, and government officials to our classrooms. It was a definite cultural experience as I taught Canadian geography with cameras flashing and translators explaining my teaching to Communist government officials. The students were incredible and did not crack under the immense pressure the principal and school owner put on them to be good students throughout the event. In the end, however, I found the entourage of press and government officials that filtered through my classroom frustrating, because it seems as though the school is more worried about public relations than the actual teaching.

March 12

It has been an intense, frustrating, and long week. My apartment washing machine and water cooler broke. I also lost my bank card. It is so difficult to replace anything around here, so I have spent way too much of my spare time dealing with all of these issues. I have also had a long week with the students. I assigned a rather long end-of-unit project. Understanding their limitations with EFL and their need for structure, I provided very detailed, step-by-step instructions for the students, yet they are still asking me how to do the project. Short of doing the project for them, there is not much else I can do. Risk is a huge challenge for the students. With so many steps and varied components to the project, the students feel like they are taking major risks with their grades.

Our principal still thinks that most of these students could handle the full Ontario curriculum next year. I have some grave doubts. The progress is quite slow in terms of curriculum. We are just finishing Unit One, whereas in Ontario we would be on Unit Four. I recently met with the curriculum director to express my concerns, taking with me samples of student work. The low level of work the students were producing surprised him, even though all of the teachers have been consistently saying that performance was a problem when considering the full Ontario curriculum.

The subtle yet ever-present differences in cultural values of the Chinese and Canadian teachers do create some tension. We have a new Chinese teacher at the school who teaches the juniors English. Yesterday she awakened her students at 5:30 a.m. and made them run a loop of the track for each mistake they made on their English test. This was very disturbing for the Canadian teachers. These students are also preparing to write the exams. The set of exams the students take in Grade 8 to determine which secondary school they will attend. If the students do not do well, it can have lifelong repercussions. These poor kids stay at the school Fridays until 9:30 p.m. and Saturdays all day to study. Sunday is their only official day off; however, many parents hire private tutors for extra study sessions that day.

March 24

It has been a day of intercultural experiences, some funny and some sad.

My senior students have been working very hard at their culminating activity for this unit of study. Their assignment is to write a proposal for a new national park in one of Canada's ecosystems. The proposal is to include graphics such as photos, tables, and charts. This morning I was scanning through the assignments, and on one of the title pages was a photograph of two polar bears having intercourse. In Ontario, you would assume the student had done this on purpose. But you can't make that assumption here. This female student would be highly embarrassed if I pointed out this indecency to her.

This morning I was sent out to purchase some games for our ESL Cafe. After being rushed out just as I finished my large coffee, I was desperate for a washroom. In the store I ran for the washroom to find only squatter toilets in stalls with no doors. I knew these wouldn't be the worst facilities I would see in my travels, so I decided to just go for it. As I welcomed the relief, I looked up to see five pairs of eyes focused on me during what many would consider to be a very private moment.

Despite one's ability to laugh at the cultural differences, there are some that prove to be too much to handle. There is one male student at the school who has become dear to our hearts, either despite of or as a result of his tendency to act out. His father was called into the school yesterday to discuss his son's poor grades in math class. The student came to the school today and showed one of his Canadian teachers the marks all over his body. His father beat him last night with a belt and a stick for 3 hours. The toughest part is that there is nothing we can do. There is no law that protects the student, and if we call the father to address the issue, there is no telling what would happen to the student. This reality is a difficult load for us to bear.

March 27

I had planned to go to Beijing this weekend but decided to hunker down with my marking work. Much of my time was actually spent responding to student e-mails about their latest assignment. I am happy to discover through these informal online dialogues that I have actually developed a good rapport with most of the students. I have trouble judging the situation in the classroom sometimes, because the intercultural communication leaves gaps in shared understanding. Many of the students were reflecting on and poking fun at our class on Friday.

On Friday, I had five cameramen, seven Tianjin education officials, five school administration officials, and one Ontario Ministry of Education representative in my classroom. It was a circus. My students proved themselves in so many ways, on so many levels, to so many people. I had been joking with the students prior to the fanfare beginning, saying they had to pretend they found me interesting, laugh at all my jokes, and seem really enthusiastic to learn. They thought this funny and put on a great show for the officials. It was fabulous.

I had an interesting chat with the ministry representative from Ontario, who has come to audit our school and, we hope, grant us permission to give Ontario credits. The representative observed one of my classes, and afterward we spoke about the ability of the students to complete the Ontario diploma. I was not going to lie, and so I expressed my concern. He then accused me of not telling the administration earlier in the year of students' abilities but then said that my oversight was excusable because I am a first-year teacher. I could not believe what I had just heard. After taking a few deeps breaths, I explained that I had been telling the administration since the beginning of the year that these students lacked the level of language and necessary skills to move successfully into the Ontario diploma program. I further explained that whatever the administration chose to do with that information was up to them. I had completed my responsibility in providing adequate assessment of the students and reported the results to the administration at regular intervals. I was so angry because I felt like the auditor was questioning the students' ability while also implying that the program was negligently being set up next year for students to complete the Ontario Secondary School Diploma because of my lack of communication with the administration. This was yet another example of the lack of communication between the administration and teachers and the willingness of the school to sacrifice the teachers for the greater good of the school's reputation. It seems ironic that I live in what many would consider a repressive Communist country, yet some of my most undemocratic experiences come from the practices of the Canadian administration of this school.

April 13

For the most part, my daily life is relatively normal (by my standards) now that I've become accustomed to the fact that I'm not at home and things are simply done differently.

It has been a frustrating couple of weeks for me and my students. We hit a pretty big wall last week that has required a lot of backpedalling. My students were to complete a research assignment on Canadian ecozones and then write a proposal to the government of Canada to develop a national park within the region. Despite my frequent and clear warnings that copying would result in failure, every single student copied from the textbook and Internet in some form or another. Some students simply printed off pages from the Internet about their ecozones and handed them in. So I failed them all.

The reactions were extreme. The students could not comprehend why I had failed them, so I had to go back to the drawing board. I have given them the opportunity to redo the assignment while I take them through the research process, step by step. We are using makeshift information cure cards to record information and are using flow charts to organize the information. These are skills that are taught in the Grade 4 Ontario classroom. Please remember this is supposed to be a Grade 9 geography class. However, even after these lessons, I still cannot get the students to move from their point-form notes to develop their own ideas. Many of the students simply want to regurgitate their research. Unfortunately, this behavior is inherent to the Chinese educational system, and I cannot expect students to perform according to the values of Western educational systems after a couple of lessons. I do not blame the students; I know they are just as frustrated as I am.

The Canadian teachers continue to be exposed to experiences we find shocking. Last Thursday, another teacher and I were witness to a local teacher hitting a student. This happened right on school property in full view of many people, including other students. The other Canadian teacher and I had to run across campus to pull the teacher and the student off each other. The teacher was fired only because we have a Canadian principal. None of the Chinese staff, students, or parents of the school wanted the teacher to be fired. They all recognized that the teacher had made a mistake but were willing to move on. So, basically, it is considered acceptable for teachers to lash out at students. This event does not surprise me. On Friday, after the teacher told the students she was leaving the school, I counseled a group of students who were completely distraught over the situation. The students told me that the student and teacher were friends, and the friends were having a fight. I am having a really difficult time wrapping my head around this experience.

On Saturday we took the whole school to Beijing for Spring Travel, leaving at 5:30 a.m. with 200 students. It was a trip that a colleague and I had planned, but we had, unfortunately, handed off the logistics to a local teacher due to the difficulties the language barrier presented in trying to book transportation and tickets. We spent 8 hours on the bus and only 3 hours out of the bus. We were told the first stop would be a park, so I packed games, fully planning on teaching the students how to play ultimate Frisbee and flags. However, the park had no rolling green hill on which to spread around and play games, even though a picture of such a hill adorned the cover of the park's shiny pamphlet. It was a large rocky mountain. Then someone decided we needed to force the students, most of whom get no physical exercise, to climb this mountain in 2 hours. At one point, we had to climb an iron staircase that was somehow secured to the side of a rock. I think I have commented more than once on my lack of trust in the durability of local infrastructures. I have done some crazy things in my day, but this one beat them all. My heart was pounding so hard, and all I could envision was all 200 kids and 35 staff members plummeting down the side of the cliff. To top it off, the school had hired a professional photographer to take pictures of the fun day for our recruitment book. So there we were, sweating to death and covered in dirt, having to smile and pretend we were having the time of our lives. We were then herded back onto our buses for the picnic lunch packed by our school cafeteria. Let me reiterate that we were at the park but had to eat sitting on the bus. Despite the disappointment of eating out of the sunshine, I was happy to be back on stable ground. As we ate our lunches, I watched students in the bus next to us toss the many plastic bags used to pack our lunches out the bus window. I went over to the next bus and told the students to pick up their garbage and find a bin. They looked at me shocked and explained, "But Mr. Xu [pseudonym] told us to throw it out the window." I have to laugh at such moments, which demonstrate my own ignorance of cultural differences. Despite the logistical nightmare and the moments of sheer panic and concern for everyone's safety, we really had a great day with the students. I feel blessed to work with such good-natured, fun students.

APRIL 15

We have about 10 bulletin boards here in the school. All of them have been assigned and divided between the English and Chinese clubs and teachers. Notices were put in everyone's mailbox to clarify which departments and teachers have the boards. I was assigned a board and was planning to do an Earth Day theme for the geography department. However, one of the local teachers had already taken the bulletin board. I sought her out and we discussed the issue, and I helped her move all of her postings to her assigned board. I then decorated the bulletin board. This morning I went to put some finishing touches on the board, and a local staff member had taken half of my postings down and put her own items up! It is really hard not to get frustrated some days.

April 19

As I have mentioned, the school is spending quite a bit of money promoting the school throughout China for recruitment purposes. The latest marketing scheme is a huge billboard on the highway to the airport in Beijing. Guess whose face is going to be plastered on it? The strange part is that I was not asked permission. I was told in a staff meeting that it was finished and was being put up this week; teacher to celebrity in 60 seconds.

We are getting the students ready for Earth Day. I have one class acting out the story, *The Lorax*, by Dr. Seuss. None of the students has ever been in a play before, so it was like pulling teeth to recruit volunteers. However, after about 45 minutes I finally convinced some of my students to take the speaking parts. This experiment could go either way.

Another one of my classes wrote proverbs about the environment. I did a lesson last week on the philosophy of the Native Americans and the holistic lens through which they see their relationship to the earth. After I shared some Native American proverbs and art, the students wrote their own proverbs. I was astonished at what some of them wrote. Some of the proverbs are quite profound. So for Earth Day, we will play some Native American music in the background while they each take a turn reciting their proverbs. There was less teeth pulling with this class.

May 19

I was lying in bed last night when I got a phone call from an old friend who is Chinese and used to work at this school. "There is a huge picture of you hanging outside the boy's dormitory at the school. You can see it from the highway!" Sure enough, I took a walk this morning to the back of the boy's dormitory to find a 10-story canvas advertisement for the school with my picture on it. I feel this situation is starting to get a little out of control and without my permission.

Things here are as usual. Major decisions are made, and the Canadian teachers are the last to know of it. Yesterday we arrived at school to find all of the students and Chinese teachers wearing their school uniforms. We, the Canadian teachers, had no idea what was going on as we watched the local morality officer and vice principal yell at the students who were not in uniform to go back to the dormitories to change. We later found out that some Chinese educational dignitaries were visiting the school to rank us for recruitment purposes, which is apparently a big deal.

Our student council has been hosting a basketball tournament every day after school this week. On Tuesday a fight broke out between two teams, leaving one boy in the hospital. Guess who was blamed by the Chinese staff? Me. Typically, the students are not even supervised in the gym after school. Most days, when you go in to throw a ball with the students, there are 50 kids and no supervision. It is the responsibility of the Chinese Physical Education Department to supervise after-school activities. On the day of the fight, the local physical-education teacher and I were there, and I got blamed. I am still trying to figure this one out and am trying to just brush it off.

As an aside, the students really are good kids. I worry that they engage in this violent behavior due to the stress they feel and the lack of outlets for stress relief.

June 7

We had our regular staff meeting on Monday, and as usual we all left frustrated and deflated. We have to work the last two weekends that we are in country. We were told this was to be a command performance and we were expected to be present, no excuses. This decision doesn't affect me so much, as I am returning next year. The teachers who are not returning, however, were hoping to have the last few weekends to do their packing and last-minute shopping and to spend time with friends they will be leaving.

We still don't have a year-end calendar that outlines how much instructional time we have left with our students. We have been told that there may be a final assembly, but the date isn't clear; teachers may be expected to contribute, but those details haven't been flushed out yet either. I do find it amazing that we teachers still react when left without a solid plan after 9 months of being here.

The student council had planned a KTV night (karaoke) for the students of the school on Thursday as a break from their intense studying. We took the appropriate measures and asked both the Chinese and Canadian administrators if this date was appropriate. We had the go-ahead from everyone. Yesterday, however, I received many phone calls from the Chinese teachers who were furious that this evening was planned for 2 days before the senior students write their nationwide exams on Saturday. Obviously there is justifiable concern about the timing, and we would not have planned this event had we known. What I found incredible was that the Chinese administration did not know about the exams. So, yet again, an event planned by the student council is moved. I am amazed at the tenacity of the students. They keep getting blocked and knocked down, but they always get back up with spirit and try again to provide a fun, community-building activity for their peers.

I submitted a request to purchase some trophies for the students who had won the various intramural sporting events organized by the student council during the year. I found it strange that the responsibility of finding the trophies was put back on me. I admit that I found this task to be difficult. How do I, a foreigner with rudimentary Mandarin at best, venture out into the local community to find some trophies and have them engraved? Remember that very few locals speak English in this community.

The last drama of the week occurred when our principal informed the teachers that our final payday would be the day before we leave for Canada. This timing does not work for anyone who is not returning. The problem is that we have to transfer our money to our Canadian account and wait 3 days to ensure that the money has arrived in Canada. We have had numerous problems with wire transfers not making it back to

Canada during the year. If the teachers left the same day they sent wire transfers home, it would be next to impossible to get in touch with the China-based banks later to remedy any problems. When we expressed concern, we were told that this was the decision of the school's owner and we would have to solve our own problems. Don't let the door hit you on the way out.

June 27

The final countdown: T minus 2 days until we board the plane for home. I admit that I cannot wait to see my family. It has been a long 9-and-a-half months.

My students surpassed my expectations on their final exams. The final question on the exam was essay form. As I watched the students write their exam for my class, I was struck by how far they had all come. Many did not pass the course in the end, but that does not mean they weren't successful in the course. I spent much of the 2 hours reminiscing about my first days in the classroom with these students. We spent the first week building vocabulary words in an introductory unit on weather. It was a steep learning curve for both me and my students. Together we went to hell and back as we struggled through the completion of their major assignments: the students trying to learn the new skills necessary to meet the expectations and me trying to learn how to teach them the skills they needed. I think that, in the process of teaching these wonderful students, I was the one who learned the most. I thank them for this gift.

End Notes

After reading about my experience, you might wonder why I would choose to return to the same school. I realized, upon reading these entries, that they do not reflect the many moments of joy I felt with regard to my teaching and the relationships with my dear colleagues, both Chinese and Canadian. I watched my students overcome great challenges in learning a curriculum that was in their second language and not relative to their own environment. They also faced challenges in gaining required skills that were foreign to their own learning culture. The growth of these students while studying at this school was phenomenal, and I wanted nothing more than to return to have another year with them while they continued to grow. Teaching is a wonderful profession, and no matter the environment in which you work, the students will always make up for the negative aspects. I chose to share my experience through my e-mails home, which often showed the frustrations my colleagues and I experienced on a day-to-day basis. I did this because working overseas as a teacher requires more than the desire and ability to teach children. It requires cultural adaptability, flexibility, self-reflection, and humor. If you cannot embrace these things while working in a different country and culture, you will not be an effective teacher. As a final note, I did return the following year. The school continued to experience severe administrative problems and almost shut down. However, I was able to witness amazing progress with my students and foster some very special relationships. This experience was incredible, and given the choice, I would do again. My time in China changed me in many ways and greatly informed the lens through which I see the world, the profession of teaching, and the relevance of culture to learning.

Carissa's Tips for Traveling Teachers

What to Bring

You can purchase anything you need in the urban regions of the country; however, you are quite limited if you end up in a rural area. That being said, in the urban areas you also may have trouble finding certain brand names. If you are picky about brand names for hair products, moisturizers, makeup, deodorant, and feminine hygiene products, you may want to bring a year's supply. The major brands readily available are Herbal Essences, Nivea, Lux, Dove, Oil of Olay, Maybelline, CoverGirl, and Red. What you bring really depends on how much luggage you want to carry. Keep in mind that clothing and shoes can be very cheap in China, and, once there, you can buy everything from high-end to bargain-basement items. Please note that the clothing in China is made for the smaller frames of Chinese men and women, so shopping for clothes may be difficult. There were a few items I was either really happy I had brought or wished I had brought:

- Long underwear (for the northern regions)
- Heavy sweaters and blazers for work
- Pens (if you are finicky; it is difficult to find good-quality ones)
- A couple pairs of good-quality shoes and boots
- A laptop with an extra battery
- Hostel sheets (two bedsheets sewn together like a sleeping bag) for when you go traveling; this item can be made once you are in China, as there are many tailors, but hostel sheets are really nice to have when traveling
- Prescriptions (some antibiotics and Diflucan, just in case)
- A first-aid kit with products specifically geared for women and stomach issues; again, these items are available but difficult to locate and are nice to have on hand
- Pictures of your family, pets, and travels to show to students and friends—everyone is very interested in your life back home
- Any English-based supplementary teaching material you think would be important for your own lessons; how much and what you need to bring will depend on the school to which you are going

Paperwork and Banking

- Leave a series of signed, blank checks at home with someone you trust in case of emergency
- Sign up for online banking
- E-mail yourself all of your important numbers and information (credit cards, bank card, passport, health insurance) and the phone numbers to call in case you lose any of these items
- Make sure you have your SWIFT code from your bank for the purpose of wiring money home
- If you can, sell everything you own that would indicate you are a Canadian resident (e.g., home, car) so that you can be declared a nonresident and not have to pay Canadian taxes while abroad
- Bring photocopies of all your documentation (passport, visa, plane ticket, health insurance) and spread these papers out through various pieces of your luggage
- Notify your credit-card company and bank that you will be overseas so they do not flag your card for suspicious spending
- Speak to someone at your bank to make sure you are able to use your bank card internationally (stick with numeric codes for the personal identification number; avoid codes with letters)
- Have enough American money available (on your person) to pay for a hotel, meals, and taxi for 2 days should there be problems at the airport (calculate the expenses using North American rates).

Questions to Ask

China can be a very difficult country in which to live and work. You must remember that it is still a Communist country and that English is spoken by very few people outside the major urban centers (Shanghai and Beijing). As such, you want to make sure that the school provides support and that you understand exactly what you are getting into, even more so than if you were going to another country. Ask lots of questions, such as:

- Does the school provide health care while in the country? Does this include visits to a Western-style hospital and medication? (Sometimes you will be told *yes*, even though that will really mean you are provided only with visits to the local Chinese doctor and herbal medication)

- What is the policy if you have to travel home for a medical or family emergency?
- If your school is affiliated with a particular Ministry of Education (ie., the Ontario ministry) does your time count toward building your teaching experience for the Qualifications Evaluation Council of Ontario (or the equivalent)?
- Are the students required to pass a standardized English test to enroll in the school?
- Where do the students go once they graduate from the school? (American or Canadian universities or local universities)
- Are students accepted into the school at any grade or must they be enrolled from the first year?
- Are there support classes for students to take prior to an Ontario (or equivalent) credit for both EFL and skill development (research, problem solving, writing, etc.)?
- What are the relationships like between the students' parents and teachers?
- Are there local teachers working at the school? What are the relationships like between the local and foreign-hire teachers?
- What are my expected work hours? What are my holidays (e.g., Christmas, Chinese New Year, summer holidays)? Will I be expected to work weekends?
- How will I be paid (local, Canadian, or U.S. currency) and how often?
- What are my living accommodations? If they are on campus, ask what degrees of freedom are allowed in regard to visitors, alcohol, curfews, etc.
- Is there someone at the school who is specifically designated to help new teachers who are getting established? (to help with things like banking, accommodations, finding the markets, learning the community)
- Will the school help with my visa applications and cover the expenses?
- What expenses will the school cover? (e.g., health insurance, visa costs, immunization costs, travel to and from the airport, extra luggage for teaching supplies, shipping once the contract is over, etc.)
- Who is my immediate supervisor? (e.g., local businessman, local government, local principal, foreign principal)
- For a first-year teacher, what kind of support or mentorship does the school provide?
- Are there other teachers at the school teaching the same subject?

- Is there a chance that I will be expected to teach other subjects or EFL classes?
- What resources are available? (e.g., textbooks, supplementary materials, access to Internet, printers, photocopiers, overhead projectors, etc.)
- May I speak with a teacher who is currently working at the school?
- Is this a school that promotes local cultural values, American/Canadian cultural values, or both? How does the school do this?
- Are there restrictions on the content teachers are permitted to teach the students? (i.e., religion, politics, sex)

WHERE IS CARISSA NOW?

After 2 years of teaching in China, Carissa returned to Ontario where she completed her master of education, focusing on international and comparative education, at the University of Western Ontario. Research for her thesis was conducted in Egypt as Carissa examined organizational culture and pedagogic values at international schools. While completing her masters, she also had the opportunity to travel to Rwanda to complete an internship working in higher education. Carissa now works as an education specialist, writing curriculum and conducting training at an international-development nongovernmental organization whose head office is in Toronto. But Carissa still travels to Africa throughout the year to conduct training and meet with partner organizations.

CHAPTER 12

TEACHING ON A CARIBBEAN ISLAND IN THE LESSER ANTILLES

Elissa Odgren

IN THE BEGINNING

I went to a tiny island in the Caribbean and fell in love with it on my first day there. I had arrived for a 1-week practice teaching placement with a Grade 3 class. By the end of the week, I was convinced that all I wanted to do was stay and teach in paradise. When I returned to Canada, I tried everything I could think of to secure a teaching position on the island. I wrote, faxed, phoned, and e-mailed the school, as well as the education department, the ministry, and even the chief minister himself. Months passed, the days got shorter, and summer was winding down, but still I had no response. I hadn't even applied to teach at any other schools; I was determined to teach there and nowhere else. In mid-August, I had my first e-mail exchange with the high school principal; I asked if he had finished hiring for the upcoming school year. He replied to me that he hadn't, so I wrote back, "Good, because you're not finished hiring until you've hired *me*." I bought my plane ticket the very next day.

I packed as much as I could fit into my two pieces of luggage, but I wasn't confident that I was bringing the right things. I flew out of cold, gray North Bay and into the warm, sunny Caribbean. Still having had no real confirmation from the principal, I armed myself with my portfolio and loitered around the high school until he showed up (no one ever answered the phone when I called the school). He found me outside under a tree one day. He was not interested in my portfolio. He told me to join the other teachers for their prep week that started on Monday. I had to ask if that meant I was hired! The following week, when he finally talked to me for more than 2 minutes, all he explained was that if I got pregnant, I had to give the school written notice at the end of my first trimester. I had secured my first teaching job—in the Caribbean.

The paperwork wasn't complicated. I didn't need a work permit because teaching was considered a government job. Driving between the education, treasury, and immigration departments, on the other hand, *was* complicated because each department thought I was the other's responsibility. This situation was made even more difficult by the hours the government offices held: 8 a.m. to 3 p.m. and closed for lunch. It occurred to me that had I been teaching in one of the elementary schools instead of the high school, it would have been very difficult to get everything sorted out.

When school started in September, it felt like chaos for weeks. The students weren't all there (some were still on vacation, or hadn't come yet), the teachers weren't all there (due to interesting hiring practices), and the conflicts in the teaching schedule were many. Even when teachers were settled in a room with their entire class, they were still in danger of being rescheduled to teach an entirely different set of students somewhere else.

The primary school students I met on my first trip were cute and little. The high school kids I met now were big and scary. My Bachelor of Education hadn't prepared me for this! I had spent so much time learning how to do lesson plans, unit plans, and report cards, but I had learned to do all those things on the computer; here I could hardly find a computer that worked. I quickly realized that this job was 110% behavior management, and all I could remember from teachers college was to flip the lights off and on to get the students' attention. Lights don't make a difference in the sunny tropics, and most of the switches in my classrooms were broken anyway!

School Environment

The first time I saw the science lab, my jaw dropped. The place looked as though it had been abandoned for years, but it had actually only been closed for the summer. There were four huge wooden tables, and the stools around the tables were of random shapes and sizes; some were missing legs, some were missing seats, and some had new seats screwed on top of the old ones. The cupboards that circled the room below the windows sat in varying degrees of decay; all had veneer peeling off in large chunks, some had no handles, and others had no doors. The windows themselves weren't really windows but just sections missing from the concrete block wall, where metal louvered shutters were installed. The louvers were all bent up, and most of the operators used to open and close the louvers were missing or just didn't work. The chalkboard was a piece of plywood bolted to the wall and painted black. The ceiling fan dangled dangerously low from a frayed electrical wire. It only had one blade left. I flipped the switch for the fan. The fan's motor made a sick buzzing hum, but the one blade didn't turn. The chemical supply room adjacent to the lab had no light, no ventilation, and no lock on the door. It did have plenty of old, dusty, unlabeled, broken bottles, though. I was relieved that I didn't have to teach chemistry because almost all of the glassware was broken, and I don't think I could have dealt with that supply room on a daily basis. It was difficult enough in biology class as I watched my students pouring acid into a graduated cylinder with a broken, jagged lip and a blob of Plasticine balancing out its shattered base. There were no safety precautions: no gloves, no goggles, no eyewash, and no chemical shower. The closest thing to a safety device was an empty fire extinguisher in the back room.

The school itself was also in poor shape. Most wooden parts were being ravaged by termites or destroyed by the students. The staff room was everybody's office. It was packed with people, old textbooks, and folders of papers. The staff bathroom had a toilet that rocked when you sat on it, a tiny mirror the size of your face, a door that was always locked, and a key that was almost always missing. On dozens of occasions that year, there was no water. No water meant I couldn't wash my hands and the toilet wouldn't flush. A couple of times I walked across the street to use the bathroom in the public library. Once, when the water had been off for days, a pregnant co-worker became very upset. She called the education department, located in a small building across the street, and demanded that we get some water in the school immediately. To my amazement, we instantly had water! Apparently the school's water supply came from rainwater caught and held in a cistern, but when it was empty someone needed to throw a switch to get the piped-in government water turned on. I guess they didn't like to turn on the government water because they had to pay for it. Most people used cistern water in their homes, so they were accustomed to running out, but I wasn't used to it, and I found it very frustrating. It is very difficult to do a science experiment without water.

Compared to Canada, there were very few resources for the teachers. On the first day of school, all teachers were issued a red pen and a blue pen. The school did give us chalk, but we had to sign for it. I never saw anyone using an overhead projector, except on rare occasion at a staff meeting. I found a dusty overhead projector stored under the front counter in one of the science labs, but I doubted that it worked. Even if it did work, I was fairly certain that the outlets in the room didn't and that I wouldn't be able to find a transparency to save my life. This electricity problem would prove especially challenging on parent–teacher interview nights. The sun would set, it would get dark in the classroom, and only then would I realize the lights didn't work.

Teaching on a Caribbean Island in the Lesser Antilles 267

Students had to buy their own textbooks, which meant that many didn't have them. There weren't any class sets, and getting one for myself, the teacher, was difficult. The bookstore across the street ran out of textbooks every year. If you were looking for a Grade 12 text at the bookstore, they probably wouldn't have it. This is when your grandmother's sister's son would come in handy, because if you knew he was going to a big island like Jamaica or Trinidad, he could pick up the book for you. The other thing was, even though the entire school was working from a specific text, nobody had the teacher's guides that went with them. I saw teachers enlarging thumbnail worksheets (and whiting out the answers) from free wrap-around teacher's-edition texts that we didn't even use, just to try and get a decent handout. Even if the students did own the required texts, they rarely brought them to school because they'd have to carry them around all day since there weren't any lockers.

The students had very small school bags. I was used to seeing Canadian backpacks and book bags that were sometimes bigger than the students. The boys were renowned for bringing next to nothing with them in their tiny, flimsy school bags. Many male students had no books in those school bags, but they always had shoe polish and a piece of foam mattress (a sponge) to keep their shoes looking clean. I would often have students show up with no writing utensils whatsoever. Students would come to the door and interrupt the lesson looking for correction fluid or an eraser. I've had fights break out in my class over pencils. There weren't any pencil sharpeners mounted on the walls, so someone's sharpener was always making the rounds. Nobody used a pencil case. They didn't used hole–punched, lined paper either, because there were no binders; they had only little black-and-white hardcover composition books, and many students kept all 10 (or more) subjects in one. If I wanted to do anything that involved cutting, I always had to precut the materials myself because the school didn't have any scissors, and the students weren't allowed to bring them to school. This rule was established after one student physically threatened another with a pair of scissors.

Although I had not previously entertained the possibility of not having enough chairs in a classroom, the school didn't have enough chairs, and many of my classes would begin with students going to look for a chair, which could take them anywhere from 15 seconds to 5 minutes. Sometimes I would enter a classroom and all the chairs would be gone because there had been a group meeting in another room, and no one had returned them. One of my classes had 38 students in it, so there was always a chair-finding frenzy at the beginning of that period.

PHOTOCOPIER CHAOS

Dealing with students fighting over limited resources was easy compared to dealing with a temperamental photocopier. I never knew so many things could go wrong with a photocopier! There was only one photocopier at my school with a staff of 80 teachers. You simply could not count on photocopying in the morning for that day's classes; only divine intervention would allow things to run that smoothly. The normal sequence of events in photocopying something really important went something like this: first you'd wait in a huge line, and when it was finally your turn, the machine would be out of paper. Then you would have to find the secretary or someone else who, in turn, had to find the key to get more paper. (There have been occasions when we simply were not allowed any more paper as we had gone over our budget). Once the new paper was located and the tray was reloaded, the photocopier would then decide to misbehave by jamming on every third page or adding black lines to the page. After that, you could run out of toner, which was even more difficult to find, and sometimes there just wasn't any more. This meant that new toner had to come over from the education department, who also sometimes ran out. If that happened, it meant there wasn't any toner on the island and you'd have to wait for a shipment to come in. Then when the toner arrived days later, someone else would get to the machine first and the photocopier would break down entirely. No photocopying for weeks. Finally, when the machine was somewhat fixed, and after waiting in line forever, you'd get your turn. And it would be at this moment that the power would go out.

LOCAL CULTURE

When asked about their future, most of my students said they wanted to live in the United States, preferably in Miami. If that wasn't possible, they'd settle for St. Thomas in the U.S. Virgin Islands. So many of the boys said they wanted to be gangstas. Not all boys thought this way of course, but many of them did, especially those in the lower achievement classes. They wanted Timberlands, Hummers, Glocks, and all the *bling bling* they could get. There were several prominent people in the community who felt that television, especially Black Entertainment Television, or BET, was to blame for the youth's focus on material acquisition and gansta behavior. Though I could understand the many reasons for the students' chronic misbehavior, there were many frustrating days when I felt like part babysitter, part police officer, and not much else.

I was surprised by the level of racism I encountered. It wasn't focused on white or black people; it was usually against Spanish-speaking Caribbean people. Many locals on this English island thought that the Spanish immigrants from other islands were beneath them. I've had classes in which students up at the front giving presentations were subjected to racist comments from their classmates. When reprimanded, the offending students would try to argue that what they said was not racist. Generally speaking, many of these children seemed to think that racism only applied to black people being discriminated against by white people; and they were black, so they couldn't be racist. There was only one Muslim family on the island, and when their youngest girl started primary school, the other students ran into the office in a panic screaming, "It's Bin Laden! Bin Laden's people are here!" I actually had a student tell me in the middle of class that all Arab people look the same. That's the kind of thing that stopped my lesson plan in its tracks.

The students also made comments about the *darkness* of each other's skin. I didn't realize that the exact shade of brown was an issue, and maybe it wasn't really, but they did bring it up any time they were teasing or insulting one another. "You and your *black* self!" they'd always say.

Few children seemed to congratulate each other on their successes. Most were quick to shout out, "You can't draw!" when a student presented their artwork or, "You can't spell!" if there was any kind of error to be seen. Students appeared to me to be highly critical of each other, though they tended to use humor to communicate this. I would hear, "Hey, Inches!" to the short student and, "You big forehead!" to another student who they considered to have a big forehead. And in French class I heard, "You? You got more rolls than a boulangerie!"

Despite this, I was delighted to realize that everyone shared food! One of my most challenging students inadvertently demonstrated this food-sharing phenomenon in my class at break time. He had a Snickers bar, and I didn't usually see the students with chocolate bars. Before he had even opened the wrapper, another student asked for a bite. And then another, and another, and each student broke off a chunk until there was only one bite left. He looked at me, shrugged his shoulders and smiled, then popped the remaining piece in his mouth. What surprised me the most was that the other students who ate from his chocolate bar were not the ones with whom he normally spent time. The same behavior held true in the staff room. If someone was eating, everyone was eating. Teachers would walk in declaring, "I'm hungry; who's got something to eat?" Then they would take a handful or a bite of a colleague's food without even asking! This was a side of the culture that I greatly respected.

The staff was great at organizing parties and dinners. Dishes were delegated in a flash, and everyone showed up at the party with something delicious to eat. I have never seen so many massive, restaurant-size pots and pans in my life! Right down to the tablecloths and little hot plates for reheating, impromptu staff luncheons were one of my favorite events. Even a group of Grade 8 students could organize a nice little feast for themselves with little effort!

As a vegetarian, eating a healthy diet was a challenge for me. The fruit and vegetable section of the grocery store was minimal and expensive, which made it difficult. Even if something looked fresh in the store, in my fridge, things went bad very quickly. There were many expired products on the shelf, and it took awhile to get used to checking expiration dates before every purchase.

There was a real sense of familiarity on the island. Their sense of genealogy amazed and impressed me; I absolutely could not keep track of whose grandfather's uncle's daughter's nephew did what. However, as in small towns everywhere, everyone knew or thought they knew everything about everybody else! This sometimes resulted in parents not respecting certain teachers and then communicating that disrespect to their school-aged children. As a result, when a parent–teacher conference was held to discuss a child's behavior, it often got very loud and very personal. Many people believed that their children would be treated better or worse, depending on their family name, or even depending on which part of the 16-mile-long island they were from. Accusations of favoritism flew easily around the school, but as I was an outsider, I was spared.

My daunting, yet enjoyable, task in September was to learn all the names of my more than 150 new students. It was quite challenging because many of the students had similar-sounding names (Kendeisha, Kenesha, Keresha, Kerisa, Kericia, Vernicia, Vanecia, Veneshaw, Delvicia, Darnecia, Denecia), while others had very unique names (Jelani, Tahira, Muriska, Ojeda, Ishini, Adonijah, Morihensi, Kondwoni, Kefentsi, Shefoo, Olufunmike, Matsimelia). In addition to these wonderful names, it seemed like everyone on the island had a nickname! The use of nicknames sometimes lead to confusion in the office when their real names were unknown by the other students. It was impossible to pull up the file on Sho-Sho, for example. A few times students had to be called to the office by their nicknames because that's all we had to go on. Hearing Boom Boom called in to see the principal at the end of assembly made everyone giggle, myself included. The only nicknames I'd ever really heard in Canada were things like Moose, Raven, or Snake, but I barely heard any animal names on the island at all.

Having been an animal lover my whole life, I had a difficult time adjusting to the way in which animals were generally viewed on the island. People tended food animals, of course; goats and chickens ran amok everywhere! Very few students had pets, and if they did, they were often yard dogs that were kept permanently tied up. I also learned that many aspects of wildlife were viewed with aversion. How is this animal aversion related to teaching? Well, one of the gifts I brought with me when I first arrived was a stapler in the shape of a green tree frog. I thought it would be a great gift for the head of the science department or another biology teacher. With my lack of cultural awareness, it appeared that I was wrong. Everybody absolutely hated frogs, including the science teachers! Frogs were often found breeding in water cisterns, which served to make them very unpopular. I ended up keeping the stapler for myself and was never asked to lend it. Snakes were also viewed with suspicion, as were geckos. They called geckos *woodslaves* and believed that if they crawled on you, they would be stuck on your skin forever. Anything that wasn't a bird and flew at night was called a bat. If I said *bat* in class, my students did not know that I meant the flying mammal. Environmental consciousness was a real challenge. Teaching biology, and ecology in particular, was very difficult when many students appeared to have little appreciation for the natural world. Students would stampede out of classrooms in fear of wasps, caterpillars, butterflies, frogs, and pretty much any other living thing. I would always catch whatever animal was stuck in the classroom and gently release it outside. I knew they had never seen anyone do that before.

Behavior in School

We had many fights at the school during my first year. The youth were quick to pick up weapons, and anything became a weapon in a time of need. To me, one of the most difficult things with regard to this ongoing violence was that every fight seemed to occur right outside my classroom. This was an open-air school with metal louvers for windows (no glass, no screens) and separate one- and two-story buildings for classrooms.

One of the classrooms in which I often taught was referred to as *the hole* because of the slope of the land. Eye-level in the classroom was foot-level on the sidewalk outside the louvered windows. When fights started at this school, they would boil over and erupt into a frenzied mass. In milliseconds, students would run from everywhere to assemble and cheer on the fight. The first time it happened, they just burst out of my classroom and ran toward the fight. The second time a fight started while I was teaching, I ran, too; I ran to the door and blocked it. I refused to let my students out. The fight was all around us. My students were screaming at me to let them out, and the boys who were fighting outside started throwing rocks at each other, which began pinging off the louvers and flying into the classroom. "Close the windows! Close the windows!" I yelled. Eventually I got used to just blocking the door when fights happened, and I acted as if the whole thing were utterly boring and uneventful. "Big deal; it happens all the time. Nothing new…" I'd say in my most unimpressed voice, even though my heart was pounding. Several times while I was teaching, I'd see little scuffles outside turn into full-on chases around the school. On two occasions, I saw students take off their shoes and throw them at the student they were chasing. Good thing girls weren't allowed to wear high heels to school.

Casually confiscating weapons from my Grade 9 students on their way into my classroom became routine. These kids always seemed to feel so much bigger when they had something in their hands. I'd stand at the door and take away sticks, broken table legs, backs from chairs, rebar, and other pieces of metal. Once I even confiscated a rusty old basketball hoop. These items were lying all over the school property and sometimes even inside the classroom itself. At the end of the year, I had quite a collection of makeshift weapons under the front counter.

When I first started teaching at the high school, we had two full-time security guards. Both of them had been or still were real police officers, but they only worked at the school. They didn't carry guns or walkie-talkies, and they were quite friendly toward the students. They had a tough job to do and were able to put names to crimes by talking so much with the kids. On the few occasions when situations arose in my classes, however, I could not find the security guards. I had to shout at students passing by my class to go find security for me. The lack of a public-address system in a school with separate buildings has incredible disadvantages and potential for disaster. One day I was giving a test to my Grade 11 boys, and the room next door started getting noisier and noisier. I soon realized that there wasn't a class in there but rather a group of students who had set up an impromptu dominoes tournament and afternoon party. They were making a ton of noise slamming the dominoes down on the table, cussing at their misfortunes, and belting out song lyrics, but I couldn't leave my class to go deal with them. I tried sending one of my students into the other room to tell them to be quiet, and I wasn't surprised when that didn't work. I remembered that I had my cell phone with me that day, and I had just learned the security guard's cell number, so I called him. My class thought it was hilarious that I used my phone to deal with the students in the next room, but it worked!

The most difficult thing for me about teaching at this school was the use of corporal punishment. My first experience with it occurred when I was in the office using the photocopier. There was only one photocopier and only one office, with a thin door separating the two. Over the noise of the photocopier, I could hear the tones of the principal's deep, angry voice and then I heard, "Thwack! Thwack! Thwack!" At first I thought someone was getting punished in there; someone was getting lashes. Licks. Strokes. The students told me they usually get them on their open palms and it's done with a thick piece of leather much like a belt. This noise kept repeating itself over and over again *very* quickly and with force, so I tried to convince myself that someone was just fixing something in the office. My mind said that the noise was far too fast and too loud to possibly be licks. But my body knew what was going on in there, because as I stood at the photocopier my heart was pounding, my kneecaps were shaking, and I thought *I* was the one in trouble. Suddenly, the door burst open and one of my students came out. It was one of my Grade 9 girls. She had a child already and the circumstances surrounding this were the subject of much debate amongst the staff. She walked out with clear eyes staring straight ahead and her head held high;

no sign of licks. I grabbed my papers and followed her out of the office. I had to walk quickly to catch up to her.

"Good morning," I said, and she greeted me in return without slowing her stride. "Was that you in the office just now getting licks?" I asked.

She barely looked at me, but her lip quivered and her eyes filled with tears, "Yes." She glanced down at her shaking, red palm held out and away from her body.

I touched her shoulder and could only muster something like, "Oh no…" We were still walking, and she was headed for the school gate. "Where are you going?" I asked.

"Away from here," she said.

I never found out why she was punished. Maybe she didn't have a textbook. Maybe she swore at another student. Maybe she didn't wear the right socks. To me, it didn't matter what she did. I could simply not justify beating a child.

What many Canadians would consider child abuse is what many of the parents on my island would consider discipline. Generally speaking, during my time there, they lived by the phrase, "Spare the rod; spoil the child," and several parents gave me permission to beat their children if they misbehaved in my class. Plenty of people my age believed in disciplining children through fear and physical punishment, but others told me devastating stories from their childhoods. In my first year of teaching, I knew this abuse was happening, but I had no idea how rampant it actually was; I saw much more of it the following years with the Grade 7 and 8 students. Throughout the next 2 years, students came to school with fat lips and stitches, and parents slapped their children in front of me during parent–teacher interviews.

Educational Challenges

I came to understand that many of the parents themselves could not read and did not know how to support their children's education. Many single parents were not home to monitor their children's activities; I often saw young students out, unsupervised, at night. Many children did not live with either of their parents and instead lived with an aunt, a cousin, a grandmother, or some other extended-family member.

There were many students struggling academically at my school. Most of them managed note taking, but discussion or any kind of group work was out of the question for most classes. I continued trying with them, and eventually they were able to branch out and attempt a few new things. For our unit on blood circulation, I made a model of the heart out of a cardboard box, and the students thought it was the stupidest thing they had ever seen. I wanted to use it because I made it with valves, so the students could get a better handle on the direction of blood flow. I also liked it because it was a box my mom had sent me as a care package, and there were stamps with shiny red hearts and horses still stuck to the back. When the day came for their circulation quiz, one of my students asked if I could put the box heart on the front bench so he could look at it while he answered the questions. The rest of the class felt the same, even though there were no labels of any kind on the box heart. I was flattered that he asked and very happy that I had finally helped them to appreciate more than just the chalkboard. After seeing the heart, they were able to make their own models of the digestive system. This gave many of the usually low achievers better grades and a bit of confidence, even though they started burning each other with the hot glue gun. The student who walked around with two pencil crayons, one yellow and one white, asking people to smile and then checking to see which one their teeth most closely resembled wasn't much of a confidence booster, though.

One of my Grade 9 science classes had so many struggling students that I didn't even know what to do with them. I spoke to the vice principal about it, and he was kind enough to set up a new class for the ones I identified. With them gone, the rest of the class blossomed into happy children proud of their achievements. A couple of months later, some of the boys started trying to sneak back into my class. I refused them entry; they had their own class to attend. That was when I found out they didn't always have a teacher and it wasn't even a real class; the vice principal was just trying to take some of the load off me. I let a few of them back into my classroom on promises of good behavior, but they didn't last. Many of them ended up dropping out of school at the tender age of 14.

In that same class, I had a real sweetheart of a child. He was brilliant, but he couldn't read at all. Letters made no sense to him whatsoever, yet he managed to keep an excellent attitude. When we had spelling tests, his words would look nothing like they should; for "ovary" he might write "mexfg." I had never seen anything like it, no one knew what the problem was, and he wasn't getting any special help. Until that year, he had been in classes with his twin sister and she would help him, but now they were separated and he was struggling to stay afloat. He remembered everything I said in class and I let him do his tests orally. We often did presentations in that class, and the first time he went up to the front, I was scared for him. He held his papers in front of his face and began, "Good afternoon. My report today is on an organ of the human body called the liver." He paused, looked down at his papers and continued, "And, well, since I can't read, I guess I won't be needing these!" and he tossed his papers over his shoulder! Then his presentation really began; he captivated the audience, taught us many vital functions of the liver, and earned himself the best grade in the class.

On the very last day of school before the summer holiday, we had a staff meeting. This was the end of my first school year, and I really wanted to say something. I had something to complain about; something that broke my heart when I realized it was happening. I was afraid to voice my opinion because I had never addressed the whole staff before, and I found some of the teachers very intimidating. I had an image of a student in my mind, the girl who had a baby at 13 and got hard licks in the office that day. Her plight haunted me and I had to say something. She always sat at the back of my class. No one really talked to her, and she didn't ever say much. She could really only write her name. This poor girl was a mother and she could not read. There was no possible way to teach someone to read with 34 other needy students in the classroom, half of them only able to read at a Grade 2 level themselves. I had tried what I could, but I needed the school, the ministry, to do something about it.

Early in the year, I had made a list of students who needed some sort of reading intervention and brought it to my head of department, but there was no such program in the school. I tried to start an extra class to help these students, but no one wanted to stay after school. I had class grades averaging in the thirties, and I was teaching Grade 9 science at what I felt was a Grade 5 level. I asked my head of department if a 32% class average was normal in a lower band, and she said yes. That was when I realized that they didn't need to pass the class! These students would all be moved into Grade 10 science next year just because they would be a year older. I tried to explain these things in the meeting, stressing that we needed to implement a reading program for all of those students who had been left behind. I almost cried when I spoke because I felt so emotional about it. I felt like I was letting the students down by being part of a school that allowed this to happen on a yearly basis to hundreds of people. Students graduated if their attendance was acceptable and their suspensions were minimal. Literacy had no impact on whether or not students graduated. It was very difficult to convince the students that education could open up different possibilities for them.

My Behavior

I don't know why first-year teachers always get the worst classes, but they do. Teaching the low-level classes in the only high school on a tiny Caribbean island was far more difficult and personally challenging than I could have ever imagined. I didn't know kids could be so difficult! These kids were 10 times worse than what my Canadian teachers in my practice–teaching placement considered to be bad, and they came by the dozen in each class. The lack of resources and administrative support served only to highlight the dilapidated conditions of the classrooms and low student morale. Though things did improve somewhat in subsequent years, the first year was all about survival, and some days were harder than others. I am not proud to say that I crashed and burned three times that year. What I did was totally unprofessional and wrong, and I know it would never have happened in Canada. When I acted like my normal self in the Caribbean, it became impossible to cope because I cared too much. I slowly began adopting the strategies of the other teachers in an effort to preserve my sanity. The staff tried their best to stay positive, but there was always a lot of negativity and heaviness in the air. So much of my personality was being swept away with the flow and vibe of the school that I ended up acting in very uncharacteristic and unacceptable ways.

The first mistake I made was to imitate a student's voice. This was totally unprofessional by my personal standards, and I knew it right after it came out of my mouth, but by then it was too late. The student in question was a boy in my Grade 10 science class, and he had a very high-pitched voice. I was in the middle of explaining something and trying to get the class to listen attentively, but he kept interrupting. He was asking questions that he would already have known the answers to had he been listening in the first place. The entire class was getting annoyed with him and so was I. The next time he asked, "But whyyyyyyy, Ms. Odgren?" I turned toward him and mocked his voice with a nasal, "Becaaaaause." Of course this was totally hilarious for the class, but I was very disappointed in myself. I apologized to him immediately. Whether or not I did damage, I'll never know, but he did listen more carefully after that.

The second thing I did was physical. I know some Canadian schools have a no-touch policy, but corporal punishment was an accepted method of discipline in this school and on the island. On this day, class was about to begin and the students were taking their time coming in from break, as usual. There had already been one fight that morning, which puts the students in fight mode for the rest of the day. One of my students started arguing with someone else just outside my classroom, and I knew exactly where it was headed. At this stage of the dispute, most kids don't hear what teachers say to them and my reaction was to grab my student by the back of his shirt and pull him into the classroom. I had never touched a student like that, and, as soon as I realized what I had done, I felt horrible. He didn't like it at all, and after he huffed and fixed his collar, he stormed out of the room and skipped the class. I went to see the head of year after class and told her about it, because I wasn't sure if I should apologize to the student or not. She didn't think I had done anything wrong, but it didn't feel right to me.

The third thing I did was totally inappropriate. I used to have this nice Grade 9 class just after a really challenging Grade 11 class, and every time I saw my Grade 9 students, I was stressed out from the management rigors of the previous period. To further complicate things, the older, bigger boys started hanging around after their class to see the Grade 9 girls. When the bell went for the end of morning break and the beginning of class, I had trouble getting these boys out of my room. The door didn't really shut all the way, or stay shut for that matter, so privacy was sometimes a little hard to come by. On this particular day, my class had just started getting down to business when I realized one of the Grade 11 boys was staring through the side window making rude gestures with his mouth to the girls. I simply walked over to the window and turned the operator to close the metal louvers so that he couldn't see in. He stuck his hand between the louvers. I kept turning. The weak metal started to bend and warp on his hand that he had jammed in the window and refused to move. I was exasperated. I flipped into nonteacher mode when I said with force, "Don't FUCK with the window, Craig!" The class gasped. I was thinking, "Oh, no. I did it again. I'm losing it here." He pulled his hand out of the window and pointed his finger at me, "I'm going to tell the principal on you!" and he left. I apologized to the class and told the principal on myself.

School Runnings

What the school didn't have, and really needed, was an attendance office. Students could be absent from classes for days, or even *weeks*, before their parents found out. If a student missed a test, I had no idea whether they were sick, skipping, or off the island with their family. Most students believed that just staying home instead of going to school was not skipping; it was only skipping if you were out with your friends and your parents didn't know about it. There were a few female students whose parents would drop them off at the school gates, but then 10 minutes later their boyfriends would pick them up. They wore their school uniforms and were always ready for their parents at 3 p.m., but as there was no attendance office, their parents had no reason to suspect that they weren't actually going to school.

Many times, it was actually the parents themselves who dropped their children off late. There were many days when it seemed like no one heeded the bell for class except me. I've practically had to pull students off the wall they were sitting on to come to class. The students were always extra late after their 10:15 morning break. There were no punishments for being late. The school further challenged this issue of punctuality by scheduling teachers to work at two different schools. The junior and senior high schools were only a 3-minute drive apart, but there was zero changeover time between classes, so the teachers would always be late no matter what. Not all teachers had cars either, which meant they had to beg rides and be really late or sometimes miss the class altogether.

Another curious scheduling item was the extra week of school at the end of the year after exams. The students were supposed to be in school and attendance was taken, but there were no classes, and there was no teacher supervision because everyone was marking exams and preparing report cards. On a related note, no real teaching happened during the month of March either. The school did a lot of sports activities and competitions to finish off second term, and there were weeks of heats that led up to a final sports-day competition. The problem was that many students were either participating in the events or skipping classes to watch the other students compete. I was thankful that the two other Canadian teachers at the school warned me about this problem in September. Although I could barely believe it, I took their advice into account while planning my second term and averted what would have been a frustrating and disastrous waste of time.

Uniforms

There was strict adherence to uniform policy. The uniforms themselves were absolutely necessary in this setting, and, as part of this policy, the school controlled how the students kept their hair. Girls could have any length hair, but they could use no more than one ribbon as a decorative hair accessory. These girls were so imaginative with the styles and patterns of their braids and plaits that I looked forward to seeing their latest masterpieces every Monday morning. The boys, on the other hand, weren't allowed to wear plaits or even have any hair at all. They had to keep their heads practically shaved, and no decorative designs were allowed to be shaved in—not even a part. The only exception to this hair-as-part-of-the-uniform-policy was that Rastafarian boys could have dreadlocks in a ponytail under a hat and Muslim girls could wear head scarves in the school's colors. However, this no-hair rule somehow did not seem to apply to the two American and Indian boys, who wore their shoulder length hair loose on a daily basis. No students were allowed to wear jewelry as it supposedly caused fights at the high school level. Students were routinely sent home for having their pants too long or their skirts too short and even for having the wrong color socks. I've seen more than a few boys driven straight to the barber shop by the principal himself to get their Afros shaved off.

Report Cards and Curriculum

All teachers had to meet every morning in the staff room from 8:15 to 8:25 a.m. for a briefing because we didn't have an overhead announcement system. After the briefing, the teachers would go repeat all the announcements to the students in their homerooms. At least once a week, the principal felt he had to tell the teachers how to behave. As in, "Teachers, please don't be late getting to your classes, but if you are late or absent, you need to call in." Or, "Please do not let your students out before the bell at lunch or at the end of the school day," and in report-card season it became, "Teachers, please hand in your report cards on time." The most difficult part of this last request was that, as a homeroom teacher, my job was to transcribe all the grades for each student from all of his or her classes onto one report card. Report cards couldn't be given out with missing grades. Every term, the date for report-card pickup by the parents was announced, and every term the report cards weren't ready until at least a week later.

This lack of attention to deadlines and time management seriously disadvantaged the students. Because everything was geared toward the Grade 11 students writing the Caribbean Examinations Council tests, which were required to leave school, the curriculum was simply to "get as far as you can in the textbook." In science, the students used the same book for Grades 9–11. I would have hoped that the teachers could manage to cover one third of the text each year and skim through a bit of the rest, at the very least. What ended up happening, however, was that the teachers did what they could in Grade 9 and again in Grade 10, but when the students started Grade 11, panic would set in. It was usually at this time that the teachers would realize they hadn't even reached the halfway mark in the syllabus. Even at the Grade 8 level, by the end of the year most teachers were only at Unit Two in a nine-unit textbook.

There were teachers at the school doing really excellent work; they coached soccer, taught after-school classes, organized theater programs, and more. I wished I could be a teacher like that! Unfortunately, many of the teachers at the school wanted the least amount of responsibility possible. The school didn't have detentions because none of the teachers wanted to stay to supervise, and the parents would be angry if their children couldn't take the bus home. I had never seen teachers flat-out refuse to do things before I taught here. Teachers would refuse classes, refuse students, refuse duty on sports day, refuse work on the weekend, and even refuse to carry a message to another teacher. Many of the teachers at the school were only there because they took a government loan to get a university degree, and then they had to work it off. Other teachers were hired straight out of Grade 13 because there was no one else available to do the job.

Once a year, the teachers wrote out comments by hand on their students' report cards. As a homeroom teacher, my job was to compile all these slips of paper and also make a comment of my own. A few times when I was transcribing my homeroom students' term grades, I would notice that all the grades in a class would look something like this: 50, 75, 60, 0, 80, 65, 80, 50, 0. It looked suspiciously like the teacher did only *one* assessment, and if the student was absent, then he or she got a zero. The school's policy on assessment was that we were supposed to get the term grade from at least three assessments, and one of those had to be a formal test. I began to understand why students were always asking me, "Is this going in the mark book?" before they did anything. I told them *everything* goes in the mark book!

Since the island was a former British colony, our school had a connection with a school in England. Every now and again, British teachers would come over to "help us out." They would do some workshops and tended to teach us strategies that would be very difficult to use in our school. It was difficult to appreciate their help, because the administration always came down hard on us, trying to complete all the new documents and policies that the British had outlined for us.

Most of the print material that we were issued was copied directly from England, without even the slightest modification for our country. For example, The National Code of Conduct stated that students must use zebra crossings (I knew what those were, but the students didn't because there weren't any; we barely even had sidewalks) and they must walk single file on their way to school. Nevertheless, they printed them in mass quantities, ready to be distributed. The students were told to read the rules and obey them. Or else.

I was probably overly critical of this help from England, as the school did benefit in many other ways, but these teachers were bringing what amounted to band-aids when the school needed a cure. The local teachers themselves had diagnosed the illnesses years ago, but papers were still being shuffled around. For example, the school and the education department had spent an enormous amount of time drafting and redrafting behavior-management policies and codes of ethics for teachers under

British pressure, but nothing actually happened. There were very simple and straightforward things that needed to be done to straighten up the school. Most teachers knew what these things were and voiced or wrote about them passionately and eloquently, but the changes never came. I was so frustrated in my first year that I actually made a list of all the things I would do to improve the school if I were in charge. Making the list was one of the only ways I could make myself feel better, and having thought about the changes I believed were needed made it easier for me to offer solutions when situations arose. I couldn't really present my ideas to anyone because I knew they would not accept anything from a first-year foreign teacher, but I did express my concerns when appropriate. I will never forget the time I ran into another Canadian teacher and shared my latest frustrations with him. I was appalled when he actually laughed at what I told him! "How can you laugh at that?" I demanded. His reply changed my mind-set instantly. He said, "It's either laugh or cry."

Because of the British teachers, the school became involved in assessing the performance of all teachers every year. It was mostly the heads of departments who had to complete this task, and at our school the heads of departments got slightly more money and fewer classes in exchange for a much greater load of responsibility and commitment. Nobody seemed to apply to be a head of department; teachers were pretty much forced into it when they became the most senior person around. Teachers could request which class the evaluator came to; meaning, you could request a visit with your Grade 12 biology class of eight university-bound students instead of your very full Grade 9 science class. I decided that I would let the evaluator choose when to come and that I wasn't going to do anything different from what I had already planned. It was the principal who came to evaluate me. I didn't ever really talk to him; he wasn't friendly, he always acted busy, and he made me nervous because I'd seen him giving beatings to too many kids. He sat through one of my classes and then gave me satisfactory on everything. I wanted to cry. Did it somehow escape him that I had 38 students in that laboratory class? No one else had 38 students in a class! When I got home, I opened my portfolio to my practice-teaching reports from Nipissing University. Reading them made me feel much better.

One thing about the school that really impressed me and always cheered me up was the sound system they used for assemblies. Assembly was outside because there wasn't a gym or an auditorium, and before assembly started they played the latest dancehall reggae, hip-hop, and soca songs—loudly! It was the students who set up the sound system and took it down at the end of the assembly. In a school with so few resources and materials, they were certainly well equipped to hold a block-party-style assembly. Sometimes I thought the songs were a little too explicit to be played at school, but the kids loved it and few teachers minded. My favorite part was when the students themselves would get up and sing at the microphone, with or without musical accompaniment. Many students were extremely talented, and it gave me goose bumps to hear them belting out their songs with such confidence.

Assembly was always first thing in the morning. Each assembly had prayers, psalms, and hymns and featured a different minister, as religion was the reason for the gathering in the first place. The ground was rough and uneven, and sometimes assembly would last up to an hour. Teachers were supposed to stand with their homeroom classes in assembly, but I didn't have a homeroom for the first few months, so I decided to help out by rounding up students who were hiding out behind the various classroom blocks. After that, I would stand guard at the side entrance, directing all latecomers into the assembly group. There were only one or two other teachers who helped. Most teachers stood off to the side in a group, and some teachers just stayed in the staff room and avoided the assembly altogether, but if some big cheering or laughing happened, they'd run out to see what was going on.

Holding outdoor assemblies was easy to do because it almost never rained. But when it did rain, moving from class to class became a challenge because the classrooms were all in separate buildings. The first time I experienced rain at school, it started during break, when I was in the staff room. It was barely raining at all by the time the bell rang for class. I gathered up my books and headed for the door. "Where you going?" the other teachers wanted to know.

"Class…" I replied, thinking this was obvious.

"But, gyal, it raining out dere!" exclaimed the first teacher.

"You'll catch cold," the next stated.

"Sit down and wait fuh de rain tuh stop!" instructed another.

As soon as I was seated, they continued their conversation. The next time it rained, I went to my class, because I felt guilty staying in the staff room. When I arrived, there were a couple of students there, but they refused to do anything until the rain stopped and the rest of the class showed up. The third time it rained, I stayed put in the staff room.

I wish we had been able to meet more often as a staff to discuss these issues. Aside from the prep week before school started, we met only three times that first year. Often these meetings were tightly scheduled information sessions and did not allow time for teachers to voice their comments and concerns. There was always a staff meeting on the last day of school, but everyone was anxious to begin their vacation, so it wasn't an optimal time for discussion. School didn't get out until early July and started up again the last week in August, so everyone wanted to maximize their vacation time. To make up for the longer school year, we did have a decadent Christmas break (3 weeks) and a lengthy Easter break (2 weeks).

The education department's hiring practices were interesting. When I started there in September, they were short staffed by at least three teachers, and every subsequent year was the same. This was very interesting considering that I practically begged for that job for months, did not receive any kind of confirmation or even possibility of confirmation, and went to the island anyway. Throughout my first year, a number of people quit and replacements took a long time to find, if they were found at all. I discovered that many teachers on staff were on monthly contracts even if they had been teaching there for years. I even knew some people who were on daily contracts, though they were not substitute teachers in any shape or form. What I finally learned in my third year of teaching was not to throw myself on their doorstep, which is what I did the first year, but to get them to hire me when I was out of the country. This gave me an actual contract with airfare, gratuity, and a year-end bonus! There were no substitute teachers in the high school. If you weren't there, your class would be unsupervised.

One thing I really liked about the education department was that they continued to pay teachers their monthly salary in the summer. This made it so much easier to work with my budget! There were a few downsides to this system, though, the biggest one being that if you weren't returning in September you did not get your summer pay. This encouraged some teachers to pretend that they were returning when they knew they weren't, just to get that extra 2-months pay. The second strange side effect of this pay system was that the education department somehow felt that they owned you, and if you wanted to go on a vacation during the summer, you were supposed to apply for permission. No one had ever officially told me about this, so I chose to feign ignorance, but I knew that it was required. In fact, any time you wanted to leave the island, you were supposed to ask permission, even during Christmas and Easter break. A colleague of mine planned to visit a high school in Florida on his Christmas break to meet with teachers running a boat-building program. This would have greatly enhanced the school's design and technology curriculum, but he was denied permission and didn't get to go.

IN THE END

Why would I want to teach in a place that I felt was chaotic and confusing? That's a tough question. I think that, ultimately, I felt like I could really make a difference there. On such a small island, everybody gets to know who you are very quickly, and they respect you for the tough job that you're doing.

The things that were important to me in a classroom were different from what mattered to most of the Caribbean teachers, and I think this difference is what the children most appreciated about me. I didn't care if the boys had the wrong color socks on, and I would not pull up their pant legs to check. I did care if someone said *shut up* in my class or called someone else *stupid*. One day, after what seemed like an eternity teaching my students to respect one another in the classroom, the vice principal leaned in the window to scold a student and she told the rest of the class to shut up. All eyes swiveled to me. The students heard this disrespectful way of speaking for what it really was.

It certainly wasn't easy teaching there. I wanted to quit within the first month and vowed I would be gone at the end of the school year. But I went back, and then I quit again at the end of that school year. Then I repeated the same pattern for a third year! I have written here about experiences from my first year only, but so much more happened after that. If teachers based their career decisions on their experiences the first year, we would have no teachers left! The first year is always difficult, and adding an international twist makes for an extreme experience. So many things bothered me about the school, but there were also so many things that I loved. Each year became easier and more enjoyable than the last. I was given higher level students and more advanced classes, but it was my experience that made me a better teacher. As I came to understand the island, I began to recognize the difference between the things I could change and those I could not. Ultimately, all I could change was my own attitude, and I eventually found the right balance for the higher good of all involved. I also learned how to deal with the harsh realities of life on a tiny island, as my students came to school affected by the latest accident, death, or murder. My experience, though traumatic at times, was an inspiring one. My students taught me courage and resilience. I taught them to see life from a different perspective and to appreciate the natural beauty of their island. I think the students appreciated my humor, my fairness, and my honesty. At graduation, an 18-year-old student presented me with a gift and a card that read, "To Miss Odgren, The Best Teacher in The World." That alone made my 3 years teaching there a success.

And now, as I sit here writing this in the safe, little city of North Bay, Ontario, all I'm doing is missing my island in the Caribbean. The island is so much a part of me now that I think often of the people there. My past students are working at the post office, the bank, and the grocery store. Some of them are already teachers. I miss driving past groups of students and having them hail me at the top of their lungs, "Hi, Miss Odgren!!!" I miss being interrupted in the middle of a lesson by an errant rooster proclaiming his maleness right outside my classroom window. I miss school assemblies with brave singers and steel drums. I miss my students and I miss my colleagues.

Teaching on a Caribbean Island in the Lesser Antilles

Elissa's Tips for Traveling Teachers

What to Bring

- All paperwork, transcripts, and so forth (in protective waterproof folders)
- Laptop, power strip to protect from surges, marks program, external hard drive, printer, and ink (not necessary, but will make life much easier)
- Cell phone (if it will work there)
- Watch, travel clock, timer (most classrooms don't have clocks)
- Sturdy school bag (be prepared for it to get very dirty and dusty from chalk)
- Water-bottle holder (so condensation doesn't drip all over your belongings)
- Insulated lunch bag
- Small notepad (to use in meetings, briefings, etc.)
- Metal chalk holders (bring extras for the other teachers!)
- Large pencil case to carry your chalk and your chalkboard eraser
- Butterfly clips for bunches of paper (hard to find, and paperclips don't cut it)
- 8-pocket plastic folder with a spiral ring (excellent for keeping class paperwork organized)
- Worksheet-type books for your subject area
- Any other school supplies you might want (as much as possible, especially a stapler, scissors, glue sticks, pencils, crayons, sharpener, ruler, calculator, stickers)
- School supplies for students (go wild at the dollar store and save to use as prizes)
- Small Canadian gifts (hold onto them until you meet the right person)
- Canadian stuff (for Commonwealth Day activities and to show Canadian life)
- Open-toe shoes, airy shirts, and skirts or pants (ladies, bring pins to keep those wrap skirts closed in the island breeze!)
- Facecloth (to carry with you and wipe yourself off when you get sweaty)
- Any prescriptions (ladies, don't forget your favorite tampons)
- Extra glasses, contacts, sunglasses
- Sunblock

Questions to Ask

- Will you set me up at a hotel or guesthouse while I look for a place to live?
- Do I get airfare, a housing allowance, or a year-end bonus?
- Do I get medical insurance?

What to Expect

- Communication breakdowns
- Missing paperwork, late or short-changed payments
- Major cultural adjustment (no matter what you think right now)
- Saying "Excuse me? Pardon me?" repeatedly because of new accents and local slang
- Massive doses of Christianity in public schools
- Homophobia, racism, sexism
- Staff who will never like you unless you work at it
- Students who will think you're rich
- Carrying everything you need in your school bag (including the chalkboard eraser!)

Important Paperwork

- Degrees, passport, police record check

Financial Considerations

- Don't expect to make any money or accumulate pension years
- Some material things are very expensive or absolutely unobtainable
- Can you afford to buy a car when you get there?
- Be sure you have enough money (or a credit card) to get back home in a pinch
- U.S. dollars are used just about everywhere

If I Had to Do It Again, I Would…

- Get hired while still in Canada
- Bring more school supplies

Things I Would Like to Have Known

- You must say *good morning/afternoon/evening* before saying anything else to a person, otherwise you will be thought of as totally rude and without manners
- The students are generally two grades below grade level in Canada
- The classrooms have no windows, so all paper things will blow off the students' desks
- Students use composition books, not three-ring, loose-leaf binders
- Phone cards are not cheaper than dialing direct

Where Is Elissa Now?

Elissa is now employed as a mathematics and science technologist in the general arts and science program at Canadore College. She is also the owner and operator of the Reptile Feeder Shop in downtown North Bay. In her free time, Elissa enjoys walking with her Great Dane and caring for her reptile and amphibian pets.

Conclusion

Learning Through Teaching

Narratives of Transcending Geographic and Philosophical Borders

Carole and Warnie Richardson

> Experience is not merely *what* we experience. It encompasses how we react, why we react the way we do, what language we use to describe it, how it changes the way in which we relate to others, how our views are subsequently affected, the concrete knowledge we gain, the questions that are answered and the new questions that arise, the physical and emotional aesthetic of the moment and how all of this frames our past and future experiences. (Richardson, 2006, p. 59)

When we initially decided to ask our students to formalize their reflections on their first-year international-teaching experiences, we envisioned general recollections of places, people, and faraway classrooms. Instead, we received detailed accounts of how decisions were made to teach so far away from home, the ways in which jobs were secured, the planning done prior to travel, and the highs and lows of teaching in unfamiliar lands. These narratives, rich with descriptions of the countries, the schools, the people, and the insights gained into personal and professional understandings, sang with the recognition of long-held assumptions and the balance to be found with a greater understanding of self. Although the stories speak specifically to teaching in various international locations, within each story are moments of profound insight that transcend borders and speak to the universality of teaching and learning.

NARRATIVE THEMES OF KNOWLEDGE CONSTRUCTION

> Narrative inquiry is increasingly used in studies of educational experience. It has a long intellectual history both in and out of education. The main claim for the use of narrative in education research is that humans are storytelling organisms who, individually and socially, lead storied lives. The study of narrative, therefore, is the study of the ways humans experience the world. (Connelly & Clandinin, 1990, p. 2)

Rooted within Dewey's concept of experience as education, and building upon the literature detailing narrative approaches to investigate teacher thinking and teacher education (Beattie, 1995a, 1995b, 2000, 2001; Carter, 1993; Carter & Doyle, 1996; Clandinin & Connelly, 2000; Cole & Knowles, 2000, 2001), these stories of first-year teachers in international venues enable us to hear the voices of these young teachers as they question their tacit understandings and explore the knowledge inherent in their lived experiences. These narratives will provide the field of education with pivotal insight into the integral importance of valuing the narrative voices of our beginning teachers as they explore the life experiences upon which their personal and professional knowledge is constructed and the transformations they experience through telling these stories in their own voices. The following narrative themes of knowledge construction; reflecting and reconnecting and reframing through relating to others speak to the ways in which these teachers build and will continue to build knowledge from their life experiences in the past, present, and future.

REFLECTING AND RECONNECTING

Through the telling of their stories, these teachers have had the opportunity to reflect on and reconnect with all aspects of their experiences, acknowledging and exploring their tacit understandings and finding a holistic balance between their personal and professional understandings. In doing so, some have identified areas in which their very way of thinking was profoundly and forever changed.

Elissa spoke of recognizing "the difference between the things I could change and those I could not" (Elissa, p. 289). Ultimately she came to the realization that "all I could change was my own attitude, and I eventually found the right balance for the higher good of all involved" (Elissa, p. 289). Amelia came to a similar realization when she spoke of finding it difficult to put aside her own ideas and accept the Thai way of thinking. In considering this challenge after her return to Canada, she mused, "It took many months of reflection after leaving Thailand to understand that life in a foreign country is far easier when one stops trying to impose one's own philosophy and ideals" (Amelia, p. 168). Erin echoed the notion of struggling to appreciate cultural differences but asked that teachers who travel "remember that all experiences, personal and cultural, will influence who you are and help to determine who you will become" (Erin, p. 158). Stephan suggested that we consider the cultural challenges to be only one aspect of teaching internationally and to expect "a holistic adventure and journey, which can only be realized if you *live* this experience" (Stephan, p. 45).

Upon her return to Canada, Miriam was surprised by the difficulty she experienced when she had to adapt to being home. "Suddenly I was supposed to be connected to the world all the time with cell phones and credit cards. It seemed to me like people were always rushing, and I missed the spicy food" (Miriam, p. 109). Nathanael spoke of his realization that he was a public face and an ambassador for both the Western world and his own country, Canada. He felt that this understanding would prepare him for teaching anywhere. "This awareness has prepared me for life as a teacher in a small town, where I will be equally noticed and monitored in public" (Nathanael, p. 203).

Rubinah spoke of experiencing a revelation that she continues to carry with her daily and that provides her with peace and patience while teaching anywhere:

> Common sense is not universal in the way that I once thought. In every culture, what is common varies. We take for granted that people will understand what we mean; people will at least comprehend our point of view even if they don't agree. This is not the case when you decide to live in someone else's world. (Rubinah, p. 19)

For these young teachers, the opportunity to reflect on their first year of teaching and to share it in their own voices has enabled them to reconnect to their experiences and to view all aspects of their journey again in a more holistic light.

REFRAMING THROUGH RELATING TO OTHERS

Other teachers reframed their experiences through the way in which they related to those around them. Experiences were viewed through the lenses of their relationships, both personal and professional, with friends and colleagues.

Neil suggested that, in order to build relationships, those who travel to a different country must embrace the culture that initially drew them there. "If you are interested in meeting other people, then get involved… there's an amazing culture waiting to be experienced" (Neil, p. 136). Kathryn spoke of education as a means of facilitating adaptation to a new home environment. "As long as you educate yourself with regard to your destination before you leave Canada, you will be able to adapt to any new surroundings. The world is not as big as it seems" (Kathryn, p. 147).

As always for teachers, regardless of where we teach, our students and the ways in which they teach us to learn inspire us to continually seek ways to engage with and celebrate our students. Paul spoke of the way in which his students enriched his learning about their country and culture:

> They teach me about the geography of the country when they explain where they traveled on the weekend and what they do outside of school for fun. My students have become one of my greatest resources for understanding life outside of the school in Mongolia. (Paul, p. 54)

Carissa reinforced the fact that the students make it all worthwhile, regardless of location. "Teaching is a wonderful profession, and no matter the environment in which you work, the students will always make up for the negative aspects" (Carissa, p. 258).

This same concern for students threads its way through many of the narratives as these teachers grapple with trying to support the special needs of learners in systems that lack an understanding of the many different ways of identifying and making adjustments for these students. Paul spoke to the moral ambiguity and practical strain of dealing with this reality:

> There are no systems in place to identify children with special needs....There are no special classes, teachers, or extra help set up for them; as a consequence, these students are expected to perform at the same level as any other student in the classroom. This puts additional stress on me, as I feel the moral obligation as a teacher to ensure the best learning environment for all of my students. (Paul, p. 53)

The same frustration is heard in Anita's narrative as she realized that, even as a first-year teacher, she was one of only two teachers in the school who had a solid understanding of students with special needs:

> It is difficult for me, knowing that some of these students could be helped immensely by spending 30 minutes each day in a

> learning-strategies session to help support them. I'm only here for 1 year, and many of my ideas are foreign to these people. So, I vow to be patient with my students. (Anita, p. 71)

Elissa's feelings of incredulity and guilt, related to her inability to provide each of her students with the strategies and resources specific to their learning needs, reflected Paul's feelings of moral obligation to his students:

> I tried to explain these things in the meeting, stressing that we needed to implement a reading program for all of those students who had been left behind. I almost cried when I spoke because I felt so emotional about it. I felt like I was letting the students down by being part of a school that allowed this to happen on a yearly basis to hundreds of people. (Elissa, p. 278)

In reframing their understandings through relating to their friends, colleagues, and students, these first-year teachers were able to consider their experiences from a different perspective. Evident in the writing of current educational researchers and philosophers is the understanding that autobiographical reflections such as these allow teachers to consider their past experiences, present situations, and future intentions as a fluid entity on the narrative continuum (Alvine, 2001; Bullough & Pinnegar, 2001; Grumet, 1990; Karpiak, 2003a, 2003b). It is also through this reflective process that teachers begin to experience empowerment (Reagan, Case, & Brubacher, 2000) as they reconstruct their personal practical knowledge based on their continuous but whole story and gain a sense of their own "text" (Connelly & Clandinin, 1990, p. 59). Giroux, in his discussion of textual authority and its perpetuation of the silencing of students' individual experiences/personal context and hence voices, brought forward the concept of voice as "self- and social representation" (Giroux, 1990, p. 91). He posited that locating the discussion of voice within a discourse sensitive to power enables people to locate and define themselves within the larger social and cultural picture. Autobiography allows students to "recover their own voices so they can retell their own

Conclusion

histories" (p. 95) and become "public actors and critical citizens" (p. 96). The insights and understandings evidenced in these narratives clearly illustrate the power of speaking with one's own voice.

Narrative inquiry begins with "experience as lived and told in stories" (Clandinin & Connelly, 2000, p. 128). It invites us to wander in amongst the words as we wend our way backward and forward through our storied experiences, thus enabling us to come to an understanding of what it is we know and how we know it. As we move in and amongst our words and invite others to wander with us, we discover new stories and rewrite old ones, even as we continue to live our stories. We have journeyed with these teachers as they have come to a greater understanding of what they know and how they know it.

Despite the challenges and moments of despair that inevitably go hand in hand with life-altering experiences, all of these first-year teachers acknowledged that their international teaching journeys changed them profoundly and irrevocably and that, given the opportunity, they would each undertake this journey again. As Anita said, in speaking so personally and powerfully to the universality of the first-year teaching experience and the demands and rewards that await all teachers, irrespective of culture, location, and classroom:

> I've had more ups and downs than ever in my life. There have been times when I've felt useless and others when I've felt pleased with my skills and compassion. There have been times when I felt a student's poor behavior was all my fault and others when I realized that I was responsible for putting a smile on someone's face. Sometimes I feel there is not enough of me to satisfy all these needy students, and other times the kids manage to do something wonderful that helps me—makes my life easier—and they give back to me. (Anita, p. 64)

This reality, so true to the heart of teaching, resonates throughout the narratives in this book and will continue to resonate in the hearts of all those who teach—regardless of geography or borders.

REFERENCES

Alvine, L. (2001). Shaping the self through autobiographic narrative. *High School Journal, 84*(3), 5.

Beattie, M. (1995a). *Constructing professional knowledge in teaching—Narratives of change and development.* New York: Teachers College Press.

Beattie, M. (1995b). New prospects for teacher education: Narrative ways of knowing teaching and teacher learning. *Educational Research, 37*(1), 53–70.

Beattie, M. (2000). Narratives of professional learning: Becoming a teacher and learning to teach. *Journal of Educational Enquiry, 1*(2), 1–13.

Beattie, M. (2001). *The art of learning to teach: Preservice teacher narratives.* Columbus, OH: Merrill Prentice Hall.

Beattie, M. (2004). *Narratives in the making: Teaching and learning at Corktown Community High School.* Toronto, Ontario, Canada: University of Toronto Press.

Bullough, R., & Pinnegar, S. (2001). Guidelines for quality in autobiographical forms of self-study research. *Educational Researcher, 30*(3), 13–21.

Carter, K. (1993). The place of story in the study of teaching and teacher education. *Educational Researcher, 22*(1), 5–12, 18.

Carter, K., & Doyle, W. (1996). Personal narrative and life history in learning to teach. In J. P. Sikula, T. J. Buttery, & E. Guyton (Eds.), *The handbook of research on teacher education* (pp. 120–142). New York: Simon & Schuster Macmillan.

Clandinin, D. J., & Connelly, F. M. (2000). *Narrative inquiry: Experience and story in qualitative research.* San Francisco: Jossey-Bass.

Cole, A., & Knowles, J. G. (2000). *Researching teaching: Exploring teacher development through reflexive inquiry.* Needham Heights, MA: Allyn & Bacon.

Cole, A., & Knowles, J. G. (Eds.). (2001). *Lives in context: The art of life history research.* Walnut Creek, CA: AltaMira Press.

Connelly, F. M., & Clandinin, D. J. (1990). Stories of experience and narrative inquiry. *Educational Researcher, 19*(5), 2–14.

Giroux, H. A. (1990). Reading texts, literacy, and textual authority. *Journal of Education, 172*(1), 84–104. Retrieved July 27, 2009, from http://roxy.nipissingu.ca:2080/login?url=http://search.epnet.com/login.aspx?direct=true&db=aph&an=9512191531&site=ehost

Giroux, H. A., Penna, A. N., & Pinar, W. F. (1981). *Curriculum & instruction: Alternatives in education.* Berkley, CA: McCutchan Publishing.

Grumet, M. R. (1990). Retrospective: Autobiography and the analysis of educational experience. *Cambridge Journal of Education, 20*(3), 321–326.

Hand in Hand to Develop a National Long Term Strategy for Road Safety. *Traffic Towards Safer Roads in the State of Kuwait.* Retrieved March 31, 2008, from http://www.undp-kuwait.org

Karpiak, I. E. (2003a). The ethnographic, the reflective, and the uncanny: Three "tellings" of autobiography. *Journal of Transformative Education, 1*(2), 99–116.

Karpiak, I. E. (2003b). Releasing the educational imagination through autobiography. *Imaginative Education Research Group*, PDF Conference Proceedings 2003. Retrieved July 28, 2009, from http://www.ierg.net/confs/2003/conf2003.php

Reagan, T. G., Case, C. W., & Brubacher, J. W. (2000). *Becoming a reflective educator: How to build a culture of inquiry in the schools* (2nd ed.). Thousand Oaks, CA: Corwin Press.

Richardson, C. (2006). *Collaborative consonance: Hearing our voices while listening to the choir. A collaborative narrative inquiry into the role of music in the lives of seven preservice teachers.* Unpublished doctoral dissertation. University of Toronto, Ontario, Canada.

INDEX

Alvine, L., 300
autobiography, 300

Beattie, M., 3, 296
Brubacher, J. W., 3, 300
Bullough, R., 300

Caribbean Island in the Lesser
  Antilles
    American, 282
    assemblies, 271, 286, 290
    assessment, 284
    attendance, 280–281
    bank, 290
    basketball, 273
    British, 284–285
    Christianity, 292
    computer, 265
    contracts, 287
    culture, 269–270
    curriculum, 282–283, 288
    discipline, 275, 278
    exams/examinations, 281, 283
    food, 270, 227
    housing, 292
    immigration, 264
    Indian, 282
    interview, 266, 275
    Jamaica, 267
    management, 280, 283–284
    money, 285, 292
    Miami, 269
    Muslim, 269, 282
    paperwork, 264, 291–292

Caribbean Island in the Lesser
  Antilles (*continued*)
    parents, 271, 275–276,
      280–281, 283
    pay/payment, 288, 292
    police checks, 292
    principal, 263–264, 274, 276,
      280, 282, 285, 289
    punishment, 274–275, 279
    racism, 269, 292
    report cards, 265, 281–284
    resources, 266, 268, 278,
      286, 300
    salary, 288
    security, 273–274
    soccer, 283
    Spanish, 269
    supplies, 291–292
    Trinidad, 267
    uniform, 281–282
    United States, 269
    vacation, 287–288
    violence, 272
    weapons, 272–273
Carter, K., 296
Case, C. W., 3, 300
Cayman Islands, 2
China
    accommodations, 261
    administration, 232, 237,
      240–241, 245, 250–251
    American, 244, 260–262
    assembly, 256
    assessment, 223, 227, 239, 251

China (*continued*)
  bank, 244, 248, 260–261
  basketball, 224, 246, 255
  Beijing, 225, 228, 250, 252, 254, 260
  clothes/clothing, 235, 259
  computer, 226, 228, 235, 244, 246
  contracts, 242
  culture, 227, 229, 233, 235–236, 258, 262
  currency, 261
  curriculum, 223–224, 227, 229, 231–232, 235, 238–240, 242, 245, 248, 258, 262
  discipline, 230
  exams, 231, 236, 237–238, 243, 248, 256–257
  expectations, 231, 234–235, 257
  food, 224, 233, 237
  foreigner(s), 238
  Gobi Desert, 57
  holidays, 242–243, 245, 261
  Internet, 223, 228–229, 232, 251, 262
  interview, 235
  Israel, 228
  management, 244
  Mandarin, 224–225, 230, 238, 256
  medications, 260
  military, 241–242
  money, 230, 239, 244, 247, 254, 256, 260
  music, 254
  orientation, 227
  paperwork, 244, 260
  parents, 224, 227, 229–232, 235, 237, 241–242, 245, 249, 252, 261

China (*continued*)
  pay/payment, 256
  pollution, 235
  principal, 223, 230, 236–238, 242–243, 245–248, 252, 255–256, 261
  racism, 245
  recruitment, 253–255
  relationships, 257–258, 261
  report cards, 235, 237, 243, 245
  resources, 231, 238, 262
  security, 244
  soccer, 224
  supplies, 223, 226–227, 229, 261
  taxes, 260
  uniform, 233, 235, 255
  vacations, 244
  visa, 260–261
  volleyball, 236
  weather, 235
Clandinin, D. J., 3, 296, 300–301
Cole, A., 296
Connelly, F. M., 3, 296, 301
constructivism, 3
contracts, 3
culture, 1–2, 298–299, 301
curriculum, 5

Dewey, J., 296
Doyle, W., 296

expectations, 1–2, 6
expatriate, 2

football. *See* soccer

Giroux, H. A., 300–301
Glaserfeld, von, E., 3
Grumet, M. R., 300

Henderson, J. G., 3

Karpiak, I. E., 300
Kirchenheim, von, C., 4
Knowles, T. J., 296
Kuwait
   American, 113, 124–126
   basketball, 126
   Christian, 121
   clothing, 118, 123, 135
   culture, 116, 123, 129–130, 136
   culture shock, 136
   dishdasha, 118
   driving, 128, 132
   Eid, 122
   exams, 133
   expatriate(s), 118, 124–125, 130
   food, 121–122, 129, 135
   holidays, 121–122
   housing, 131
   immigration, 124, 128
   India, 122–123, 128
   Internet, 116
   interview, 113–116, 119
   Israel, 119–120
   Japan, 114
   management, 121
   Mecca, 122, 127
   medications, 135
   money, 117
   Muslim, 121–122, 124, 132, 136
   netball, 136
   paperwork, 120
   parents, 129
   pay/payment, 119
   police check, 117
   principal, 118–119, 133
   Ramadan, 121–122
   report cards, 133

Kuwait (*continued*)
   resources, 119
   rugby, 125, 136
   security, 119, 125
   soccer, 125, 127
   United States, 115
   vacations, 122, 133
   vaccinations, 117
   violence, 115
   visa, 128
   wasta, 128
   weather, 123
   westerners, 126

Mexico
   accommodations, 46
   administration, 34,
   American, 32–33, 35–36
   British, 36–37
   clothes/clothing, 44
   computer, 39, 42
   contracts, 42, 44
   culture, 32–33, 46
   currency, 44
   curriculum, 40
   discipline, 32
   extracurricular, 34–35, 40
   holidays, 45
   management, 32
   Mismaloya, 38
   money, 34–35, 45
   music, 39, 44
   paperwork, 35–36, 44
   parents, 33, 35
   pay/payment, 35–36, 44–45
   principal, 32–33, 35
   Puerto Vallarta, 32, 34, 36, 42, 44
   resources, 45
   salary, 44

Mexico (*continued*)
  security, 32–33, 35, 38, 44
  soccer, 31, 33, 36–39
  Spanish, 31–32, 36, 39, 41–42
  supply teach, 34
  United States, 32
  vaccinations, 44
Mongolia
  American, 48
  clothes/clothing, 56
  culture, 54
  currency, 55, 58
  curriculum, 51–52
  discipline, 53
  expectations, 55
  food, 56–57
  gers, 50, 52
  hockey, 56
  holidays, 69
  interview, 48
  Japan, 50
  music, 56
  paperwork, 57
  parents, 42, 50, 53–54
  pay/payment, 55, 57
  resources, 53–54, 56, 299
  soccer, 50
  special needs, 52
  supplies, 50, 52–53
  Tuul River, 51
  Ulaanbaatar, 48–49, 52, 54–55, 57
  United States, 49
  visa, 57
  weather, 52, 55–56

narrative(s), 4–6, 295–297, 299–301
New Zealand
  administration, 65–67
  American, 82

New Zealand (*continued*)
  assembly, 75
  assessment, 68
  Auckland, 60
  bank, 81–82
  basketball, 75
  British, 70, 78
  clothes/clothing, 82
  computer, 82
  culture, 62, 75–76
  curriculum, 59, 78, 83
  discipline, 64
  exams, 66
  extracurricular, 33
  food, 81
  haka, 75, 77
  immigration, 79, 83
  Internet, 59
  interview, 78, 83
  management, 66
  Maori, 60–62
  money, 63, 66, 69, 72, 78–82
  paperwork, 62, 79–80, 83
  parents, 61–62, 64, 69, 73, 75, 80
  pay/payment, 78–81
  police checks, 80
  Powhiri, 61
  principal, 60, 67, 78–79, 82–84
  punishment, 72
  rugby, 61, 74
  special needs, 67, 70–71
  supplies, 82
  supply teach, 59, 78, 83
  taxes, 81–82
  uniform, 62, 74
  United States, 80
  visa, 60, 79, 83
  weather, 63, 74

Index 309

New Zealand (*continued*)
  waiata, 77
  Whangarei, 75
Nigeria
  American, 15–16
  assembly, 24
  bribery. *See* corruption
  British, 12, 14
  Catholic, 10–12, 20, 22
  Christian, 10–12, 22
  clothes/clothing, 20, 28
  corruption, 9, 26
  culture, 9, 11–12, 17, 19, 21, 24, 26
  currency, 16, 25
  curriculum, 10, 12, 19
  discipline, 20–21
  Ebo, 10
  Eid, 17
  expectations, 9, 13–14, 21
  food, 13, 16–18, 20, 23, 26
  gender, 13
  hijab, 18
  Ibadan, 17–18
  immigration, 15
  Indian, 11, 17–18
  Lagos, 14
  malaria, 20, 26–27
  medications, 27
  money, 16, 23–25, 27–28
  mosquitoes, 27
  Muslim, 10–12, 17–20, 22
  naira, 24
  Oyinbo, 19, 21, 27
  orientation, 17–18
  parents, 22, 24
  pay/payment, 25
  pollution, 18
  principal, 11–12, 18, 21–23

Nigeria (*continued*)
  salary, 25
  security, 16
  supplies, 27
  vaccinations, 27
  violence, 15, 25
  visa, 14, 27–28
  weather, 15
  Westerners, 11
  Yoruba, 10

parents, 3
pay, 4
Pinnegar, S., 300

Reagan, T. G., 3–4, 300
reflect. *See* reflection
reflection, 1–5, 43, 168, 176, 225, 244, 246, 250, 258, 295, 297–298, 300
reflective practice, 2
reflected. *See* reflection
reflecting. *See* reflection
relationships, 2, 5, 298
Richardson, C. A., 4, 6, 295
Richardson, W. J., 4, 6
Rhie, W., 188

self-esteem, 4
self-efficacy, 4
self-reflection. *See* reflection
St. Vincent/Grenadines
  accommodations, 87
  Amazonia guildingii, 96, 108
  assemblies, 91, 95, 98–99
  Barbados, 88–89, 101
  Barrouallie, 96–97, 103
  Bequia, 93, 101, 105–106, 108
  Calliaqua, 91, 96, 103

St. Vincent/Grenadines (*continued*)
  clothes/clothing, 85, 87, 92, 101
  computer, 87, 92, 94
  Cuba, 91
  culture, 91, 96, 103, 109
  culture shock, 109
  currency, 89, 110
  curriculum, 90, 99
  driving, 89, 96
  expatriate, 86
  food, 89, 93, 96, 106, 109
  Grenada, 86
  holidays, 100–102, 107, 117
  immigration, 88
  Indian, 89–90
  Internet, 92, 110
  interview, 85–86, 107
  Kingstown, 86, 89, 91–92, 108
  money, 86, 105, 107–109, 111
  mosquitoes, 93
  music, 91–92, 94, 96
  orientation, 85
  parents, 90–91, 98, 102, 105, 107
  pay/payment, 87, 105, 107
  police check, 87
  principal, 88, 90, 99
  report cards, 98–101, 107–109
  resources, 87, 91
  special needs, 91
  St. Lucia, 85–86
  supplies, 87, 90, 110
  supply teach, 95, 110
  uniform, 90
  United States, 87, 91, 101
  visa, 105
  weather, 92, 94–95, 99, 101, 103
South Korea
  accommodations, 197, 199, 212
  American, 184–185, 192, 209

South Korea (*continued*)
  banks, 207, 217–218
  clothing, 186, 207, 218
  computer, 213, 215, 219
  contracts, 203, 213–214, 221
  corrupt, 185
  culture, 181–182, 184–185,
    187–188, 202, 204, 221
  currency, 208, 217
  curriculum, 192, 197
  Daegu, 186, 193
  discipline, 192
  driving, 217
  exams/examinations, 188–190,
    192
  expectations, 182, 185, 193, 195,
    200, 212–213
  extracurricular, 181, 189
  food, 184, 207, 216–217
  foreigners, 185, 187, 193,
    202–204, 209–210, 212,
    217–218
  gender, 203
  hagwon, 181, 191–194, 198, 203,
    210–211
  hierarchy, 188
  holidays, 184, 204, 214
  immigration, 215
  Internet, 207, 212–213, 215–216,
    218
  interview, 211
  Japan, 182–184, 206
  management, 192, 194, 198
  medications, 219
  military, 192
  money, 192, 202, 207–208,
    213–214, 217–219
  MoonKkang, 193, 211, 221
  music, 190, 206, 208, 220

Index 311

South Korea (*continued*)
  paperwork, 214
  parents, 187, 189, 191–192, 194–196, 209
  pay/payment, 211, 213–214, 217, 219
  punishment, 198, 208
  relationships, 203–204
  salary, 182, 208, 211, 213
  security, 218
  Seoul, 186, 206
  supplies, 207
  taxes, 213
  United States, 184–185, 193, 213
  vacations, 193, 213–214
  vaccinations, 215–216
  visa, 215
  Westerners, 185, 187, 192, 203
special needs, 299

Thailand
  accommodations, 152, 158
  administration, 154, 161, 168, 178, 179
  American, 151
  assembly, 167
  basketball, 167, 169–170, 174
  Bangkok, 151–152, 155, 158–159, 161, 164, 166, 172–173
  Buddha, 155
  clothes/clothing, 155, 156, 158–159, 173
  computer, 160
  culture, 154–155, 164, 168–169, 171, 174–176, 178
  culture shock, 168, 171, 175–176
  curriculum, 152–153, 155, 159, 168, 172, 175, 178
  expatriate(s), 163

Thailand (*continued*)
  expectations, 167, 155, 171–172, 178–179
  farang, 166
  food, 158, 173
  foreigners, 151, 166–167
  gender, 167
  hierarchy, 154
  housing, 158
  Internet, 151
  Japan, 151, 161
  Klong Toey, 173
  Lertlah, 163–164, 166–167, 170, 172
  mai pen rai, 156, 175
  money, 155, 159–160, 176, 178
  music, 151–153, 165, 167
  orientation, 152
  paperwork, 159–160, 172
  parents, 155–156, 173
  pay/payment, 154, 160, 178
  pollution, 166
  principal, 161, 174
  report cards, 153
  resources, 152, 158–160, 173, 178
  salary, 159, 171
  security, 176
  supplies, 154, 159, 178
  taxes, 160, 178
  United States, 153, 156
  vaccinations, 163
  visa, 172
  wai, 155
  Westerners, 159

United Kingdom
  accommodations, 150
  administration, 144, 150

United Kingdom (*continued*)
   American, 146
   assessment, 140
   attendance, 145
   basketball, 46
   banks, 149
   Catholic, 141–143, 145
   Dagenham, 141, 143
   clothing, 143
   curriculum, 148, 150
   Essex, 139–141, 143, 150
   exams/examinations, 142
   extracurricular, 145
   food, 149
   housing, 149
   Internet, 141
   interview, 140
   London, 139, 146, 150
   money, 148–149

United Kingdom (*continued*)
   netball, 146
   paperwork, 49
   parents, 144
   pay/payment, 149
   principal, 144
   punishment, 144–145
   recruitment, 140–141
   rugby, 146
   soccer, 146
   supply work/teachers, 140–141
   TimePlan, 140, 146, 149–150
   Uteach Recruitment, 141
   violence, 143–144
   visa, 149
   weapons, 143
   weather, 150

Vygotsky, L., 3

www.ingramcontent.com/pod-product-compliance
Lightning Source LLC
Chambersburg PA
CBHW060943230426
43665CB00015B/2042